Praise for *Peak Integration*

"*Peak Integration* is a brave and brilliant quest for wisdom in our broken world. It is shot through with a painful honesty and hard-won hope. Pierce J. Brooks is a force worth reckoning with!"

> —DR. CORNEL WEST, philosopher, author, and public intellectual

"A thoughtful and focused exploration of the internal disconnect many of us carry and what it means to create and live an integrated existence, fully tapped into the wholeness and greatness of who and what we truly are as powerful and perfect emanations of the Divine. *Peak Integration* is a masterclass and a guide to reclaiming the harmony within and is a must-read for anyone ready to understand their purpose and step into their full potential."

> —MICHAEL BERNARD BECKWITH, founder and CEO, Agape International Spiritual Center; author, *Life Visioning* and *Spiritual Liberation*; host, *Take Back Your Mind* podcast

"In *Peak Integration*, Pierce's authentic voice reveals how his life experiences serve as a backdrop for well-researched theories, illustrating how childhood trauma and family dysfunction shape disruptive relationship patterns. Through thoughtful examples, exercises, and his groundbreaking energy chart framework, he offers a path to deeper emotional connections in romance, intimacy, and beyond."

> —ANN M. MCNEIL, MSW, retired psychotherapist

"*Peak Integration* couldn't come at a more important time. When masculine and feminine energies fall out of balance, life unravels. Pierce provides a powerful road map to reclaim your wholeness through harmony, healing, and honest self-reflection."

—JESSA WHITE, MA, licensed therapist

PEAK
INTEGRATION

A Blueprint for
Harmonizing Masculine
and Feminine Energy to
Rebuild Purpose and Connection

PIERCE J. BROOKS

WONDERWELL
PRESS

Published by Wonderwell Press
Austin, Texas
www.gbgpress.com

Distributed by Greenleaf Book Group

For ordering information or special discounts for bulk purchases, please contact Greenleaf Book Group at PO Box 91869, Austin, TX 78709, 512.891.6100.

Design and composition by Greenleaf Book Group
Cover design by Greenleaf Book Group and Jonathan Lewis

Publisher's Cataloging-in-Publication data is available.

Print ISBN: 978-1-963827-17-0

eBook ISBN: 978-1-963827-18-7

To offset the number of trees consumed in the printing of our books, Greenleaf donates a portion of the proceeds from each printing to the Arbor Day Foundation. Greenleaf Book Group has replaced over 50,000 trees since 2007.

Printed in the United States of America on acid-free paper

25 26 27 28 29 30 31 32   10 9 8 7 6 5 4 3 2 1

First Edition

For Dad, Mom, Tati, Tayla, and my brothers.

For Nana, Kim, and Edwin too.

And for those who have hurt me, and more importantly those I have hurt.

May all of us find and sustain peace.

Contents

Introduction

"Integration is a basic law of life;
when we resist it, disintegration is the natural result,
both inside and outside of us."
—NORMAN COUSINS

There have only been three moments in my life when watching television left me truly shaken. The first was HBO's *Euphoria*, when a teenage Nate discovered his father's hidden sex tapes with his mistresses. That same season, one of my real-life ex-girlfriends appeared as an extra (I had to stop watching the show for months—it hit too close to home). The second was the 2022 Oscars, when Will Smith exited the stage saying, his voice sharp and trembling with anger: "Keep-my-wife's-name-out-your-fucking-mouth!" I replayed that moment obsessively, not for the drama, but because something in his tone—his face, his aggression—felt disturbingly familiar. The last was *Love Is Blind* season 6, when Clay, a former athlete, revealed how his father had forced him to tag along on his infidelity escapades. I recognized the weight of what he carried, even as the show reduced it to a subplot. These moments—raw and unfiltered—became mirrors, showing me the disconnection I carried within myself. It's true what they say: Art imitates life.

When you witness your private wounds played out on-screen, it's an unsettling kind of exposure. But when the initial discomfort fades, a strange comfort emerges; you realize you're not alone. That realization can be a lifeline, but it's also an invitation—a call to look inward and confront the disintegration that so often defines us.

Disintegration is the slow unraveling of our balance, the chaos that takes hold when we disconnect from ourselves. It's in the fractured relationships, the self-destructive patterns, the unspoken grief we carry. And for many of us, it's so familiar that we hardly notice it. This book is about learning to notice—then to heal, and ultimately, to reconnect. It's about reclaiming the balance that I call *integration*, the state where our masculine and feminine energies work in harmony to create wholeness. It's the antidote to the entropy that leaves us lost, fragmented, and void of meaning.

I didn't always have the words for what I now call integration and disintegration. Growing up, I wrestled with what it meant to be a man. The world around me offered one set of answers—stoic, tough, dominant—while something deeper inside me longed for a more expansive truth. The musician Prince gave me a glimpse of that truth. He blurred the lines between masculine and feminine with a grace and confidence that felt both radical and undeniable. Prince didn't just perform; he *embodied*. His artistry wasn't about rejecting masculinity or femininity but about blending them into something transcendent. His symbol, his sound, his presence—they all whispered to me that there was another way to exist in the world. A way that felt true.

My path toward integration has been messy, marked by missteps and revelations. It's taken years of reflecting on my own story—on the choices I've made and the pain I've endured—to understand how these energies have shaped me. Only when I began to reassess my understanding of masculine and feminine energy did I realize how deeply this disintegration had shaped my choices. Along the way, I realized that the mainstream models for understanding masculine and feminine energy weren't enough nor accurate. Too often, these ideas were reduced to superficial clichés, used in conversations about dating or attraction, without the depth needed to apply them to life. So, I created a new framework—one that maps these energies against the states of integration and disintegration, showing how they manifest in our emotions, beliefs, choices, and actions. It's a framework designed not just to analyze but to empower, offering practical tools for real change.

This book isn't just my story, though. It's for anyone who's ever felt the weight of disconnection, who's struggled to make sense of the push and pull between their internal world and the expectations of the external one. It's for anyone seeking alignment—not perfection but coherence. Masculine and feminine energy aren't about gender; they're about the universal forces that shape us all. Integration isn't something you achieve once and for all—it's a practice, a process of becoming.

The path isn't easy, and the subject matter can be heavy at times. We'll confront intergenerational trauma, personal and relational failures, and the lingering impacts of disintegration. But we'll also celebrate moments of transformation and the breakthroughs that come with integration. As you move through these pages, I encourage you to engage deeply. Let this book be more than something you read. Write in the margins, underline what resonates, challenge what doesn't. Each chapter is like a track in a curated playlist, with its own rhythm and tone, building toward something greater than the sum of its parts. Some chapters will speak to you immediately; others might take time to reveal their meaning. That's okay. Like your favorite songs, the lessons here will evolve with you.

This isn't just a book—it's an invitation. To reflect. To grow. To reclaim the harmony within you. And perhaps to see your own story in a new light. Together, let's begin the work of integration.

PART I

The Ethos of Integration

Understanding the Feminine and Masculine

Within each of us exists a primordial polarity.
The integration of these yin-yang forces aligns our
feelings, thoughts, and actions in harmony.
Through self-awareness, intention, and execution,
we manifest our internal state in the world around us.

CHAPTER 1

The Energy-Integration Axis

"I must choose between despair and energy—I choose the latter."
—JOHN KEATS

A few years before I wrote this book, I ruined my own life. My former best friend, the son of a famous singer who had been like a father to me since childhood, found out his wife and I were having an affair. My girlfriend at the time was then told I had cheated, and word spread like wildfire throughout my community. My friends heard about the double life I had been living behind everyone's backs, as did my family. In one fell swoop, I damaged most of my close relationships and set my reputation on fire. This was all my doing.

You may be wondering why I would take such a risk with that affair, considering there was so much to lose. I wondered, too, after I got caught, steeped in the shame of that rock-bottom moment. Why had I done that? Cheating had always been second nature to me, long before the affair with my friend's wife, but why? Why was I so addicted to it? How had I let myself get to that place?

Maybe it had to do with my trauma around my dad's womanizing and eventual suicide. Maybe I was compensating for the fact that I never reached the NBA—the dream I had dedicated my entire life to, only to fall short after playing college basketball. A red thread of inner turmoil and confusion stretched all the way back to my earliest days of life, but I had no awareness of the subconscious dynamics underlying my actions. I needed to figure out the *why* behind the *what* so I could change course and start becoming the man I wanted to be.

My road to recovery began with treatment for sex addiction, a path that led me to therapy, the support of a 12-step community, and the unwavering care of my uncle. In facing the darkest parts of myself, I also found a deeper understanding of masculine and feminine energy—the push and pull that had shaped all of my choices. As I began to piece together the parts of myself I had long ignored, I found clarity not just in recovery but also in life. This understanding became the foundation of my purpose—speaking, sharing my story, and mentoring young people (especially men). Through this lens, I discovered how to navigate life's challenges with intention and balance.

I now invite you to embark on the same inner work, to master these forces and find your own clarity.

This book hinges on two primary principles:

1. The full spectrum of masculine and feminine energies exists in everyone.
2. Our human experience revolves around how we manage these polar dynamics, both personally and interpersonally.

In our patriarchal society, we're judged based on our masculine energy—our actions that can be seen—but what's happening on the surface can never fully encompass our stories. Behind each of our

choices lies the feminine, the vast sea of emotional and mental information that drives us to live as we do. We can all act on that information
from a psychologically integrated place—masculine and feminine
together—rooted in connection, empathy, and love.

Many of us strive to live in that state by developing our conscious
awareness and learning to regulate our emotions. The easier choice in
the short term, however, is to live in a fear-based state of disintegration
wherein we react without empathy, disconnected from ourselves
and others, making impulsive or hurtful choices we later come to
regret. The more we gear our intention toward integration within
ourselves, the closer we align with our vision of the person we want
to become. To pass up this opportunity robs us of our ability to live
a life of deep fulfillment.

What Do We Mean by *Energy*?

Known as *prana* in Hindu literature, energy is the force behind all
happenings in the universe. It is the divine intelligence that beats our
hearts, moves the Earth around the Sun, and urges plants to grow. It's
the warm feeling we get from spending time with someone we love
and the bad vibe we pick up on when a coworker no one can stand is
at the office. It's the biofield, the aura, permeating and surrounding us,
perpetually changing based on our thoughts, emotions, and actions. It
is the unseen—underlying the veil of the physical dimension, present
throughout every moment of our existence.

All energy, including that of our bodies and minds, is subject to
certain universal laws. The first law of thermodynamics, also known
as the law of conservation, states that energy is neither created nor
destroyed. When we use it, it doesn't disappear but instead converts
into another form of energy. The food we eat contains energetic

components we convert into heat, motion, and more. We convert the feminine energy driving our emotions—described by some as "energy in motion"—into the masculine energy that drives our actions.

The second law of thermodynamics describes the workings of entropy, a measure of the disorder of the universe. In the 1860s and '70s, Austrian physicist and philosopher Ludwig Boltzmann and German physicist Rudolf Clausius conducted research that showed everything in nature flows from a state of order to disorder, and focused energy is required if order is to be re-achieved. Every system in the universe will naturally be found either in a state of maximum disorder, or in the process of moving toward it. By applying this theory to our own energy, we bring awareness to our tendency toward disintegration. Integration is only possible when we consciously and consistently focus our feminine and masculine energies on maintaining order between our emotions, thoughts, and actions.

Masculine and Feminine Energy Defined

Our gender significantly impacts how we experience life, and society's sex-based stereotypes often influence how we manage our energy, which we'll discuss more in the next chapter. Throughout this book, we'll explore cultural trends and anecdotes related to how *most* men and women feel about their masculine and feminine energies, but I push back on the notion that feminine energy is for women and masculine energy is for men. In pursuit of peak integration of the masculine and feminine, we must accept and embrace all the different energetic parts of ourselves, then learn to unite them for the highest good of ourselves and others.

Masculine energy is defined by external activity and has to do with taking action. It knows what to do and how to move. It's decisive and committed. It creates stability and structure. The masculine is focused on *doing* and comprises that which can be seen. Feminine energy is defined by internal activity. It has to do with emotion, thought, and intuition. It creates passion and flow. The feminine knows how to *be* rather than *do* and comprises the unseen. These energies complement each other, unable to exist independently. The feminine is input. The masculine, output. The feminine is vision, and the masculine is mission. The feminine is questions, the masculine is answers. Between this duality we seek connection, union, balance, and harmony. Our survival depends on this integration and how we balance the polar energies involved.

We humans are not separate from the sea of energy that comprises our universe. Our intuition, the voice of our higher consciousness, connects us to the protection and guidance of the divine. That voice works to prevent us from doing and consuming things that harm us while urging us to do the things necessary for our survival, like resting or eating certain foods. Human intuition is based in emotion, the realm of the feminine, which our psychologically disintegrated society devalues as weak. When we follow the guidance of our higher consciousness and don't abandon our authentic self, life becomes straightforward. We no longer feel lost or wonder which path to take.

Our society is currently anchored in a deeply disintegrated phase, and we've all been forced to take notice of the disconnection plaguing us in our public discourse. Union can only be reached when we learn to create the safety we need in order to express these energies in their healthy, integrated forms.

I'm far from the first person to write about these dynamics, but learning about them resonated with me deeply. These days I can't help but notice them playing out everywhere, all the time, in every situation, and I have noticed some critical issues in our discussions about masculine and feminine energy. The first is that more clarity and consistency are needed if we're to move forward with a construct that works. Many people still fall into the trap of equating masculine/ feminine with male/female. We need to bring more nuance to these discussions so we can explore our masculine and feminine energies in ways that are expansive rather than limiting or oppressive.

Modeling the Masculine and Feminine

I model masculine and feminine dynamics using the following energy chart, which you'll see throughout this book. We can think of the horizontal axis as "sea level." Below it lie the disintegrated expressions of the feminine and masculine being pulled down toward rock bottom. Above sea level are expressions that reflect a more psycho-spiritually integrated state that gears us toward connection.

THE ENERGY CHART		
FEMININE *FEELING & THOUGHT*		**MASCULINE** *BEHAVIOR*
• Compassionate • Secure • Trusting • Creative • Peaceful • Calm • Insightful • Perceptive	• Reasoned • Contemplative • Mindful • Objective • Thoughtful • Aware • Clarifying	• Committed • Supportive • Structured • Disciplined • Consistent
• Anxious • Insecure • Lonely • Worried • Numb • Angry • Impatient • Overthinking	• Doubtful • Skeptical • Obsessive • Pessimistic • Paranoid • Confused • Irrational	• Aggressive • Dismissive • Withdrawn • Hostile • Isolated • Manipulative • Controlling • Forceful

The Masculine and Feminine Energy Chart

The top-left quadrant of this chart displays expressions of every-one's—men's and women's—integrated feminine energy. In this state of *being*, we feel compassionate, secure, trusting, creative, peaceful, calm, and inspired. Our thoughts are positive, constructive, reflective, and grounded in logic. The top-right quadrant reflects the integrated masculine. In this state of *doing*, we handle our actions in ways that are committed, supportive, structured, disciplined, and consistent.

Below sea level in the bottom-left quadrant, disintegrated feminine energy manifests fear as feelings of anxiousness, loneliness, anger, worry, numbness, and impatience. Our thoughts there are negative, distorted, or rooted in insecurity. In the bottom-right quadrant, disintegrated masculine energy manifests as behavior that is aggres-sive, dismissive, withdrawn, hostile, manipulative, controlling, or forceful. Connection becomes more difficult the closer we get to rock bottom.

Looking at the chart, we can begin to see how masculine/femi-nine differs from male/female. Cooking, for instance, has long been associated with femininity but, being an *action* that requires us to do something, it is based in masculine energy. The same can be said for parenting children. Though this (hopefully) is informed by the intangible compassion of our feminine energy, it is accomplished through consistent, committed, structured action in the external world.

In a recent moment of clarity, I found myself questioning the traditional view that logic and thought are traits of masculine energy. This realization was a profound aha moment for me as I began to see how these intellectual qualities aligned more closely with the feminine. Deep understanding is the essence of internal reflection—hallmarks of feminine energy. This shift in perspective allowed me to embrace the feminine as a powerful source not only of emotion but also of intellectual insight.

Our What, Why, and How

Our actions can be seen and judged by the outside world. *Why* we do those things can never be seen, but the foundation of our reasoning is emotion, the language of the subconscious mind. We can utilize the energy chart as a GPS of choice, helping us navigate our way toward integration by identifying our *whats*, our *whys*, and ultimately our *hows*. This tool can serve us well when we're feeling lost.

ENERGY CHART

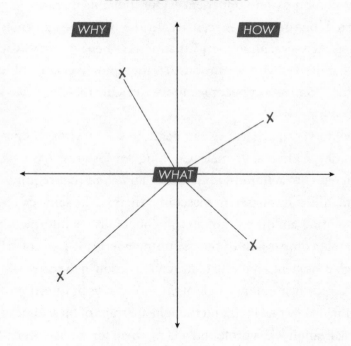

At any given moment when we have a choice to make, we can figure out what to do by assessing where we currently are on the chart. We can ask ourselves, "What am I experiencing? What am I feeling or doing? Am I above or below sea level?"

Say, for example, you get into an argument with your spouse and blow up at them in anger. This situation is your *what*. Energetically, you're in your disintegrated masculine, the bottom-right quadrant of the chart. *Why* you blew up stems from disintegration happening with your feminine energy in your bottom-left quadrant of the chart. Perhaps internally you're feeling insecure in the relationship or worried you'll be abandoned. Once you've identified the fear-based *why* motivating your undesirable *what*, you can elevate above sea level by healing the feminine energy behind your actions. You are able to do this by acknowledging and confronting the unseen parts of yourself, transforming fear-based motivations into intentional ones—a process we'll explore in greater depth in the chapters ahead. From the calm, compassionate top-left quadrant of the integrated feminine, you can identify your *how*, move into your integrated masculine, and act from a place of empathy, resulting in a stronger connection with your spouse.

By using the chart as a GPS of choice, we can act more consistently from a place of awareness. Becoming conscious of the context driving our behaviors results in more mindful behavior overall, allowing us to pursue our personal mission and ultimately fulfill whatever we believe to be our life's purpose.

When we neglect, ignore, or repress the feminine, the masculine wanders through life unmoored, impulsive, and confused, unclear about its purpose and often inflicting collateral damage on those who come into contact with it. Healthy action is rooted in healthy intention. Consistent integration of these elements aligns us with our ideal, authentic self. This is, again, the more difficult mode of living. Disintegration is easy to achieve, and we spend much of our time there, but it's not where any of us want to be. Integration is the path to growth and connection rather than destruction and loneliness.

The Pros and Cons of Each Quadrant

To access a state of peak integration, we must master how we manage the energies of all four quadrants on the chart, all of which offer their own benefits and drawbacks. Developing true integrity requires us to see, hear, and acknowledge our shadows—the hidden parts of ourselves we suppress or deny, not just the aspects of ourselves that we readily accept or find desirable.

Let's take an individual look at each of these quadrants and how they can move us forward or hold us back.

Top Right: The Integrated Masculine

THE PROS AND CONS OF THE INTEGRATED MASCULINE *UNCONSCIOUS COMPETENCE*	
PROS	**CONS**
• Committed	• Ignoring areas of life that don't revolve around achievement
• Supportive	• Overinflated ego
• Structured	• Arrogance; overconfidence
• Disciplined	• Complacency
• Consistent	• Inflexibility; rigidity
• Accomplishments	• Aversion to change
• Leadership	
• Alchemy	
• Manifestation	

Society revolves around the energy of the top-right quadrant of the chart. Collectively, we celebrate external accomplishments that can be seen, noticed, and experienced by all. When someone new meets us for the first time, they don't usually ask how we are. They ask what we *do*. The beneficial, connective, love-rooted actions we take are the metric used by the world to judge whether we're up to par.

Good leadership is derived from integrated masculine energy. We admire people who are willing to step up and take on roles of greater responsibility to benefit the collective. Commitment, support, structure, discipline, and consistency are all required if a leader is to succeed. The top-right quadrant is made up of the energy that transforms feelings and ideas into action. It's the alchemy that manifests our feminine desires and intentions into tangible impact in the real world. This is how we finally come to see and enjoy the positive changes in our lives that were once only dreams. Without integrated masculine energy, nothing would ever get done.

Mastering this energy builds confidence within us. When we make a habit of operating in our top-right quadrant, we become adept at getting out of our head and moving seamlessly into a flow state. A steadiness develops, and we stop second-guessing ourselves, giving others the impression that we achieve our accomplishments effortlessly. When we spend enough time and effort acting within a framework of proven success, we can stop overthinking and move forward with clarity. This can be described as a state of "unconscious competence" wherein we function from an integrated place without having to think much about it.

Once we've entered this energy, we must actively do the work to remain there in order to reap its benefits. Let's look at the example of Eddie Murphy's stand-up comedy career. As a cultural force who redefined comedy in the 1980s and beyond, Murphy left the stage when his Hollywood career took off and hasn't returned to stand-up since. While he's expressed interest in performing again, stepping back on stage would mean revisiting the challenges he once overcame—grappling with emotions, doubts, setbacks, and the discipline required to master his craft. Unlike comedians like Chris Rock and Dave Chappelle, who stayed active in stand-up, Murphy would need to rebuild his confidence and rediscover his rhythm. To do so, he must embrace both masculine energy—action and outward performance—and feminine energy—reflection and internal growth—to fully reclaim his mastery.

No matter how skilled we become, sustaining peak integration demands staying grounded in the purpose behind our pursuits.

While society values the healthy masculine above all the other energies, an imbalance toward the top-right quadrant can lead to problems if we're not careful. Spending all our time in our integrated masculine quadrant can cause us to ignore other areas of our life. We see an example of this in people who construct their identity around their accomplishments at work and derive confidence from their career but ignore their family and the responsibilities required for a healthy home life.

Another risk of relying too much on integrated masculine energy is developing an inflexibility toward change. When we find a mode of operation that works for us, it's tempting to want to stay there, never again having to question whether we might be able to improve. This can manifest as stubbornness and frustration over time, pulling us down into our bottom-right quadrant where we demand that others do things our way. Disintegration waits in the wings anytime we're rigid rather than curious. Our existence relies on the living, breathing, dynamic impermanence of all things. When we're not moving and making progress, we stagnate to the point of irrelevance.

Bottom Right: The Disintegrated Masculine

PROS AND CONS OF THE DISINTEGRATED MASCULINE *UNCONSCIOUS INCOMPETENCE*	
PROS	**CONS**
• Immediate results/feedback • Pleasurable feelings of power; intoxication • Potential for drastic change • Protection from pain • Ego boost	• Self-destructive tendencies; addiction; self-harm • Behavior that harms others; aggression • Loneliness; withdrawal; isolation • Ruined relationships • Legal or career problems • Physical illnesses

The bottom-right quadrant, while harmful to others and universally condemned, provides us with immediate results. Mean or aggressive behavior is felt by others right away and gets us feedback on where they stand in relation to us. We can get what we want by exerting power through manipulation, intimidation, and force. This proved useful in our species' quest for survival along the path of evolution, getting us access to food, territory, mates, and the protective action needed to ensure offspring could live long enough to reproduce. Without this caustic energy, none of us would be here.

Disintegrated masculine energy is also sensually intoxicating. A 2008 study at Vanderbilt University in Nashville[1] suggested that indulging in aggression activates the same neural reward pathway in the brain as sex or cocaine, flooding our bodies with pleasurable dopamine. Fighting excites us, as evidenced by the growing and widespread fascination of violent movies, music, video games, and pornography. Unfortunately, this behavior can become an addiction that keeps us hooked on the worst aspects of our nature, making it hard to move on. Social media companies rely on our disintegrated masculine energy and its intense desire to feed on others. This is a state of "unconscious incompetence" wherein we function from a disintegrated place, largely unaware of the *why* behind our *what*.

It can also feel natural to live in the bottom-right quadrant because the brain is wired to scan the world for threats so we can survive. To view our own aggressive behavior as righteous massages our ego, convincing us we're doing the right thing by fighting back in a dog-eat-dog world. We fixate on this darkness, telling ourselves that doing otherwise would expose us to vulnerability and potential doom. We double down when we're in disintegrated masculine energy because the entire world, pulled below sea level by society's imbalance toward bottom-right quadrant energy, makes it exceedingly easy for us to do so. "Look out for yourself," it tells us, "because no one else will." This protection feels necessary, and on certain occasions, it is. The only way to deal with aggression from others, in rare cases, is to match that aggression ourselves in self-defense.

The biggest downside of the disintegrated masculine is the obvious harm it inflicts on our relationships. Indulging in the energy of the bottom-right quadrant can swiftly ruin our reputation, as Will Smith discovered when he doled out that infamous slap at the 2022 Oscars. We lose our connection to others because this energy cuts us off from our empathy. All people see is the slap from the outside, but not the mixture of inner pain, turmoil, and fear that sparked that reaction. Even if others could see what's happening with our feminine energy, adding context to our disintegrated actions, it wouldn't justify the harm we have caused. We're viewed as erratic, threatening, untrustworthy, and unworthy of respect when we react to life's challenges without reflection or compassion. To operate from the bottom-right quadrant sets us up for criticism, resentment, and abandonment.

Top Left: The Integrated Feminine

THE PROS AND CONS OF THE INTEGRATED FEMININE *CONSCIOUS COMPETENCE*	
PROS	**CONS**
• Compassionate	• Lazy
• Secure	• High on toxic positivity
• Trusting	• Addicted to escapism
• Creative	• Stagnant
• Peaceful	• Stuck in denial
• Calm	• Comfortably numb
• Inspired	• Analysis paralysis
• Confident	• Targeted for attack by the
• Fearless	disintegrated masculine
• Free	
• Ethereal	
• Enlightened	

The energy of our top-left quadrant provides the fuel our integrated masculine uses to manifest action. This is the energy of conscious, clear logic and emotion. It imbues us with a relaxed air of confidence that allows us to coexist peacefully with others. Competition is enjoyable here; we can readily compete with others without stepping on anyone or pushing them beneath us. The healthy feminine is creative, inspired, fearless, free, and motivated to pursue whatever actions lie ahead in the top-right quadrant.

In the top-left quadrant, we audit our internal world, constantly checking in on our thoughts and feelings, evaluating them against whatever is happening externally. This allows us to continually recalibrate our strategy from a well-grounded place of awareness while keeping the big picture in mind.

To me, the best thing about this quadrant is that we tend to spend the least time there, making its coveted energy rare and special. It's difficult to consistently embody the integrated feminine, but its energy creates an internal radiance that comes with knowing one's worth and intrinsic value. Ever met someone who shifted the energy of an entire room in a positive way just by being there? One so strongly connected to the loving source energy of the universe that they lived as its open conduit? Those rare humans did the internal work required to live in the top-left quadrant.

Integrated feminine energy pervades our most pleasurable, relaxing experiences. The top-right quadrant entails enjoyment but also requires effort and risk to be sustained. While work is required to reach the top-left quadrant, we feel incredible while we're there, riding the highs of enlightenment, able to create and connect unhindered. Professional artists use the masculine to carry out their craft but channel the feminine to show us the contents of their hearts. This is a state of "conscious competence" wherein we function from an integrated place through deep awareness.

While the integrated feminine is pure and divine, it can harm us to lean in to it to the point of imbalance. Attempting to feel good all the time, emotionally bypassing any resistance from our external reality, traps us in a dream world of fantasy, causing us to stagnate. It's not enough to brainstorm and write to-do lists or create vision boards. We must *do* in order to manifest the ideas channeled by the top-left quadrant. By becoming too comfortable in our integrated feminine energy, we can fail to follow through, thus losing faith in our abilities over time.

Another drawback of living in our top-left quadrant is that the integrated feminine attracts external attack. Calm, loving energy flies in the face of how most people think they have to be in the world. "Who do you think you are?" they might say, envious and ready to take all that happiness down a peg, wondering why you're seemingly unfazed by the weights pulling everyone else below sea level. We live in a world where the wounded masculine seeks to dominate the feminine in all things. Individuals who are truly comfortable in their own skin threaten everything wounded masculine energy stands for.

What contemporary society refers to as "toxic positivity" is another risk of spending too much time in the top-left quadrant. This term describes the tendency to dismiss or invalidate negative emotions by insisting on maintaining a cheerful facade, even in the face of genuine hardship. While it might seem like an attempt to stay positive, toxic positivity actually denies the reality of life's challenges—such as bills, breakups, war, and natural disasters—by encouraging avoidance rather than engagement. By turning away from these realities, we risk pulling ourselves below sea level into a disintegrated state, numbing ourselves or denying the truth. True growth and resilience come from acknowledging and addressing these difficulties, not from masking them with forced optimism.

Bottom Left: The Disintegrated Feminine

THE PROS AND CONS OF THE DISINTEGRATED FEMININE *CONSCIOUS INCOMPETENCE*	
PROS	**CONS**
• A loud internal alarm • Potential for transformation • Creation of inner awareness • Space to reframe limiting beliefs • Catharsis • Leaps in wisdom and emotional maturity	• Anxiousness; worry • Insecurity; shame • Loneliness • Numbness • Impatience • Feeling invisible • A scarcity mindset • Pessimism • Hopelessness

Though being in the bottom-left quadrant of the energy chart is never enjoyable, it does deliver benefits. The disintegrated feminine provides us with the loudest, clearest internal alarm that something needs to be addressed. Anxiety, shame, loneliness, and worry tell us in no uncertain terms that something is wrong. Lack of clarity in our logic causes us to seek knowledge. Without awareness of these feelings, we will act on impulse and be stuck in our disintegrated masculine, leaving destruction in our wake.

Another benefit of our disintegrated feminine energy is that it often leads us to places of powerful and purposeful transformation. A lot of great art is created by people who have been hurt and worked through their trauma by turning it into creative gold. The process of healing the wounded feminine creates deep internal awareness and understanding of self, providing the best lessons and the biggest leaps in the attainment of wisdom. There is growth in confronting our shadow.

There's also catharsis in the energy of the bottom-left quadrant. We have to feel to heal, as they say, and there will always be a time and a place for being in our pain so we can release it as we make our way back out of the darkness. This is a state of "conscious incompetence" wherein we function from a disintegrated place, with awareness of the *why* behind the *what*.

One of the biggest drawbacks of getting stuck in our disintegrated feminine is that people can't see what we're going through emotionally. They'll never fully appreciate the intricacies of our *why*, and this can create judgment or confusion, leading to further disintegration and disconnection.

Another big problem with an imbalance toward the disintegrated feminine is that we can learn the wrong lessons in that space. Feeling numb, depressed, or hopeless causes us to focus on what we lack. Our mindset revolves around scarcity, and we can convince ourselves that the world can't provide whatever it is we desire. "There's not enough. Not for me, anyway," we say, keeping ourselves stuck in isolation and powerlessness.

What Is Peak Integration?

Peak integration is our optimal state of being as humans, a place where being and doing become one. Here we become fully present, almost as if time didn't exist; we operate with awareness, fearless and engaged. The structure and skill we develop through our masculine energy creates a safe space where our healthy feminine can be free. We see peak integration at play in musicians who've spent thousands of hours working to master their craft so they can be comfortable playing live for audiences of thousands of people, unhindered by distractions. We spend too much time and energy fighting what's happening in the present. "I want *this* to be different and *that* too." Peak integration is about relaxing in our feminine energy, accepting whatever comes our way with grace and capability.

This state becomes accessible when we master how we navigate the masculine and feminine energies modeled by the chart. To reach that state on a consistent basis provides us with the most expansive and rewarding life experience available to us. When we're able to seamlessly integrate the complementary aspects of our polar energies, we are free to live in our authentic truth, leading to a clear consciousness and sense of purpose.

Peak integration is not about perfection or avoiding mistakes. There will always be moments when we falter, lack answers, or drop the ball. When Kobe Bryant scored 81 points in a single game against the Raptors in 2006, he didn't do it without missing shots or turning the ball over. We still go through those experiences, but they no longer throw us off track. We can pivot to meet the situation at hand and embrace the moment in spite of whatever's happening around us.

For me, peak integration is the key to delivering a powerful and impactful speech. I dedicate significant time to mastering my material, ensuring I know it inside and out. But it's not just about the content—it's about connecting with my audience. I take time to understand who they are, what they need, and the expectations they bring with them. As an inspirational speaker, I specialize in guiding people toward personal growth, resilience, and empowerment. This deep connection with both my message and my audience allows me to speak with clarity and conviction, creating a transformative experience that resonates long after I've left the stage.

Peak integration is also not about the ephemeral pleasure that comes and goes when we're disintegrated and living below sea level. Synthetic, temporary, superficial happiness is easy to find, but it's built on a foundation of sand. Deep, enduring fulfillment and satisfaction take time and hard work to create in our lives, but those sacrifices pave the road to a future we can take pride in. By achieving peak integration, we access the "god state" inherent within us all. No one can live there all the time, and that's okay, but the more work we do within ourselves, the more quickly and easily we'll be able to get there in the future.

The opposite of peak integration is the rock-bottom sea floor of disintegration. There are several common trajectories for people who eventually reach this state. Many who get stuck in their wounded masculine (like me or my dad, whom you'll read about later) organize their entire world around hedonism and domination over others. They dive into addictive vortexes of drinking, sex, or the thrill of their own anger, giving up on themselves and their lives in the process. This leads not only to crippling emotional isolation but also eventual depression, when they look back on how much they didn't accomplish because they didn't want to put in the work. All the chances they didn't take. All the relationships they ruined. All the love and fun they missed out on by feeding a monster that can never be sated.

An infamous example of rock-bottom disintegration occurred on January 6, 2021, when extremist supporters of Donald Trump stormed the US Capitol. Driven by a deep fear of losing their identity and control, many surrendered to irrationality, behaving in ways disconnected from their integrated selves. At rock bottom, we often act erratically—fueled by anger, resentment, and self-righteousness, even when our actions harm others and ourselves. In this state, we may believe our behavior is just or noble, but without connection and integration, we risk becoming the very force of destruction our higher self would seek to heal or avoid. In less extreme cases, people living in disintegration can often appear successful from the outside. Many make a decent living and command respect but feel spiritually empty, bouncing from situation to situation because they can't connect with others. They prioritize their own desires and comforts above all, have few close relationships, and hold back from doing any internal work that would require them to head down a path without knowing its exact destination. They stagnate, paralyzed by the prospect of emotional risk, and find themselves "free" but alone.

If we choose at some point to make the hard choice and embark on our personal journey toward peak integration, we allow ourselves to focus more on process than results. Our healthy feminine may have a specific vision in mind, and our healthy masculine can embrace rather than control how it manifests. Rather than thinking, *This must happen*, we can remain calm and think, *Let's see what happens*. The reward is ultimately a life full of connection, accomplishment, love, intimacy, satisfaction, and purpose. Choosing to do the work in search of peak integration is no small feat. It can mean the difference between a future of light or a future of darkness.

Core Masculines and Core Feminines

The vast majority of people identify more closely with one end of the masculine/feminine energy spectrum than the other, finding more comfort either in their capacity for feeling or doing. This "default setting" determines whether we are core masculine or core feminine individuals and often aligns with our biological sex, but not always. Many men feel more comfortable residing primarily in their feminine, and the same is true of women who prefer to live in their masculine energy.

Core masculine individuals tend to be action-oriented initiators, go-getters, and extroverts, assertive and driven by external metrics of success, like accolades and respect from others. They feel comfortable embodying the intense, fiery energy of the sun, the yang to humanity's yin. Core feminine individuals tend to be observers, dreamers, visionaries, and introverts. They're emotionally centered, measured, and inspired by internal metrics of self-discovery, peace, harmony, connection, and nurturing. They are sensitive, guided by emotion, intuition, logic, and instinct. They are the moon and regenerative energy of rest. Yin to the yang.

Whether we identify as a core masculine or core feminine impacts how we show up in the world. For example, parenting for a core masculine might look like preparing a child to be independent and take on the external world with "tough love," while a core feminine person might have discussions around their child's feelings. People who resonate primarily with core masculine energy in relationships often prefer to take the lead in choosing a mate, while those with core feminine energy may feel more aligned with being chosen. The core masculine focuses on freedom, while the core feminine focuses on connection.

The work of integration acknowledges that all of us, regardless of which label we identify with more, desire at least some of the experiences of the entire energetic spectrum. A core masculine will never feel whole without emotional connection and understanding. A core feminine will never feel whole without freedom. Through integration of these dynamics, the masculine and feminine can unite and show each other the workings of their respective sides in ways that are safe and expansive. By bringing together all parts of ourselves in alignment with our highest, most authentic version of ourselves, we become something greater than any of those individual parts could be on their own.

You might find it difficult to identify whether you're a core masculine or core feminine. This is entirely normal, as many of us find ourselves somewhere in the middle, leaning right or left on the chart 60 percent of the time, for example. (Few people, if any, would say they inhabit one end of the spectrum 100 percent of the time.) The core energy we experience can also be situational. You might feel like a core masculine at work but feel more like a core feminine at home. You may find your core energy shifting over time as you age and evolve.

To lean core masculine or core feminine is a matter of both nature and nurture. Nearly all of us begin life in our feminine energy because we're dependent on our connections with others for survival. During childhood, our unique personalities reveal themselves as certain kids step up to lead while others follow. Many children who are hurt by their parents or friends are forced into a disintegrated state, driven by their fight-or-flight instincts. We can never predict exactly where our experiences will lead us and how they'll influence our "default state," but life tends to beat the creative, expansive power of the healthy feminine out of many of us by the time we reach adulthood. We must reclaim this part of ourselves and foster its energy if we're to bask in its benefits.

The Emotion-Belief-Choice-Pursuit (E-B-C-P) Pipeline

When we become integrated, the energetic flow between our emotions, beliefs, choices, and pursuits is free and unhindered. Take the example of driving a car. To do so with unconscious competence—integrated masculine energy—we have to develop confidence in our driving abilities. This takes repetition and frequent positive results, leading to positive emotions.

As we get more practice, we cement the belief that we're a good driver, which opens us up to the many choices available while we're on the road. We can merge onto the freeway, switch lanes, parallel park, and handle all other challenges that come our way effectively thanks to the knowledge we've gained through practice. Driving becomes second nature, freeing us up to pursue our transportation goals.

Getting into an accident can harm our confidence, however. After that, we go back to square one, intently focusing as we practice rebuilding our belief in our abilities. No matter how good we get at executing a certain skill, we can always be knocked off our game, back to a disintegrated state. Our feminine energy (our emotions and beliefs around the knowledge we've gained) must be integrated for our masculine energy (our choices and pursuits) to maintain integration.

When disintegration occurs, we find fractures in one or more of the bridges between what I call our Emotion-Belief-Choice-Pursuit pipeline. This usually comes down to how we connect our emotions to our beliefs, or our beliefs to our choices.

In my work as a coach, I see a lot of people who try to grind their fractured emotions into integrated choices by hammering positivity into their beliefs. *Mindset, mindset, mindset* is their mantra, and while that's certainly important, we can't willpower our way past the reality of a fractured emotional state. This is why forcing ourselves to quit an addiction cold turkey, for example, rarely brings lasting success. Our choices are rooted in the subconscious emotions driven by our feminine energy. The only way to reprogram those emotions is through repetition of more integrated patterns of thought and emotion.

For many disintegrated core masculine individuals, the furthest they delve into their feminine energy is the realm of belief, causing them to intellectualize everything while ignoring their feelings because the realm of emotion feels too uncomfortable. They turn to their thoughts for solutions to problems but avoid making choices informed by emotion unless absolutely necessary.

Mastering integration of our masculine and feminine energies helps fix the fractures in the bridges of our pipeline so we can be honest and intimate with ourselves. The process of mastery here is far less limiting than going through our lives either doing without feeling or feeling without doing. This is most relevant to disintegrated people who, for instance, feel a lack of fulfillment and satisfaction but lack awareness of why they feel that way. They look outside themselves, blaming the external world for the disconnection in their relationship to self and others.

Our choices are overloaded with contexts unique to each individual. We're biased in the choices we make because, well, we are us. But the next person comes with a different, unique context of their own, informed by their own combination of thoughts and emotions, and we spend too much time judging the choices and pursuits of others without the compassion of understanding why they behave as they do.

Disintegration lies at the heart of our most painful struggles. The more we can integrate our feminine and masculine energies from a place of love, the better our experience of life becomes. Through mastery of our dualistic energies, we open ourselves up to moments of peak integration, where we can operate at our full potential. I've written this book to guide you through the work of integration so you can design your life from a place of authenticity and purpose.

Much of the disintegration we see between the masculine and feminine stems from messages we've received from society that warp our concepts of these energies. Next, we'll discuss how this framing has impacted how we view the masculine and feminine within ourselves.

Key Takeaways

- The full spectrum of masculine and feminine energy exists in everyone, and our human experience revolves around how we manage it.

- Energy that is not maintained or managed mindfully tends toward disintegration over time.

- Masculine energy relates to action and the external world while feminine energy relates to emotion and our internal worlds.

- Integrated energy is based in love, lifting us "above sea level." Disintegrated energy is based in fear and pulls us "below sea level" toward life's rock-bottom moments.

- Both integrated and disintegrated masculine and feminine energies have their pros and cons. The key to mastering our energies is to integrate them effectively.

- Peak integration is our optimal human state where being and doing become one.

- People who feel most comfortable in their masculine energy are known as *core masculines*, while *core feminines* feel at home in their feminine energy.

- Integration allows our energy to flow freely through our Emotion-Belief-Choice-Pursuit (E-B-C-P) pipeline. When disintegration occurs, we find fractures in one or more of those connections.

Reflections

- Do you consider yourself more aligned with core masculine or core feminine energy?

- How does that influence where you spend most of your time on the energy chart?

CHAPTER 2

Conceptualizing the Feminine and Masculine

"You, man, should not seek the feminine in women, but seek and recognize it in yourself, as you possess it from the beginning. . . . You, woman, should not seek the masculine in men, but assume the masculine in yourself, since you possess it from the beginning."

—CARL JUNG, *THE RED BOOK: LIBER NOVUS*

Let's address the elephant in the room: A part of you is still thinking about this in terms of biological sex. You hear *masculine* and *feminine*, and your brain links those concepts to men and women. You may also find it hard to access either your masculine or feminine side, or you may deny that both energies exist within you at all. I often meet resistance to this concept when I introduce it to people for the first time. Often, feminine energy in men is linked with weakness while masculine energy in women is viewed as unattractive, evil, or intimidating. We're shown in all manner of ways from the moment we're born that only certain forms of expression are acceptable for our sex. The truth is that both energies are intrinsic to our being, and we must master them in order to live an authentic, fulfilled life.

This is not to say our biological sex has no impact on our energy or experience. We can observe that most core masculine individuals are male while most core feminine individuals are female. These trends stem not just from how we're socialized as we grow; they are instinctual, reflecting deep roots in the natural world. We can liken the concept of masculine and feminine energy to the cocktail of hormones driving our reproduction. All human bodies need a mix of estrogen and testosterone to function, but most healthy female and male bodies have far more of one than the other. This largely influences the "nature" factor of where we fall on the chart at any given time. The "nurture" factor comes into play as we gain life experience and interact with external energies, such as those of other people. Our environment and experiences can go a long way in pushing us toward a masculine or feminine core in different areas of life.

These concepts only become oppressive when we deny the full spectrum of these hard and soft, hot and cold, passive and active energies to everyone. The discrimination, gaslighting, and violence experienced by gender-nonconforming men and women has served as one of the most consistent sources of suffering throughout history. Outdated paradigms that seek to pigeonhole men and women into self-limiting boxes are no longer needed for our survival as a species, if indeed they ever were.

The intention of this book is to examine the energetic duality present in all things, not to reinforce sex-based stereotypes or make dogmatic proclamations about male and female behaviors. We all operate along spectrums of energy spanning polar yet symbiotic states, subject to the rhythms of night and day and the impacts of peace and conflict. Without the dark, we can have no light. Without hate, love has no value. I prefer to view these dynamics through the lens of humanity, as concepts are easier to absorb and process when we personalize them for ourselves.

As human beings, we see and feel this polarization embodied in the form of the masculine and feminine. In this chapter, we'll examine the presence of this duality in nature, religion, psychology, and other areas of life. We'll also talk about how masculine and feminine dynamics have influenced the course of history and where we find ourselves today.

The Feminine Within Men, the Masculine Within Women

I want to speak directly to any men reading this who have a hard time coming to terms with their feminine side. You've probably been taught to see that deep, vulnerable, emotional part of yourself as shameful. We're told that in order to survive this world, we must suppress and hide everything about us that could be viewed as soft, sensitive, or weak. I've been there. For most of my life, until I went to therapy in my thirties, I was too lost to face my deepest emotions. I couldn't let myself examine the *why* behind my actions because I feared what I found there might break me. My ego simply couldn't handle it until I hit a rock-bottom moment in my personal life that resulted in the dissolution of several close relationships.

Long term, neglecting the feminine within puts us men on a one-way path toward self-destruction. Our external world will always mirror what's happening within us. What you see around you is the direct result of the combination of fears, desires, and strategies that brought you to this point. The true key to surviving this world, then, is to become conscious of the *why* underlying our actions and heal the wounded emotions behind our disintegrated behavior.

How do you view the relationship between your actions and intentions? How efficient are you at accomplishing what you want to accomplish each day? For most core masculines, disintegrated behavior results from emotions we're often not even aware of, keeping the true nature of our problems hidden from our consciousness. Take the example of an alcoholic who can't stop drinking. Nothing apart from an external stimulus can stop a person in such a state from pursuing their addiction. Once their rock-bottom moment comes and they decide to get help, they may enter a program like Alcoholics Anonymous and discover there that their issue didn't stem from alcohol at all.

In the 12 steps to recovery, it's all internal work until the addict reaches out to make amends with those they've hurt in the past. The first 8 steps focus entirely on healing the disintegrated feminine through journaling, self-reflection, and spiritual surrender.

This journey of healing the feminine is a process we must all go through at various points in our lives. The only way to rise above sea level toward integration is by going within to examine the unseen.

While masculine energy within women is often labeled unattractive or negative, it is necessary for survival. All women must make choices in order to make their way in the world, just as men do. Those with a high degree of agency are viewed by some as too tough or even aggressive, but there's nothing combative about taking action with autonomy. It is built into our experience as free human beings. It's optimal for women to stand in the integrated version of their masculine energy without shame, able to make clear choices without having to depend on others.

Reframing the Feminine

If you're a core feminine reading this, you may hesitate to label certain traits or behaviors as "feminine" or "masculine." While I'm a core masculine myself, my conversations with core feminines have revealed their struggles in relation to how the feminine is viewed by society. They shared that they're sick of being equated with weakness and told their masculine aspects should be disowned or suppressed. They've been pressured to make themselves smaller or disappear altogether to appease domineering expressions of masculinity. They've been judged as off-putting or unattractive for leaning into their masculine energy, but leaning into their feminine energy got them branded as silly, pathetic, or overly sensitive at times too. I want to offer a perspective of feminine energy that surpasses these limiting stereotypes.

The Wheel of Emotions[1] is a model created by psychologist Robert Plutchik that offers a logical way to make sense of our feelings. It

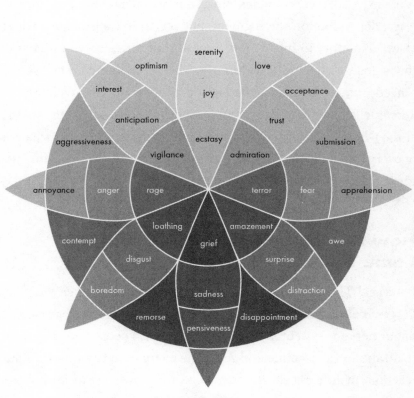

The Wheel of Emotions

displays[2] our eight basic emotions at the core of a flowerlike structure—ecstasy, admiration, terror, amazement, grief, loathing, rage,
and vigilance—organized in relation to their opposites. The vertical
dimensions of the "petals" of the flower show additional emotions that
stem from the eight basic ones, which lessen in intensity the further
out one goes. Between each petal are "combination emotions" we
experience when our core emotions blend. Contempt, for instance,
is a combination of rage and loathing, while love is a combination of
ecstasy and admiration. If left unchecked, the weaker emotions can
intensify into the core emotions at the center of the flower.

The Wheel of Emotions provides a visual representation that can
help us simplify the countless levels of nuance our feminine energy
contains. All of these emotions impact our masculine energy in different
ways, depending on the segment, but certain ones provide a wider
channel to move us into action. Rage, for instance, is a feminine trait
that signals a vital block within us—whether a boundary crossed or
a need unmet—and fuels the energy to confront and overcome it.
Terror tells us we're in danger and can help us seek safety. In looking
at the wheel, it's clear that feminine energy determines the behavior
of every human being; we all experience these feelings while moving
through the world.

How the Feminine and Masculine Come Together

Polyvagal Theory, a framework introduced in 1994 by Dr. Stephen
Porges,[2] connects the emotions behind our behaviors to the responses
of our nervous system. By applying Polyvagal Theory to our conceptualization of masculine and feminine energy, we can link it to our
reactions in different situations. When we perceive that we are safe, we
remain in the green zone at the bottom of the chart: calm, connected,

POLYVAGAL CHART

The nervous system with a neuroception of threat:

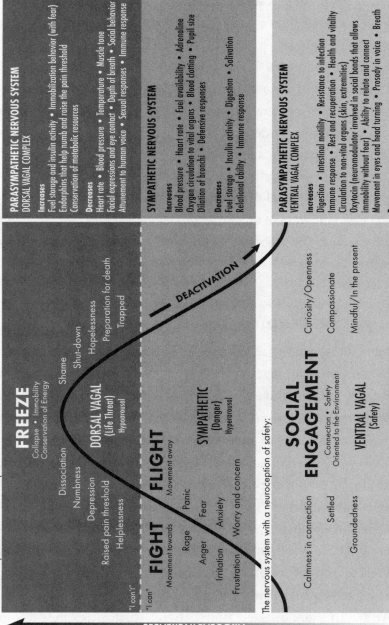

FREEZE
Collapse • Immobility
Conservation of Energy

Dissociation
Shame
Numbness
Shut-down
Depression
Hopelessness
Raised pain threshold
Preparation for death
Helplessness
Trapped

DORSAL VAGAL
(Life Threat)
Hypoarousal

"I can't"

FIGHT
Movement towards

FLIGHT
Movement away

Rage
Anger
Panic
Fear
Irritation
Anxiety
Frustration
Worry and concern

SYMPATHETIC
(Danger)
Hyperarousal

"I can"

The nervous system with a neuroception of safety:

SOCIAL ENGAGEMENT
Connection • Safety
Oriented to the Environment

Calmness in connection
Curiosity/Openness
Settled
Compassionate
Groundedness
Mindful/In the present

VENTRAL VAGAL
(Safety)

DEACTIVATION

AROUSAL INCREASES

PARASYMPATHETIC NERVOUS SYSTEM
DORSAL VAGAL COMPLEX

Increases
Fuel storage and insulin activity • Immobilization behavior (with fear)
Endorphins that help numb and raise the pain threshold
Conservation of metabolic resources

Decreases
Heart rate • Blood pressure • Temperature • Muscle tone
Facial expressions and eye contact • Depth of breath • Social behavior
Attunement to human voice • Sexual responses • Immune response

SYMPATHETIC NERVOUS SYSTEM

Increases
Blood pressure • Heart rate • Fuel availability • Adrenaline
Oxygen circulation to vital organs • Blood clotting • Pupil size
Dilation of bronchi • Defensive responses

Decreases
Fuel storage • Insulin activity • Digestion • Salivation
Relational ability • Immune response

PARASYMPATHETIC NERVOUS SYSTEM
VENTRAL VAGAL COMPLEX

Increases
Digestion • Intestinal motility • Resistance to infection
Immune response • Rest and recuperation • Health and vitality
Circulation to non-vital organs (skin, extremities)
Oxytocin (neuromodulator involved in social bonds that allows
immobility without fear) • Ability to relate and connect
Movement in eyes and head turning • Prosody in voice • Breath

Decreases
Defensive responses

VVC is the beginning and end of stress response.
When VVC is dominant, SNS and DVC are in transient blends which promote healthy physiological functioning

Adapted by Ruby Jo Walker from: Cheryl Sanders, Anthony "Twig" Wheeler, and Steven Porges.

rubyjowalker.com

grounded, open, compassionate, and mindful. When we perceive we're in danger, arousal increases as our nervous system decides how to respond. If we believe we can deal with the threat effectively, we feel rage or terror, leading either to fight or flight. If we believe we can't deal with the threat, we freeze and submit in a state of collapse. Awareness of how we're experiencing safety or danger in relation to Polyvagal Theory can help us understand how our feminine and masculine energies are interacting at any particular moment.

Our polar masculine-feminine energies can be viewed as manifestations of existential divinity. These complementary opposing powers drive the ways of the universe, shaping our environment and everything in it. For proof of this, we need only look out the window at the great outdoors.

Integrated Nature, Disintegrated Society

In nature, the dynamics of masculine-feminine duality are fully integrated and operate in concert. The sun and moon exist independently, offering unique gifts and experiences, yet work together to give life to the energies unfolding on earth. Day and night alternate seamlessly and without resistance to each other. The cool of darkness gives way to the warmth of light. Creation and destruction accompany birth and death, yet nature doesn't go to war with itself over this. Predators kill and consume prey to survive another day. Those same aggressive predators nurture their families with compassion so life as a whole can continue. All are interconnected, and while each individual organism experiences wins and losses, the overall system sustains itself beautifully, returning to relative balance after imbalance occurs.

We see far more disintegration between dualistic expressions in society than we do in the natural world. Ego and power struggles open the pathway for disconnection to ensue. At home, the pillars of

Mom and Dad are frequently at odds, oscillating between love and their individual fears. I remember my dad telling me in anger, "You're just like your mother when you act like that," beating it into me that being compared to Mom was always a bad thing and passing down his disintegrated ideas about women.

In government, we watch Democrats and Republicans (the Mom and Dad of politics) squabble like defensive parents fighting at the dinner table. They appeal to our sense of morality, telling us we must join their side not only by voting against those on the opposing side but by hating them outright as well. We are *good*, they say, and those *other* people are *evil*. Wealth and poverty tear the masses apart, pitting us all against one another in a war for social control. Our public successes and failures define our legacy in the eyes of others, leading the world at large to get the impression we either "have our shit together" or not. We are all caught in the middle of these dueling forces, steadfastly carving out paths of our own, walking the tightrope between living to please ourselves and living to please others.

To reach peak integration is to live like the moon and sun in a divinely powerful state of seemingly effortless balance, able to move smoothly between energetic polarities, making the most of everything available to us. We all inherit society's dualistic conflicts in life, but we ourselves are direct descendants of oneness. The expansiveness of uniting the masculine and feminine is what has brought us this far in history. The same unity will be required of our species in the future if we're to survive.

The Feminine and Masculine in Intimacy

The complementary energies of the masculine and feminine are felt most acutely in the areas of love and sexuality. This is the case in both hetero and homosexual relationships, as even same-sex couples need a core masculine and core feminine dynamic to survive long term. Our differences—the energetic space between us—draw us together like magnets with opposing charges, while too much energetic similarity dulls our interest. This theory aligns with the evolutionary theory that we seek trait variety while looking for someone to pair-bond with (a.k.a. dating); we're attracted to people who possess traits we suppress but admire within ourselves. This is because we seek to attach to those who make us feel safe and meet needs that have gone unmet thus far, both by others and ourselves. By uniting with them and reaping the benefits of their unique gifts, we not only boost our chances of survival but also quiet the inner voice that tells us something is lacking (like assertiveness or emotional nourishment) when we're on our own. Together as one, we can finally feel whole.

Many modern yogis, energy healers, and self-development gurus like Tony Robbins teach that opposing masculine and feminine polarity is responsible for creating the "spark" of sexual passion in relationships. The deeper the difference in energy, the stronger the attraction will be. In the same way that we can't know light without darkness or love without hate, we can't see our core end of the energetic spectrum with clarity without the contrast of our polar opposite personified. By way of their presence, our own unique powers and traits are magnified, allowing us to learn about ourselves and evolve toward greater integration. Our lovers, whether our relationships endure the test of time or not, unwittingly end up serving as our best spiritual teachers. They are the mirrors that reflect the quality of the energy we're putting into the world. Disintegration repels those we're close with long term. Integration inspires trust, emotional safety, and a desire to stay.

While core masculines and feminines want similar things in life, they tend to focus on different priorities. Core feminines crave affection, attention, and understanding, all of which lend themselves to feelings of internal safety. They want to be seen and cherished. A core masculine's experience of safety is more often externally validated by respect from others. They want to accomplish feats that garner them praise as proof of their worthiness. This was the case for my father, Dexter, for whom respect was everything. His martial arts background gave him a hardened exterior that made others fear him, though he never explicitly tried to look tough. He just was, and people knew not to mess with him. Fear, respect, and safety were intertwined essentials in his life.

When core masculines and feminines miss out on these experiences in intimacy, their relationships risk depolarization. Core feminines who feel unseen, unheard, or unloved often make up for it with more masculine tendencies. Core masculines who feel disrespected, questioned, or controlled can become indecisive and lose direction. Courage and vulnerability are required on both sides if a couple is to heal its friction and polarize once more.

Duality in Religion and Spirituality

Themes involving duality lie at the heart of ancient religion and spirituality. The Spiritual Law of Correspondence,[3] an ancient esoteric principle derived from Hermetic philosophy, states there is constant resonance between our inner and outer worlds. Our relationships and experiences reflect the state of our mind and spirit. There is always a correspondence between the laws and phenomena of the various "planes" of being and life, the seen and the unseen, which I equate to masculine and feminine energy.

> **"Gender is in everything; everything has its Masculine and Feminine Principles; Gender manifests on all planes."**
>
> **—THE KYBALION**

The Bible echoes this sentiment as the Creator is described as creating men and women in its own likeness, implying we are all energetically polar expressions of the Divine itself.

> **"And God said, Let us make man in our image, after our likeness: and let them have dominion over the fish of the sea, and over the fowl of the air, and over the cattle, and over all the earth, and over every creeping thing that creepeth upon the earth. So God created man in his own image, in the image of God created he him; male and female created he them."**
>
> **—GENESIS 1:26–27 (KJV)**

When it comes to our personal lives, we can harness the Law of Correspondence while working to manifest whatever it is we seek. Our everyday lives demand that we constantly work through the process described in this book: balancing the health of our internal and external worlds in order to get what we truly want. Spiritual practitioners accomplish this by creating an intimate relationship with the Divine so their feminine energy can receive its wisdom as visions, ideas, and intuition. They then move into their masculine energy to bring that wisdom to life on the physical plane. You might feel called to start a business, for instance, daydream about it constantly, and then move into the state of action needed to make it a reality once your inner world is ready. Manifestation is not magic. Anyone can master alchemy provided they're willing to get honest about the quality of their energy. What we emit, we will receive.

The external world does not mirror our higher self or the self-image we believe represents who we truly are. Instead, it mirrors *everything* within us, including our emotional wounds, limiting beliefs, and fearful assumptions. If you're confused about what you're looking for, you'll create and experience confusion during your search. If you feel chaos within yourself, you'll find yourself surrounded by it over time. Understanding this allows us to clearly see the positive and negative effects of our thoughts and emotions on the world around us. By mastering how we use our energy, in turn making integrated choices, we empower ourselves to resolve personal paradoxes.

Ancient Chinese philosophers also formed their discussions around the existence of reciprocal, interconnected forces. In Chinese cosmology, the universe is believed to arise from a primordial energy that then organizes itself into two complementary forces: yin—the feminine, receptive principle; and yang—the active masculine. These dual principles manifest in various cycles and natural processes, such as the contrasting rhythms of winter and summer, or the interplay between harmony and disruption in the world around us, and the chemistry between core masculines and core feminines. If you look at the yin and yang symbols, each side contains a small part of the other. Amid the light, yang, masculine side is a black dot of yin. Within the dark, feminine, yin side is a dot of yang. This signifies the presence of both within us, regardless of which core energy draws us more. The term *tai chi* refers to what I call "peak integration" in this book, a transcendent state of infinite potential created by the unification of masculine and feminine forces. The universe, itself existing as oneness, desires oneness between its energetic yin-yang creations. Taoist practitioners strive to achieve this oneness with the universe throughout life, knowing that an appropriate balance of yin and yang is needed in all things.

In Tantric traditions, yin and yang are represented by Shiva, the Hindu god of destruction, and Shakti, the goddess of divine feminine power. In oriental art, these deities are often portrayed embracing each other in unbridled affection. Shiva and Shakti are said to exist in our bodies as well, calling all Hindu worshippers to worship the masculine and the feminine in one another. This intimate worship is not meant to justify the mistake of placing one another on a sacred pedestal. Instead, an element of surrender is involved, embodied as an opening of the chest and expelling of suspicion. Tantric practitioners focus on breathwork and rituals of embodying energetic connection not only to boost their sexual passion, but also to expand their consciousness by experiencing the unity of the masculine and feminine in all aspects.

Western religions like Christianity rely on more moralistic concerns than on the kind of conversations surrounding our internal and external realities found in Eastern religions. The dual concepts of good and evil underlie discussions of sin and salvation, which determine whether believers are destined for Heaven or Hell. God and the Devil are said to influence our thoughts, feelings, and actions at all times, exposing us to the whims of external forces of control. Unlike polytheistic religions that represent the masculine and feminine through reverence for both gods and goddesses, the Christian God offers us one all-powerful male figure. The feminine, by contrast, appears in Christianity trapped in its own expressions of duality—the virgin and the whore, for instance.

Oppressive religious movements have long used sex-based stereotypes to justify harm, particularly against women and gender-nonconforming men. We now find ourselves in a place where, spiritually speaking, we feel lost in relation to those stereotypes because they seem not to reflect who any of us truly are. Getting back to our roots as complementary, equally powerful forces of nature is crucial if we're to feel at home in our world and live in harmony with our individual purpose. Again, without proper reverence for the feminine, the frequency of the spiritual realm, the masculine will always feel lost, confused, and lacking in purpose.

The Masculine and the Feminine in Psychiatry

Carl Jung, the twentieth-century Swiss psychiatrist and founder of analytical psychology, introduced the concepts of the anima and animus. These words describe the subconscious feminine side of a man and the subconscious masculine side of a woman, respectively. According to Jung, these elements combine to form the archetype of the Self and influence our perceptions of and attitudes toward the opposite sex. He theorized that constant exposure to members of the opposite sex fosters an inherent understanding of each other. However, Jung noted that men often repress their sensitivity, making the anima one of the most significant and challenging human complexes. This repression can lead men to project disdain for their own feminine side onto the women around them. Similarly, women may project their disdain for their own masculine side onto the men in their lives. Jung urged individuals to carefully discern between the anima or animus within and the real men and women around them. This suggests that, upon deeper reflection, both men and women may discover that their disdain is a projection of unresolved tensions within their own internal feminine or masculine composition.

Jung represented the human psyche through the concept of the Self, which he believed consisted of the conscious mind, the unconscious mind, and the ego. From birth, the Self is whole, but with our development, a separate ego-consciousness crystalizes. This process of ego differentiation often determines the first half of our lives. Once it has been achieved and we're anchored in the external world, a new task arises as we enter the second half of our lives—a return to, and rediscovery of, our original Self. Jung referred to this return as "individuation," which occurs once the ego reaches an impasse of some sort.

**"The actual processes of individuation—the
conscious coming-to-terms with one's own
inner center (psychic nucleus) or Self—generally
begins with a wounding of the personality."**

**—JUNGIAN PSYCHOLOGIST MARIE-
LOUISE VON FRANZ**[4]

Individuation begins when the ego embarks on a journey to align with the Self, the inner guide that orchestrates our psychological growth.[5] Along the way, the ego encounters archetypes that represent key aspects of the psyche, gradually revealing a fuller picture of who we are. The first archetype to emerge is the shadow, a mirror of our unconscious mind that holds the traits and emotions we've suppressed or denied. As the process continues, the ego engages with the anima or animus, archetypes that reflect our inner feminine and masculine energies and help bridge the divide between the ego and the Self. Finally, the *mana* figure—often portrayed as a wise old man or woman—appears, symbolizing the collective unconscious and its vast reservoir of wisdom, drawing the ego closer to a state of inner wholeness.

The archetype of the Self is the final destination on the path of individuation. Jung claimed at that point "the Self embraces ego-consciousness, shadow, anima/animus, and collective unconscious in indeterminable extension. As a totality, the Self is a *coincidentia oppositorum*; it is therefore bright and dark and yet neither."[6]

In the same way that Jung's individuation process hinges on the blending of light and shadow, living above sea level requires us to integrate all parts of our authentic self, including those we've blocked out or would rather not identify with. Until we can get to know and love our true self once more, our ego will demand that we wear a mask so we can feel accepted by the external world. As you continue to read this book, I invite you to shine the light of your consciousness on the aspects of yourself currently hidden in the dark. For the integrated feminine and masculine to work in concert, you will need awareness of your disintegrated fragments. To self-reflect in this way can feel terrifying, but it puts you on the path to personal freedom.

You Don't Have to Choose Between Polarities

We perceive the Self within us as one coherent entity, but this is an illusion created by the mind. The "us" we know is composed of fragmented yet interconnected pieces of largely subconscious programming. Our memories and self-perception are inaccurate. We often don't know what we truly feel or need. Our personality can fall apart in a single moment of trauma. We change our minds all the time. The Self is an integrated system of body, mind, and spirit continuously impacted by internal and external energies. The fact that we're such complex beings can be difficult to conceptualize and accept. We feel shame over the vulnerability that results from our inconsistent feelings and ideas, afraid we'll be branded hypocrites or incapable. You might worry if, for instance, you find yourself feeling introverted in certain situations and extroverted in others. You might think you're bad for wanting to be in your feminine energy at home when you spend the majority of your time in your masculine energy elsewhere. In truth, nobody is ever one thing all the time—and that's okay. In fact, it's advantageous. To integrate all parts of ourselves empowers us to utilize the full potential of our energies in order to meet the present moment from an optimal place.

Building integrity isn't about playing it safe by jumping into the "right" boxes. Life's not about to let you get away with that.

Masculine or feminine.

Liberal or conservative.

Healthy or toxic.

Successful or failing.

Happy or sad.

Mean or kind.

Generous or selfish.

Fortunate or cursed.

Creating an identity around any of these labels, despite protestations from your intuitive feminine, will also likely lead to friction, disappointment, and cognitive dissonance. The prospect of integration, leading to greater energetic unity and overall connectedness, goes against the nature of the disintegrated masculine forces dominating our world today. They won't give up without a fight, but we can all choose to resist their brainwashing and ignore their attempts to make us follow their way. It is our birthright to navigate the energies of duality as we see fit. Be the night and day at once. Be the moon and sun.

"If any human being is to reach full maturity, both the masculine and feminine sides of the personality must be brought up into consciousness."

—M. ESTHER HARDING[7]

To sum up: pigeonholing yourself on either end of the spectrum of the masculine and feminine will cause you to wall off an integral part of yourself. You'll never be able to tap into your true purpose or potential when you prohibit yourself from operating in an expansive mindset that makes use of all your personal power. Releasing dogmatism toward your own energy will provide you with a wider perspective of your vision (the feminine), your actions (the masculine), and the internal relationship between the two.

In this chapter, we talked about how we can reframe our conceptualization of masculine and feminine energy in ways that align more closely with its original roots. As I've stated, our society is currently undergoing a period of growing disintegration driven by disintegrated forces. Next, we'll examine evidence of that disconnection and different aspects of what's at stake if we don't turn things around soon.

Key Takeaways

- Examining masculine and feminine energy isn't about reinforcing sex-based stereotypes. Rather, it's about studying the energetic duality present in all things.

- Core masculines and core feminines are taught by society that certain energies are off-limits. Integration requires us to harness all energies available to us.

- The natural world exists in a harmonic state of integration, while human society struggles with worsening disintegration between energetic forces.

- It's said that energetic polarity between core masculines and core feminines drives attraction and chemistry within relationships.

- Duality lies at the heart of spirituality, most religions, and our collective moral codes. Most faith-based practices honor the feminine and masculine as divine creative forces.

- Psychologists like Carl Jung have studied masculine and feminine energy via archetypes that live in the minds of all people and collective societies.

- According to Carl Jung, integration leads to individuation, which allows us to come home to the Self.

- We do not have to choose between polarities. To experience peak integration more often, we must learn to embrace, honor, and master all parts of ourselves.

Reflections

- How have societal expectations about masculine and feminine energy impacted your personal experience?
- How does this relate to your views on energetic duality?

CHAPTER 3

Societal Expressions of Disintegration

"Where there is no vision, there is division."

—MICHAEL BERNARD BECKWITH

Feminine and masculine dynamics have been playing out since the dawn of time, woven throughout history at micro and macro levels. Everywhere we come together—in families, schools, communities, churches, workplaces, and areas of commerce across generations—these polar yet complementary energies tell the ongoing story of the duality of life. We can think of the classical era of ancient Greece as a period of peak integration in which democracy, philosophy, math, drama, architecture, and overall innovation flourished. The masculine and feminine were united in society, to the benefit of humankind. Humanity has been through countless rock-bottom periods as well, including the Middle Ages, where the Plague brought untold loss and destruction. As in all things, the universe seeks to restore balance and equilibrium.

In the United States, the past century has been characterized by examples of these dynamics and their influence on society. For a clear sense of the impact of our masculine and feminine energies, we can apply these events to the energy chart introduced in the first chapter. The integrated feminine manifests as an expansive sense of freedom, opening of our inner worlds, and the uninhibited expression of personal choice.

The first walk on the moon, the end of segregation, the sexual revolution, and the proliferation of the internet all filled society with feelings of infinite possibility. Events driven by the integrated masculine centered on creating more freedom of choice, efficiency, and opportunity for the masses in the external world. The civil rights movement and the passing of *Roe v. Wade* expanded our freedoms in society. Events driven by the disintegrated feminine, like the Great Depression and the COVID-19 pandemic, put the masses in fear for their survival and create persistent feelings of existential dread. The disintegrated masculine, by contrast, drives events characterized by systematic control, restriction, and limitation. This includes World War II, the war on drugs, and the creation of the Jim Crow laws in the late nineteenth century.

As history unfolds, the collective moves toward greater efficiency and ease due to advancements in technology and invention. Much of what we consider disintegration today would likely seem like integration to our grandparents. Not having access to things like working plumbing, antibiotics, birth control, or the internet leads to differences in goals and expectations. These generational shifts in perception are relative, but the emotions and actions involved are identical across time. The disintegrated feminine and masculine have always behaved as they do.

Although the collective moves toward greater capacity for freedom, choice, and opportunity as the years pass, capable of accessing an increasingly better quality of life, we are more disconnected from one another than ever before. Various surveys have shown feelings of loneliness to be on the rise globally.[1] Disintegration pervades modern society, jumping out at us from all sides, echoing louder throughout the zeitgeist as time goes by. It can feel nearly impossible to escape the chaos and destructive pressure of the influences striving to pull us below sea level, driving wedges between us and thereby drowning us in our own emotional disempowerment.

People these days are choosing disintegration in response to our individual and collective trauma despite our deep desire for connection and emotional intimacy. In this chapter, we'll take a broad look at how disintegration between our masculine and feminine energies is showing up prominently in today's America.

Disintegration in Music

Music has always had a powerful influence on my personal life. My dad worked as a bodyguard at Death Row Records and was an avid Prince fan, drawn to the oversexualized style Prince boasted in his earlier years. Wanting to get closer to Dad, I was drawn to his interests and soon fell in love with Prince's hard jazz era. When Dad gave me a hard time as I rode next to him on car rides, music would fill the silence, soothing my deep feelings as I processed how I was being treated as a kid. To this day, I go on long drives when I seek solace and the healing power of my favorite records.

Mom had music in her blood as well, with a cousin who once worked as president of Motown Records and manager of acts such as Marvin Gaye and Lionel Richie. There was always something playing at our house, teaching me about the world. I learned about topics like love and racism through music—things they never mentioned at my school.

The entertainment industry is geared toward teenagers and held my attention during my adolescence. When I was in fourth grade,

K-Ci & JoJo released *All My Life,* and I'd belt it out from the depths of my soul, indulging in my infatuation with my first crush. Most '90s R&B embodied a spirit of pure, unbridled devotion. This echoed the influence of twentieth-century artists like Stevie Wonder and Michael Jackson, symbols of Black joy who called for radical love all over the world. Their music aimed to boost the vibe above sea level. Artists like Curtis Mayfield and Prince explored all four quadrants of the energy chart in their work, employing their full spectrum of masculine and feminine energy.

As I grew older and started going through puberty, the mainstream music on the radio seemed to become more and more driven by the disintegrated masculine. Artists like Nas and Tupac were eclipsed by Eminem and 50 Cent. The softness of Jill Scott and Erykah Badu, which brought balance to the airwaves during the gangster era of Snoop and Dr. Dre, received less focus. Record companies homed in on algorithms and proven formulas for catching the interest of the greatest number of listeners. The explorative experience of music was hammered into hyper-structured equations of *verse/hook/verse/hook/bridge/chorus.* Songs longer than five minutes became rare, leaving eight-minute tracks from bands like Funkadelic or Led Zeppelin in the past. The labels wanted bite-sized bits of, as quoted by Dr. Cornel West in his speech at Edward Waters University of Jacksonville, "G-string music."

I've never been against sexual expression or the raw power of disintegrated masculine energy in entertainment, but the imbalance I've perceived brings with it a feeling of soullessness. I see videos of people twerking with their asses out in Walmart and can't help but think there's a direct thread leading back to what's being pushed by labels these days. In the 1980s, conspiracy theories spread about the crack cocaine epidemic that had begun plaguing communities of color in LA, linking the power of the cartels trafficking the drug with the CIA.[2] The government was working from behind the scenes to keep us down, people said. Today, the same whispers permeate the music industry, alleging certain artists are uplifted above others to dumb the population down and keep us materialistic. I have to wonder.

Your experience with modern music may differ, but have you noticed we don't hear about love, unity, or fighting the powers that oppress us as often these days? Do you feel instead like your attention is being drawn to violence, drugs, clubbing, the gangster life, or calls for exploitation? Powerful, uplifting artists who integrate their masculine and feminine traits are certainly out there, like Kendrick Lamar, Taylor Swift, Anderson .Paak, and Cleo Sol, but positivity is not where bread gets buttered by the industry gatekeepers of popular music anymore. There seems to be less space for devotion and sacred expressions of sexuality.

Even some core feminines, abused and taken advantage of for far too long, are being pulled into the corner of the disintegrated masculine under the guise of empowerment. Artists like Cardi B and Coi Leray boast that women can play men and inflict the kind of trauma that wounded them. *We're done being used. Now we will use you.* Hurt people hurt people, and the downward spiral of society continues. None of this is new, of course. Arrogance, control, and dehumanization have existed in music since before Frank Sinatra sang "Luck Be a Lady," ordering his date never to leave his sight. The issue is the imbalance. Frank also sang about love.

As social creatures, we need models for how to show love, be romantic, and value those important to us, especially when we're young. We lack templates for connection, especially when we come from disintegrated families. Life gets dark quickly when we start emulating people who think abuse is acceptable or will lead us to favorable outcomes. At the end of the day, we all want love and acceptance, but we isolate ourselves from those treasured realities when we consume disintegrated content and throw our psyche off balance. There's still room in the music industry for expansive expression, but until we correct this energetic balance throughout the collective, we're less likely to see it as the norm.

Disintegration in Our Algorithms

Algorithms want us predictable, placing us in one box or another so they can hook us with content that resonates emotionally. These algorithms massage our collective cognitive bias for black-and-white thinking, sparking our anger and passion for justice. We find ourselves sucked into rabbit holes of extremism and violence, enraged over stories we heard five minutes ago, unaware of who may be profiting off that rage—financially or otherwise. Even those of us who see ourselves as peaceful, decent people can feel the tug of radicalization at the edges of our fury, coaxing the worst versions of ourselves out into the world. Dehumanization and normalization of hatred endure as primary goals.

Algorithms fueling sites like Pornhub work in the same way, luring softcore users into dark pockets of harder intensity and degradation of the feminine in short order. You can be the most vanilla person in the world and soon find yourself wading into the deep waters of allegedly consensual depictions of rape and torture. The algorithm wants us there feeding the beast, pushing our own limits and those of others through sex acts we weren't even there to search for. When post-nut clarity kicks in, we blink and cringe at the screen staring back at us. Shame then ensues, causing us to doubt ourselves, as if the algorithm knows us better than we know ourselves. *How did I end up here? This is what men are supposed to like, but this isn't who I am . . . or is it?*

The Second Law of Thermodynamics states that all closed systems, such as our internal echo chambers, maximize entropy, tending toward disorder and disintegration. To reverse this tendency requires an input of energy, which is what makes tasks like housekeeping so tiring. When we don't maintain our home or our car, they eventually fall apart. Our minds work in the same way, requiring inner work if we're to stay above sea level. The algorithms we fall into work against us in this way, rooting us so firmly in certain interests or beliefs that we disconnect from our true nature and abandon ourselves. We offer up our souls as sacrifices on the altars of greed, bigotry, and abuse. Anyone who speaks up in protest from outside our bubble of choice is sprayed with prejudice and dismissed. Harmony and peace aren't sensational enough to tickle our fancy when we're treading the waters of disintegration, so we search for dopamine hits rooted in taboo, eschewing the safety of healthy connection.

I was raised in Los Angeles and went to college in San Francisco. Growing up in California's liberal strongholds led me to assume the rest of the world would be just as diverse. Living in Texas and North Dakota showed me how different life could be. In America's redder states, I found people's judgment stemmed from lack of exposure to people like me, just as my judgment was due to my lack of exposure to them. When I sat down in conversations with those people, we were eventually able to appreciate one another's views. This desire to connect with those with differing views and backgrounds seems to be rapidly slipping away from us in recent years. As social media has come to command more of our attention, we've become isolated in rigid, narrow bubbles of belief programmed by algorithms that urge us to judge and condemn those we don't align with. They are *evil*, we're told, and must therefore either be avoided or destroyed.

There is potential for algorithms to feed our integration by addicting us to sources of stimulation that feed our light rather than our shadow. What we're seeing in social media is far from organic. There's a concerted effort to keep us trapped in the lower realms of emotion where we're easy to hook and control.

Disintegration in Politics

Our dueling political parties demand that we hate, judge, and criticize those who oppose our stance. Flexibility of belief or attempts to "reach across the aisle" are ridiculed and chastised. It feels like there's no place left for the truly engaged, educated citizen who craves new knowledge and a blend of each side of the spectrum. The voices of those in the middle are drowned out by the loudest people at both ends of the spectrum. We feel that to fit in somewhere, we must take on a dogmatic worldview and accompanying set of beliefs that may not have anything to do with how we feel as individuals. Here again, we struggle to see ourselves. *This isn't me.*

Objectively speaking, value exists in both progressivism and conservatism. Evolution is served optimally when we adapt in the present for the sake of a better future based on what's worked well in the past. Tradition and change both have their place in our lives, but our echo chambers prevent us from attempting to unite them in harmony. The universe seeks balance, as do the hearts of the people, but we are trained to embrace and create polarity through a political climate of fear, scarcity, and shame.

Skepticism is crucial if we're to develop an educated, well-rounded understanding of politics. These days, most of us fall prey to the whims of The Algorithm, trusting its sources without question and suspending our own need for further investigation. We read the headline but tell our brain we've read the whole article. We rile ourselves and others up over a superficial understanding of issues we've never taken the time to consider from other angles. The pervasive lack of trust in our media and political institutions imbues us with a sense that no one quite knows what's true anymore anyway. Forming a well-educated opinion doesn't matter to us as much as our desire to *feel* like we're in the know. The Dunning-Kruger Effect—a cognitive bias that prevents us from realizing how little we know about something—plays out in our minds as we speak like experts about topics we lack any deep knowledge about. Yet we judge, argue, and block one another over these things all the same, insisting we have the answers.

It wasn't long ago that Americans were able to agree on fundamental facts and values. Republicans and Democrats alike could agree that Nixon had broken the law after the Watergate scandal came to light. The intensifying polarization ripping apart modern society is keeping us from getting things done together. Disintegration in politics leads to disintegration in families as we struggle to make ends meet, buy homes, or have kids. We have fewer in-person conversations about the things that matter, making us feel isolated and less willing to talk about potentially triggering ideas.

The pendulum can swing the other way, however, when we hear others lash out in ways we wish we could. We may go mask-off on social media to vent our frustrations in similar ways, but we fail to find true interconnectivity there. Fostering social integration requires us to master the art of speaking our truth while respecting those who oppose us.

Our two-party system offers a sturdy foundation for fruitful democracy in America, provided we're willing to hear one another out and work together through the hard conversations. Until we learn to work together to find common ground, we will remain at war with one another, yelling too loudly to listen.

Disintegration in Dating

With the rise in app-based dating, hookup culture has overshadowed our cultural traditions around courting. Our need for intimate connection is commodified by apps like Tinder that urge us to forge fast-food closeness with strangers. We are judged, accepted, and rejected based on first impressions of profiles that can never fully encompass who we are, leading to feelings of powerlessness. To approach people who interest us in the wild feels increasingly intrusive, as we've grown used to controlling our bubbles and the energy we expose ourselves to. The illusion of abundance around hookup culture makes us feel like we're shopping rather than building relationships. Entitlement ensues. Boundaries are crossed. People are used, discarded, and traumatized in their quest for the enduring spark of magic we all seek in our hearts. In response, many people have reportedly given up on dating entirely.

Broadly speaking, men and women across the globe are choosing to stay single in greater numbers. Governments increasingly concerned about plummeting birth and marriage rates offer tax cuts to parents and couples who tie the knot but have thus far failed to enact effective solutions. We can all agree economic factors contribute to this problem, with individuals struggling in the midst of rising inflation to support themselves, let alone a whole family. But truly confronting these trends will require societies to acknowledge the elephant in the room: The power imbalance between the masculine and feminine has been laid bare in modern times for all to see clearly, and swaths of women are choosing to opt out of the game rather than risk being abused.

A number of studies have shown that marriage increases the lifespan of husbands but decreases the lifespan of wives.[3] They've also shown while women make up roughly half the workforce in the United States, those who are married still pick up a heavier load when it comes to household chores and caregiving responsibilities.[4] Their husbands, by contrast, continue to pour the same time and attention into their jobs and hobbies that they always have. Throughout the lockdown period of the COVID-19 pandemic, women in the US workforce faced steeper job losses and slower job recovery than men, choosing to sacrifice their careers to care for their children at home while their husbands took less of a hit.[5]

Men haven't yet stepped up to close the gap in domestic or emotional labor to make raising a family easier on women. Paul Dolan, an author and professor of behavioral science at the London School of Economics, cited data in 2019 that showed unmarried, child-free women were the healthiest and happiest subgroup among the adult population. "Married people are happier than other population subgroups, but only when their spouse is in the room when they are asked how happy they are. When the spouse is not present: fucking miserable." He concluded by saying, "If you are a man, you should probably get married; if you are a woman, don't bother."[6]

Sexually speaking, heterosexual women consistently report far lower satisfaction in the bedroom than men. The *orgasm gap*, a term coined to describe the disparity in orgasms between couples, illustrates the fact that heterosexual men orgasm more than 90 percent of the time in their relationships while women only climax 39 to 65 percent of the time, depending on the sexual dynamics of the couple.[7]

When we look at the big picture and see that women are working harder in their relationships but are rewarded with far less pleasure or time for leisure in their lives, it's easy to see why women would pass on marriage and children. Until we learn to approach marriage and parenting in ways that protect and honor the feminine, disintegration in this area is likely to continue.

Disintegration in the Workplace

At its best, capitalism provides society with ample room for a vibrant free market that inspires friendly competition in business. Our masculine-oriented hustle work culture, however, has focused so intently on exploiting the labor force in the name of greed that workers are left with little room to breathe. The quest for profit among investors and those in the C-suite squeezes those on the front lines, demanding that those putting up with bare-minimum compensation sacrifice even more than they already are. CEOs cut benefits while giving themselves raises. HR equips employee computers with spy tech to oversee every click while asking those same employees to give their all. Stable, long-term, well-paid contract positions seem to be increasingly rare. "Gig work" floods the job market now, while recent graduates struggle to piece together cohesive careers. Not able to make ends meet? You clearly need to hustle harder.

The COVID-19 pandemic forced many to stop and reflect on their priorities in life and where they wanted to devote their time. The Great Resignation soon followed as employees were called back to work by employers before they could be given any guarantee of safety from exposure to the virus. Personally speaking, 2020 flipped my approach to my career on its head. I don't stay up answering emails at night or log hours during weekends anymore. Had the pandemic not happened, I might still be working without strong boundaries around my personal time. Looking back, I wonder, *What was I thinking?* My old habits are tinged with the same unpalatable feeling of awakening from a nightmare. *They're working me to the bone, yet I stay. I don't actually want to be doing this.* This again is an area where our fear can end up serving us, inspiring us to let things fall apart when we're feeling called to build something entirely new.

Providing consumers with quality products and services requires mastery of both masculine and feminine energy. Working for another person or organization allows us to insert ourselves into the protective structure of the masculine. We can tap into the feminine energy needed for creation on a consistent basis, but flexibility is needed if we're to be successful. The disintegrated masculine energy of corporate culture and hustle addiction pushes the impression that we humans are machines. Among the labor force, we've all arrived at the conclusion that life should involve more than working tirelessly until we die, particularly as younger generations of Americans realize they may never be able to afford to retire.

As a species, we're in dire need of greater balance and integration in the areas discussed in this chapter. Our future hinges on our ability to reconnect and heal our emotional wounds together. This change must begin with us on the individual level, beckoning us to examine what's currently happening at the deeper levels of our hearts and minds.

Now that we've looked at the big picture of how the masculine-feminine energy construct reflects disintegration in our society, we're going to zoom in on how these dynamics impact specific areas of our individual lives. We'll examine the workings of masculine and feminine energy through the lens of my lived experiences and those of others. Analyzing the disintegration in our personal stories can help us lay the foundation for integration moving forward.

Key Takeaways

- Each period of history is characterized by its energetic dynamics. Collectively, our societies experience prosperous eras of peak integration and rock-bottom times of despair.

- As history unfolds, the collective rises to a better quality of life, but we're currently more disconnected than ever before.

- Disintegration exists in the mainstream music sphere, our online algorithms, our political parties, our dating scenes, and our workplaces.

- The destructive nature of disintegration threatens our survival as a species. Our collective future hinges on our ability to bring balance to the masculine and feminine dynamics driving our world.

Reflections

- Where do you see masculine and feminine energy at play around you in society?

PART II

Disintegration in Our Lives

Before we learn to integrate, we spend much of our journey
below sea level, striving to navigate the waters of disintegration.
Through our experiences in the major areas of
life, we gather energetic knowledge.

Identity Through the Masculine and Feminine Lens

PEAK INTEGRATION: KNOW YOURSELF
SELF-ACCEPTANCE, SELF-WORTH, EMBRACING UNIQUENESS, PERSONAL GROWTH

INTEGRATED FEMININE
LOVE-BASED FEELING

- Accepting of one's uniqueness
- Having pride in oneself
- Feeling self-assurance and confidence
- Maintaining consistency of self; integrity
- Keeping an openness to change and expansion of identity

INTEGRATED MASCULINE
LOVE-BASED ACTION

- Acting with integrity
- Demonstrating self-discipline
- Examining one's inner world
- Shining light on the uncomfortable parts of oneself
- Doing personal work around identity

DISINTEGRATED FEMININE
FEAR-BASED FEELING

- Holding self-hatred, self-pity, or shame over one's appearance or story
- Desiring to be someone else
- Internalizing others' labels or judgments (even if they're untrue)

DISINTEGRATED MASCULINE
FEAR-BASED ACTION

- Attacking, dismissing, or excluding people who are different
- Isolating oneself from others
- Behaving inauthentically to fit in
- Resisting personal growth
- Changing one's appearance to gain acceptance

CHAPTER 4

Identity

"What is your answer to the eternal question, 'Who am I?'
Your answer determines the part you play in the world's
drama. Your answer—that is, your concept of self—need
not conform to the external reality to which it relates."

—NEVILLE GODDARD

In part II of this book, we will be exploring the *why*, the feminine energy that fuels our actions, as it reflects through various lenses. Our *why* in life, commonly referred to as our purpose, is what our identity looks to in order to make sense of itself. When we're born, we subconsciously search for the answers to the *whys*. *Why am I here? Why is all this happening?* The voice of our purpose serves as our invisible guide throughout life, justifying and motivating our decisions. Everything we do in the present moment either brings us closer to or pushes us further from the purpose we seek to fulfill.

During our earliest years, we're primarily in our feminine energy, constantly absorbing information and focusing on our internal experience. We are open-minded, curious, emotionally expressive, intuitively connected, and willing to explore new ideas. As we grow and form relationships with others, we start moving into our masculine energy more often, focusing on the external world and the existing structures that seemingly determine how things work. The experiences we go through during those formative years, along with how we're labeled and judged by society, come together to influence our sense of identity. By developing a big-picture understanding of the factors that contribute to our overall experience of self, we can become conscious of what's been happening for us subconsciously, empowering us to take agency over how we utilize our energy. Our whole lives can change following even slight shifts in perception.

Our experiences in the area of identity culminate to determine our status quo on the energy chart. We all come into existence at sea level with souls yearning for connection. Our energy is then influenced by a series of factors that are out of our control, causing us to rise or fall. Children born into disintegrated environments feel the quality of the energy around them, and their brains begin adapting immediately, searching for coping mechanisms that create some sense of internal stability in the context of external instability. Disintegrated identity constructs hidden in the subconscious are notoriously difficult to unveil. We can accelerate this process by finding alternative ways of looking at ourselves, our thought processes, our behavioral patterns, and the choices we make.

Why are you—*you*, specifically—here in this universe, living the life you're living? What is it you're here to accomplish? How will you know when you're on or off track? Until we discover our answers to those questions for ourselves, balance and harmony elude us. We may find ourselves spiritually adrift, searching for our place in the world, unable to hear our intuition speaking on behalf of our higher self. Our true purpose is not goal-centric; it aligns with the contributions we make to society as we take each step of our journey. To discover and fulfill it can take a lifetime of soul searching and personal work, but it doesn't have to, and the work required to make it happen is worth the effort. With our life's purpose comes a moral code that brings our boundaries into sharp focus. When we're clear about our path, where we're headed, and why it's important, our yeses and nos speak for themselves. Anything not in alignment eventually sees itself out.

From here, we'll be exploring how identity and our *why* intertwine as we grow and what this means for our energy. With an informed understanding of what we need in the area of identity, we can form an integrated template for navigating life.

Identity on the Axis

Let's view our experience of identity through the lens of the masculine and feminine energy chart. In each chapter of part II, we will move clockwise from the bottom-right quadrant (see the Identity table at the beginning of this chapter), starting with the disintegrated masculine. We will then move through the bottom-left, top-left, and top-right quadrants of the chart. This order of movement aligns with the Emotion-Belief-Choice-Pursuit pipeline. To rise from rock-bottom living characterized by disintegrated masculine behavior, we must move into our feminine energy to gain clarity and healing around our emotions and beliefs. We then move back into action, entering our integrated masculine energy, when we're ready to make choices and seek out our pursuits.

We come into existence at sea level—that axis or baseline from the chart, dividing integrated states of being (above it) from disintegrated states (below it). But our environment, experiences, and the labels we're given can cause us to get stuck in a particular quadrant, often below sea level. We solidify our unique perspective in our minds as "the way things are." If we grow up in survival mode, we come to view others as tools for survival, whether consciously or not, and create a defensive, false self through which to express ourselves. This pulls us further and further below the surface, away from authentic connection with ourselves and others. We think we're loving ourselves by feeding the ego until we land at rock bottom and see the extent of our misery.

In the bottom-right quadrant of the disintegrated masculine are examples of fear-based actions people take in relation to their identity. When our ego—the inner voice that defends our self-esteem to protect our sense of self—is fragile or wounded due to past trauma, we attack, dismiss, or exclude people who differ from us in certain ways. We may also isolate ourselves from the world, telling ourselves we're different from everyone else in some way. We may run from the reality of who we are, afraid to get a good look at our shadow, and behave inauthentically to fit in. Patterns of resistance to change or personal growth may keep us stuck, holding us back from where we want to be. We may also mimic other people's templates of beauty to feel comfortable in our own skin, even to the point of plastic surgery. We mislead ourselves when we follow the identity templates of others. Our external expression of self will always mirror the inner universe that only we experience.

In the bottom-left quadrant of the chart, the disintegrated feminine rules us with fear-based feelings about how we perceive our identity. We feel self-hatred or shame over our appearance or our story. We pity ourselves and feel a desire to be someone else, as if we must change to be acceptable or lovable. We accept how others judge us, even if those reflections aren't true. This all fuels the fear-based actions of the disintegrated masculine. The subconscious story we create around our identity makes up who we are in our own eyes. What we tell ourselves internally manifests in our external world. It's an energy we carry with us everywhere we go.

The Stories We Need

To live well, it's essential that we connect with, acknowledge, own, and express our story through a frame that honors our humanity. We don't have to love our story, but to break through the walls that hold us back, we do have to embrace it. Often, the darker parts of our story plant the seeds of the purpose we came here to fulfill. Our purpose is the unique fingerprint of how we bring more love and connection into the world. It is through our feminine energy that we connect with the collective.

When we confront and deal with the fear-based feelings we hold in relation to our identity, we can elevate above sea level into the top-left realm of the integrated feminine. Spiritual work is required for this ascension, as we must start telling ourselves new stories about ourselves. We must all go through this process several times throughout life, adapting as we lose loved ones, move to new cities, or make career changes. When we're willing to do the inner work of healing our emotional pain, we can connect to ourselves so securely that we can be ourselves in any room, whether anyone there likes us or not. We can stop people-pleasing and feel comfortable in our own skin. The energy of the integrated feminine is the good stuff. It's the pride, self-love, and earned confidence we're all chasing whether we know it or not, and it's the hardest energy to get to and maintain.

When we connect to our identity through love-based feelings, we can take love-based action through the energy of the integrated masculine. Here, we act with integrity, behaving in ways that align with the self we project outward to others. We courageously examine our inner world and shine light on the parts of ourselves we're not comfortable with, knowing that we're safe to explore our shadow. With one choice after another, we balance our energy from a place of self-discipline, choosing to remain consistent with our vision of the person we want to be.

> **"It takes more courage to examine the dark corners of your own soul than it does for a soldier to fight on a battlefield."**
>
> **—WILLIAM BUTLER YEATS**

Self-examination is the hardest work we'll ever do in life. We would much rather point fingers at the external world than look with honesty at the part we play. In the area of identity, this approach lays the path toward peak integration. If, as Socrates once said, "the unexamined life is not worth living," then examination of the self holds the greatest potential for enrichment. By exploring and owning our stories, including responsibility for our mistakes, we can return to the essence of who we really are.

Moving into action from the top-left quadrant of the chart can be achieved by following the pipeline of Emotion-Belief-Choice-Pursuit. When you feel yourself, you believe in yourself. When you believe in yourself, you choose yourself, making sure to fill your own cup first so you can fill the cups of others. When you choose yourself, you act in ways that love and honor yourself. This results in an unwavering identity that stems from a love-based place. Secure attachment to our self is the fertile ground for expansion of the soul. Life presents us with countless identities to mirror in exploration of the powerful beings we are at our core. With an integrated identity, we can stop doubling down on what keeps us defensive, knowing that it's okay to be wrong, learn, and grow. By developing awareness around our story, change and accountability become less frightening.

My Story: Dreams of Basketball

From early childhood, my identity revolved around being tall. In elementary school, I was always the tallest kid by about a foot and a half, towering over my peers in the back row of every class picture. Doctors predicted I would end up growing to more than seven feet as an adult. Because of all this, people in my life assured me the NBA was in my future, and I went through childhood believing my purpose had been decided by fate. "Remember me when you get into the NBA!" Everyone, from my family to teachers to strangers at the grocery store, treated me like a future basketball star. I accepted this vision as my destiny without question, feeling on some level like I might not even have to work hard for it. By middle school, I was already better than everyone else without having to try like they did, and I had no reason to believe that would change.

Still nationally ranked and the tallest in my class, I joined a champion varsity high school team, playing alongside Jordan Farmar, who would later gain fame with the Lakers. Crowds came to watch him play, but soon they started noticing me too—freshman starters on the varsity team were a rarity. When Jordan moved on, more eyes were on me, and the pressure kicked up a notch. It would be "my" team from then on, or so I thought.

My identity around basketball played a significant role in my relationship with my dad. In his eyes, my success or failure was a reflection of his own. While he valued willpower, he, like me, lacked self-discipline, which shaped his path in adulthood. He earned a reputation for his resilience, never tapping out during MMA sparring sessions. To challenge himself, he'd deliberately start in tough situations, like being trapped in a chokehold, only to flip the script and make his opponent submit. In his professional kickboxing career, he faced Billy Blanks of Tae Bo fame three times, defeating him every time. Yet, despite his skill, his failure to stay disciplined and fully committed kept him from reaching his true potential.

Like many people of exceptional intelligence, he struggled with the volatility of mental illness, and this kept him from getting out of his own way. It bothered him to see the same patterns developing in me. I was quick to quit or give up in the face of challenges, which drove him to try to toughen me up by being hard on me when we practiced together on the court. Like him, I was distracted by women—and he could see it. He wanted to drill into me a work ethic he had never been able to model due to his own lack of boundaries. There were also moments, however, when he would soften up and get vulnerable with me. "You don't need all this, Pierce. I know you'll do great things even if basketball doesn't work out. I'm not worried about you." Those blips of kindness meant the world to me every time.

Basketball players with my projected height trained differently back then. If you were destined to be seven feet or above, you trained to play the center position like Shaq. However, I stopped growing at six feet, five inches and was unable to keep my game up to par as teams transitioned away from assigning traditional positions to players. Following my freshman year in high school, someone told me if I wanted to play Division 1 basketball, I'd need to change my game; I would no longer be able to solely play center. So I switched up my practice to more of a guard's game, focusing on ball handling drills. The only problem was that I lacked the foresight to practice against defenders. I practiced alone during the off season, scoring consistently, but the skills I picked up didn't translate into games with real opponents. When I came back for my sophomore season, I took the first shot of my first game and airballed. I took my second shot and airballed again. After airballing for a third time, I lost all confidence and stopped shooting.

The year ended up being a disaster. My game never improved, and as people lost hope in my skills, my dad started leaving my games early. While playing, I'd be distracted, glancing up into the stands to see whether he was still there. My game was good enough if he stayed, but not on the days when he left, and my identity as the tall kid destined for the NBA abruptly dissipated. At a loss, I found myself questioning my worth. I had made choices around basketball for so many years, but it wasn't the destiny I was made for. The question of who I actually was at my core, untouched by the opinions of others, came to the forefront of my attention.

In spite of my losses, I value those early years and the experiences they provided, all of which informed the basis of who I am today. Discovering my true identity required me to unlearn much of what I'd been taught about myself. When disintegration ruled my world, I was a different person in every room, changing how I expressed myself based on whom I was talking to. To feel comfortable being my true self in every room, I had to learn to remove the layers that weren't me while keeping the good stuff I'd picked up along the way. Forming a clear idea of what that looked like was integral to finding my way there.

We often know exactly what we *don't* want in life, but when it comes to what we *do* want and the details of that vision, we're hazy on the specifics. Finding our unique expression of integration takes time, experience, and for some of us, a fuck-ton of inner healing.

Aspects of Identity We Can't Control

My identity came to revolve around being Black, though it took time for me to connect with that aspect of myself. I went to a Southern Baptist school as a kid, and while the student body was diverse, race was never a topic in the curriculum. By eighth grade, I was nationally ranked in basketball and was sent to different areas to play. As a middle-class kid from the burbs, this was my first exposure to inner-city culture. The kids there who looked like me spoke and lived differently, which came with a sense of tension that eased over time as they got to know me. I didn't quite feel comfortable hanging out with the Black kids or the White kids, but I tried to get along with everyone equally. I started becoming resentful of the fact that I had never learned about

Black history growing up, particularly as I started experiencing racism while traveling the country. Topics I had heard of in Prince's music and read about in relation to figures like Malcolm X suddenly felt more relevant to my life.

Much of the pain we experience in relation to our identity stems from oppression aimed at traits we cannot control. We don't choose our hair, skin, or eye color. We don't choose our sex. We don't choose the country where we're born or the religion (or lack thereof) passed along to us. The disintegrated forces of society don't care that we lack control over these things. They judge us regardless, labeling us with stereotypes. Women born with brown hair may be told "gentlemen prefer blondes" and feel as if they don't measure up to conventional beauty standards. Blonde women, by contrast, may be judged as dumb or ditzy and feel pressure to prove their intellect. Such stereotypes tend to have a deep impact on how we view ourselves, along with the opportunities offered to us. With hard work, we can step into our own expression of things like beauty or intelligence in defiance of the limitations placed upon us.

How we're treated due to stereotypes about aspects of our identity we can't control directly influences our beliefs about the world, what we fear, what we value, and so forth. As a Black man, I feel a need to be on guard around the police, for instance, but I also know there are people who feel a need to be guarded around *me*. Many women, by contrast, feel they have to be on guard while hiking by themselves or walking alone at night. Clearly, these kinds of fears have justifiable roots in our psyche. We all strive for caution in the interest of survival. I would never tell another Black person to trust all White people or tell any woman to trust all men. The entirety of the energy chart is relevant to our journey, including our need for fear.

We can learn to respond to the disintegrated energies of the world by getting past the fear that disconnects us from one another. By finding common ground, we create paths of connection, and the labels separating us disappear. At the end of the day, we all experience the masculine and feminine dynamics of the energy chart. We are all subject to the full spectrum of integration and disintegration in the areas of emotion and action. Focusing more on our points of commonality than our differences is a habit to hone if we're to create more integration in society.

Case Study: Shein
THAT Haitian

I went to an inner-city middle school in the sixth grade. While it was a fun time, I had to be ready to defend myself. I'll never forget when my classmate Q and I were going at it in Ms. Hicks's class, hurling insults at each other. He suddenly said, " . . . and you a Haitian!" It took a few seconds to process that he was insulting me, and in the spirit of clapping back quickly, the words that came out of my mouth were, "My *parents* are Haitian," as if to say, *I* wasn't Haitian, only *they* were. The moment those words slid out of me, I felt myself shrink. I had never been ashamed of my heritage. I quite loved and was proud of it, but Q threw me off guard with the vitriol in his voice.

I remember reeling about my response for months, returning to that moment and replaying it in my mind. I wanted so badly to right this wrong, so I set out to do just that. April rolled around, and I commissioned a family seamstress to make me a matching two-piece set out of Haitian flags. In May, I glided through the halls beaming in the regality of my wardrobe. I wanted everyone to know who I was—THAT Haitian. The respect I got from my peers for the pride I displayed was more than enough.

Shein's feminine energy was reflected in her aim to win her showdown with her classmate. She felt vulnerable about her identity, caught off guard that people would criticize her for it. Through

continued

masculine energy, she feigned indifference and distanced herself from her heritage initially, misaligned with her inner self-concept. When she took time to acknowledge her true feelings, she was able to redirect her masculine energy to visibly align with her pride in her culture.

Identity Issues Around Gender Stereotypes

As a core masculine, stereotypically male roles have felt natural to me, but the expectation that men should bury feelings and embody stoicism created disintegration in my life. Before I started my healing journey in my thirties, I was disconnected from my feminine energy and as a result, didn't know what my purpose was. I had no solid *why* from which to make decisions because I shut down the channel to my intuition. Instead, I made choices from a place of hedonism and a desire for external validation, leading to mistakes I still regret. Integrating my feminine energy into my identity required me to go against the template my father had modeled around what it meant to be a man: womanizing, being addicted to porn, lying, and cheating.

If I could talk to my younger self today, I would tell him his problems had nothing to do with women, porn addiction, monogamy, or cheating. The emptiness he felt was spiritual. He was searching for fulfillment in a template he assumed would bring him power but brought something else entirely. When we're lost in the fog of disintegration, we're blind to the true source of our issues and end up repeating the same cycles, finding "solutions" that do nothing to address the true problem.

Rather than asking questions like "What should a man be?", we can focus on questions that honor the truth of our energy. I don't believe a *man* should necessarily lead, protect, or provide. However, a *core masculine* will do these actions most of the time, because that's where they'll feel most comfortable. Core feminines, by contrast, feel more comfortable connecting to their intuition and the voice of their inner guide. It can be difficult for core masculines to get practice in the intuitive lane, with all their focus on the external world. This is especially true for men who only allow themselves to access feminine energy through their interactions with women. The solution is not to cut men off from their feminine, but to acknowledge that masculine and feminine energy exist in everyone whether we choose to own them or not. Denying inherent parts of ourselves will only keep us disintegrated.

Trapped by Our Limiting Beliefs

It's easy to learn the wrong lessons from our experiences, especially the most painful ones. In response to trauma, we can get stuck in our disintegrated feminine energy, convinced we're inherently terrible or unacceptable.

I'm ugly.

I'm stupid.

I'm lazy.

There's something wrong with me.

People don't like me.

I'm always doing something wrong.

I'm not worthy of the life I want to lead.

We can also get stuck in the energy of the disintegrated masculine, stewing in anger and resentment that we then project onto the world.

I can't trust anyone.

I have to control others so I won't get hurt.

People will see me as weak if I don't act tough or happy.

They're the problem, not me.

If I have to suffer, so should they.

These frames of reference become the lens through which we view life. We cement limiting beliefs into our subconscious mind and carry the wounded energy they create with us everywhere we go. We all deal with feelings of hatred toward ourselves and others at times, but some people get so far below sea level that they feel they can't get out of it. Disintegration is deeply felt but invisible, woven intricately through our identity. We tell ourselves things like "Everyone hates me" or "I'm bad with money" and live our lives as if those ideas are facts.

Leaving our limiting beliefs unchallenged can feel safe, but it causes us to miss out on important information. Our confirmation bias—where we interpret any new information as confirming rather than challenging our existing beliefs—keeps us trapped in our disintegrated algorithm, cutting us off from a more expansive life perspective. We stop asking questions. If we truly want integration and connection across all planes, we need to move out of our bubbles.

At the root of our limiting beliefs is fear, which often manifests as the labels, stereotypes, and categories we assign to one another's traits. When you're born into a world that tells you, "You're like *this*," it can feel impossible to leave that place. Pulling the contents of our subconscious mind into our consciousness can help us find comfort in our authentic selves. When we see the beliefs underlying our behavior, we can begin to rewire our mind and heal what's plaguing us. Ideally, we can get to a place where our inner self aligns with what those around us experience—a place where we can feel comfortable being ourselves exactly as we are.

Regardless of how we show up in the world, someone will give us shit. The world is changing its optics on our identities all the time. We need roots within ourselves so we have something consistent to hold on to in the midst of our disintegrated world.

Evaluating our connection to our identity can give us a clearer sense of how our experiences and beliefs are influencing our masculine and feminine energies. When we reach integration, we no longer need to play the chameleon, shifting through personalities in different situations. We can find safety in expressing our truth from the place of our highest good. The *why* around our motivations will always determine our *how*.

In addition to our individual sense of identity, our generational identity can have a dramatic impact on the status quo of our energy. We inherit the emotional work our childhood caretakers both did and didn't do. Next, we'll explore disintegration in relation to family.

Key Takeaways

- The experiences that influence our identity determine our status quo on the energy chart. How we think of ourselves, particularly in relation to our purpose, impacts our energetic template for how we approach life.

- We can connect to our identity from a place of love or a place of fear. This determines where we find ourselves on the chart. An integrated identity allows us to evolve spiritually and psychologically.

- We're often oppressed based on aspects of our identity we can't control, like our race or our sex. This creates fear we must process and conquer if we're to find common ground and integrate with others.

- Our identity issues often arise from gender stereotypes that create a spiritual void within us. We can learn the wrong lessons from those experiences and cement them as limiting beliefs.

- Evaluating our identity can show us how our experiences and beliefs are currently influencing our energy.

Reflections

- Do you connect to your identity from a place of fear or love?
- What factors led to this?

Family Through the Masculine and Feminine Lens

PEAK INTEGRATION: LOVE-FILLED MEMORIES AND TRADITIONS
FEELING YOUR FAMILY, BELIEVING IN FAMILY, CHOOSING FAMILY, LOVING FAMILY

INTEGRATED FEMININE
LOVE-BASED FEELING

- Feeling aware in a high-context household
- Having a desire to nurture your family
- Feeling loved by your family
- Feeling that you can be yourself
- Being curious about who your family members are as individuals

INTEGRATED MASCULINE
LOVE-BASED ACTION

- Helping a child to explore their identity and potential lifepaths
- Establishing and modeling a code of conduct for how to behave
- Creating a safe and stable household environment
- Seeing your child for who they authentically are
- Establishing a unique and special bond with each child

DISINTEGRATED FEMININE
FEAR-BASED FEELING

- Feeling unsafe in your home
- Feeling unloved, uncared for, or confused about dysfunction happening in the home
- Feeling confused in a low-context household
- Feeling like you have to hide something from your family or be someone other than who you are
- Feeling family fear patterns (finances, health, xenophobia, politics, racism, etc.)

DISINTEGRATED MASCULINE
FEAR-BASED ACTION

- Choosing a lifepath for your child against their will or consent
- Causing instability in the household
- Talking back or not respecting your parents
- Creating division or unhealthy competition between family members
- Parenting in a disengaged manner
- Teaching dogmatic ideologies

CHAPTER 5

Family

"Like branches on a tree, we all grow in different directions yet our roots remain as one."

—SUZY KASSEM

According to Terence T. Gorski, author of *Getting Love Right: Learning the Choices of Healthy Intimacy*, 70 to 80 percent of people come from dysfunctional families.[1] When fear, confusion, resentment, manipulation, projection, avoidance, anger, denial, gaslighting, immaturity, and emotional chaos rule the home, we learn that these behaviors are acceptable and effective. We may also believe our parents' emotions are our fault and wonder why we cause so many problems without trying. Abuse, addiction, and mental illness go unacknowledged and untreated in many dysfunctional families. The presence or lack of such dynamics in the home is the single most important factor in how we process our lives. Until we take a close look at our caregivers and our earliest experiences with them, we continually search—whether consciously or not—for answers about how we're showing up in the world and why.

We don't see our parents subjectively. As kids, we idealize them as gods who always know the way, copying their patterns and cementing them as our own. All parents do, of course, make mistakes, but in dysfunctional households, which I call "eggshell households," children are molded into believing something is wrong with them and their feelings. We believe the world functions according to our family's ways, only to have the veil lifted bit by bit as we grow. We see how integrated families are living and begin to ask questions. "Do I not deserve the same kind of love? What's going on in my family?"

Our family provides our first template for interaction between our feminine and masculine energies. These are the choices available to us for how we can handle our feelings and actions. If there's an imbalance between these forces in our family, we're likely to inherit that balance internally, identifying more strongly with the feminine or masculine within us. We must learn to channel, navigate, and utilize both in order for peak integration to occur. Action and emotion are needed for wholeness. In this chapter, we'll explore how family impacts our energy and whether we begin life above or below sea level.

Family on the Axis

Our experience of family determines the masculine and feminine dynamics we experience energetically. Our caregivers create our first impressions of values, rules, and emotional strategies for getting needs met. Disintegrated, fear-based feelings and actions pull the whole house below sea level, while integrated feelings and actions raise everyone up.

The bottom-right quadrant shows a sampling of ways the disintegrated masculine expresses itself. This energy is responsible for the majority of the trauma passed down through generations. Parents who are overwhelmed, addicted, or mentally unwell often default to authoritarian coping mechanisms to employ control. They yell, hit, threaten, and force. They ignore, dismiss, and disconnect. They avoid and allow TV or the internet to raise their kids for them. They are consistently absent or abusive in some way, whether physically, emotionally, or psychologically. Growing up in an eggshell family under the curse of the disintegrated masculine is a dark way to enter the world.

The bottom-left quadrant captures the fear-based feelings of the disintegrated feminine. There, we feel victimized, unsafe, overwhelmed, unloved, uncared for, and confused about what we've done to cause such dysfunction. We feel like we have to hide behind a mask, unable to show our family who we actually are. We may struggle with confusion in the setting of what I call a "low-context household," where parents provide little to no information about their own history due to shame or other factors. We can also inherit the fear patterns our parents have around things like money, politics, or xenophobia. These feelings are all repressed, leading to more isolation, lack of connection, and feelings of being unseen.

In the top-left quadrant, the integrated feminine creates feelings of love, safety, curiosity, and the desire to nurture. This energy often shows up in what I call "high-context households," where people have fewer secrets and communicate easily. There's a willingness to listen on all sides for the sake of connection, allowing everyone to process emotions together out loud. Parents in these families are curious about who their children are as individuals from the get-go. They have an active interest in how their kids learn and a willingness to listen to how they express their feelings.

In the top-right quadrant, we see how the integrated masculine shows up in families. Parents who thrive in this energy create safe energetic containers for their kids to explore the world and figure out who they are. They establish a respectful code of conduct for how to behave and model it for their children consistently. They protect their children and each other from harm, whether it's physical, emotional, or psychological. The environment is one where honesty, stability, and open communication can flourish. Each child enjoys a special bond with each caregiver, feeling seen and valued for who they are authentically.

Peak integration within a family unit is about consistently creating positive memories together. At the end of the day, memories with the people we love are all we have, and if the majority of those memories are dark, it can taint the whole picture. Being present with one another through a series of love-filled traditions allows everyone to be safe and share. We demonstrate love by showing up for and deeply connecting with one another while honoring boundaries. It can take lots of practice living an integrated lifestyle to get there, but these are the moments that center family in our hearts.

My Story: Family Dynamics

I always felt I had two sides, but it took time to see the value in uniting them in friendship. The dark and light within me are often caught in a tug-of-war, and I've learned to better integrate both. This tug-of-war existed between my masculine and feminine energy before I found my healing path. The seeds of disintegration were planted during my childhood, at home with my family, as is the case for most of us. When your parents are caught below sea level, dysfunctional templates of masculine and feminine energy are all you have. As a collective, we're in desperate need of integrated models for living well. Intergenerational trauma is keeping too many of us asleep, blind to the *why* fueling the ghosts inside us.

My mom and dad were both the eldest of three children in their families. Mom's father—my grandfather—had a heart attack and died when she was eleven. Because he died on his day off, her family didn't receive any government aid. My grandma didn't have a car, license, or job, and she ended up cooking for a Catholic church within a month, which she went on to do for forty years. Mom had to grow up right away, foregoing the life of a normal teenager. That Christmas morning, her mother woke her up to say, "There's no Santa. Come help me wrap these gifts." Sheltered and innocent, Mom ended up in an abusive first marriage but left after her spouse got violent. A year later, she met my father.

My dad also lost his dad at the age of eleven. He had looked up to him in spite of the frequent violence against his mom, who was an alcoholic and frequent customer at the local bar. Grandpa once pulled a gun on a man, in front of my dad, who'd been talking to Grandma, and he often would get into fights with the neighbors. In his final argument, Grandpa went next door with a lead pipe, started beating a man, had a heart attack during the fight, and died. My dad witnessed the entire event through the front window. After trying to revive him, my dad asked his two younger brothers to help carry the body inside. They laid him on the living room floor and waited. His body stayed there for hours until their mother came home. Now fatherless, living with a drunk single mom and two violent brothers, he was aimless until he met Steve Muhammad.

Steve Muhammad, a Black Muslim and martial arts expert, opened a dojo in LA back in the '60s during the civil rights movement. Bruce Lee once said Steve had the fastest hands he'd ever seen. Steve would bring Black and Brown kids into his dojo and teach them martial arts so they wouldn't be fighting each other on the streets. My dad was one of those kids and ended up being a phenom karate fighter, traveling the world with the other kids from the dojo during the 1980s and 1990s. Over twenty years, they never lost a single tournament. After that karate rockstar stint, Dad started working as a nightclub bouncer.

Around that time, he met my mom, they got married, and eventually she became pregnant. He showed excitement for fatherhood, even making plans and attending tests—but when she became pregnant, he ultimately asked her to have an abortion. Mom, a devoted Catholic, told him that wasn't happening. Her mother, my nana, even called him to explain, "We don't do that in this family. Do whatever you like—you don't have to be involved—but she's having the baby." Soon after, I was born. Four years later, my mom got pregnant with my brother, and again after being proud, Dad eventually told her to get an abortion, but she refused. From the get-go, he was a reluctant father, but he seemed to like us once we were in the world. My mom found him staring down at me in my crib at the hospital the night I was born and asked what he was doing.

"Just wondering what he's gonna think of me."

I've heard stories of the early days when my parents allegedly got along and were sweet to each other, but I don't remember any of that. What I remember, even from my earliest days, were all the women Dad had around. He would bring them to the house while my mom worked during the day at the hospital. They were woven into my life, but I was trained to be silent about it, as if none of those women who played with and babysat me existed. When I was two or three, I remember having an imaginary conversation on my plastic play phone with Julie, one of the women he spent the most time with. Most of the women in my dad's sphere had no idea he was married, but Julie did.

"Hi, Julie! Bye, Julie!"

Dad spanked me for that—for repeating his own words. The threat of his temper constantly lingered in the air throughout the house, creating unpredictability, fear, and confusion for the rest of us. The rage, yelling, and violence escalated over time. I hated his cheating. I hated lying to my mom and the fact that he forced me into it. I knew in my gut it was all wrong, but I didn't know how to handle it. My mom, avoidant and frozen in her own trauma, did whatever she could to minimize conflict.

I remember loving my dad deeply, always looking forward to the good moments that punctured the fear in our family. From the outside, he appeared calm and self-assured; but he wore different masks depending on whom he was with. In the presence of women, he was charming and soft. In public, he was an observer and a good listener who knew how to tune into the energy of others, being calm and present. His own experiences with pain gave him the empathy he needed to show up for others. He would say everything was going to be okay in times of crisis—and people believed him. The masculine shell of safety he provided allowed others to open up and trust him.

With me, he was more vocal and played the role of teacher, showcasing his intelligence. I wanted to dig into the many layers of his personality, and my strategy was to ask questions, which he appreciated. Urging me to form an analytical mind, he would ask me questions in return, helping me break down situations after the fact. "Why do you think that person made that decision? Use your head." He was full of riddles for me to solve, always testing me. "If I had a thousand pounds of metal in one hand and a thousand pounds of feathers in the other, which would be heavier?" Four-year-old me would say, "Um . . . metal?" He loved tricky stuff like that. He was also obsessed with chess and would play it every day, and he taught me to play along with him.

But above all, Dad wanted to teach me to handle threats by preparing me to be tough. His experiences had taught him the world was a cold and dark place and that I would have to figure things out by myself. No one was coming to save me. "You're on your own," he would say frequently, but I knew it was out of love. I became good at reading the energy of every room I entered, a skill I later learned did not come naturally to everyone.

On my mom's side, there was a running joke that Dad didn't exist because no one ever saw him. She usually picked me up from school, but on the rare occasions when Dad showed up in his yellow Jeep, a symbol of his uniqueness, I felt a happiness I would carry with me for the rest of the year. My favorite childhood memory is a family reunion we held where he actually showed up. I had begged him to join us, and he said, "We'll see," which always meant no. But this time he came, and joy exploded in my heart. I felt so proud to be around him and show everyone he was real. We connected deeply through music as he expanded my knowledge of the arts. My family ate international, cultured foods that my friends and their families weren't eating.

I remember my excitement when he would order for us at sushi restaurants. He took me to places that blew my mind, and while there was always some woman tagging along, it was usually fun . . . for a while.

One night when I was twelve, my parents got into an argument that got out of hand. Dad was in a bad mood, playing chess near the kitchen, when my mom approached him hesitantly about a bill they'd gotten in the mail.

"Dexter, can we talk about this?"

"No."

"You overdrafted the account."

He got up to look at the bill and lost it. "This is about twenty dollars! Do you want twenty fucking dollars?"

"No."

"Then shut the fuck up. Get out!"

My mom froze in shock as Dad poured himself a glass of orange juice from the fridge. He saw her standing there, still looking at him, and threw the open carton at her. It fell to the floor as she turned to run up the stairs. He picked the carton up and threw it again, splattering orange juice across the walls. I ran after him as he followed my mom. When he got upstairs, he picked up the vacuum cleaner, and I stood in front of him.

"Dad, STOP."

Thankfully, he put the vacuum down, grabbed his keys, and stormed out of the house. Things had gotten heated between them before, but it wasn't until that moment that I realized how bad their relationship really was. That was the last straw for my mom.

When my parents got divorced, I started hopping back and forth between their homes. Though Mom made good money, she started getting panic attacks, at times waking me up in the middle of the night in tears, saying she didn't know how we would make it. I would console her and tell her we could make a plan together. We never did. Instead, she'd buy lottery tickets and consult her tarot cards. Every number she saw would be a sign of some omen. For a while, the roof was falling apart, and when the rain came, we'd be filled with anxiety, rushing around the house to catch the water in buckets. Again, I offered to help figure out a plan to get a new roof. That plan was usually the lottery until years later I ended up getting a job and buying one for her.

Through it all, Mom made continuous sacrifices for us kids. She worked full time and still managed to pick us up and drop us off from school, make our meals, take us to sports practices, and keep our spirits up despite the trauma she endured. She took us to Mass every Sunday, making sure we never missed church. I would look at her in awe, proud to be her son. Her faith kept our family afloat. Through her selflessness and dedication, every bill was paid, and our needs were met in abundance. It's astonishing how a woman from Pomona, California, who mostly grew up without a father, could overcome such adversity to achieve and give all that she did.

At Dad's house, there was freedom . . . too much freedom. *Playboy* magazines were strewn everywhere, sparking my initial interest in porn. I also came across the sex tapes he'd made with his mistresses when I was an adolescent and abruptly became aware of his more vulnerable side. This was all happening while I was starting to get involved with girls, and I had trouble understanding the boundary between friendship and infatuation. I started experimenting sexually around then and was keenly aware that my friends weren't living similar lives. I kept all of it inside, ashamed of my dark, double life, knowing people would find the whole thing weird. "Let's hang at your house," I'd tell them. I didn't want them seeing what was happening at mine.

My parents' templates for how to handle feelings and actions created an imbalance toward the disintegrated masculine within me. I was expected to feel nothing and act tough in order to survive my childhood by aligning with the whims of my father's mercurial temperament. I had to put my true self aside, the one who told the truth and felt *everything*, to become the empty vessel Dad needed to store his secrets.

I don't write this out of vengeance; I have compassion for the pain he experienced in his own disintegrated life. He didn't inherit the right templates from his parents either. He was a charismatic but tortured soul for whom life had always felt heavy, and I assume he did his best to get through it. My mom, stuck in her disintegrated feminine, was doing her best too. Though the lottery tickets, tarot cards, and miracles never solved the avoidance issue, she was seeking the integrated feminine influence of hope and inspiration. She taught me how to believe in what seemed impossible. The airy, spiritual part of her shows up in me when I choose hope over despair.

To love myself, I've had to unconditionally embrace the people my DNA came from. Integration requires us to own where we have come from and seek balance where imbalance once reigned. Your family and story are a significant part of you, but they don't have to determine who you become.

The Workings of Intergenerational Trauma

Children born into functional, integrated families have the greatest likelihood of growing into competent, confident, well-adjusted adults who thrive in interdependent relationships. They know who they are, trust their instincts, and generally feel safe in the world. Kids from disintegrated families, by contrast, often struggle in a number of ways. They may have addictions, phobias, anger problems, compulsive urges, or lack self-esteem. They are also more likely to end up in abusive relationships, either as victims, perpetrators, or both.

Children who are treated poorly by their parents must adapt to their situation in order to survive. They may choose primarily to fight, flee, freeze, or fawn—making them aggressive, avoidant, dissociative, or codependent. Above all, they must keep their connection to their parents, causing them to idealize and justify the dysfunctional behavior around them. To believe Mom or Dad might be truly unsafe, incapable, or unwell would equal existential oblivion. While being hit, screamed at, or neglected can strike abject terror into the heart of a child, it's impossible for them to expect or seek out anything else. They create stories in their minds about why such treatment was acceptable or even desirable, telling themselves they're evil or unlovable as they are. When they grow into adults, they reflect their parents' words and actions in some way, usually by either becoming a bully or someone too afraid to stand up for themselves.

The roots of trauma inheritance aren't just psychological, however. Researchers have found that children of mothers with PTSD can be born smaller than usual and those born after a famine can be at higher risk for heart disease.[2] External influences that occur while babies are in utero can also alter the way their genes later function, which lies at the heart of a modern field of study known as epigenetics. In 2014, researchers Brian Dias and Kerry Ressler reported an epigenetic pathway that ran through sperm.[3] They gave a male mouse a mild electric shock as it smelled a cherry blossom. The resulting fear response to the scent was passed down for two generations, causing the son and grandson of the mouse to associate cherry blossoms with danger. This suggests we may inherit our parents' associations to trauma as an evolutionary adaptation, feeling the memory of fear and stress caught in their bodies even before we were born. The more trauma there is in our bloodline, the more likely we are to struggle.

Case Study: Anita
She Was There All Along

My father was a drunk who, I was told, tried to kill my mother and us four girls. He left when I was six months old. Soon Mom left, too, leaving us kids with our grandparents in the countryside. Later, my older sister fell ill, and our doctor recommended she go live with my mom. The memory of my sister leaving with the doctors haunted me for years. I never knew whether I would see her again and felt as if she had died. This was the third of many losses I endured from a young age and the start of my downward spiral. Feeling alone and abandoned, I went into survival mode. I worked hard to succeed and stay one step ahead of everyone because I couldn't count on anyone but myself. I found ways to numb myself, to stop the pain I felt. Trouble followed me as I learned to manipulate people, places, and situations to get my way. My grandparents responded with a hard stance that included a lot of whippings, resulting in more trauma.

After years of this vicious cycle, I could no longer live with the results I was creating for myself. I quit drinking, found the goddess spirit inside me, and started loving myself unconditionally. Through self-care, hard work, tears, yoga, meditation, setbacks, and betrayals, I was able to address my core issue: abandonment. Today, I adore the woman I am inside and can see she was there all along, suppressed by trauma. Finding her has been my life's purpose.

Born into a disintegrated family system, Anita discovered her feminine energy had been wounded from a young age. Through disintegrated masculine energy, she responded to life with defensive, manipulative behavior. After hitting rock bottom, she was able to heal her feminine energy by addressing her core wound of abandonment. From there, she rose above sea level, found self-love in the integrated feminine, and turned that love into purpose.

Roles and Wounds in Dysfunctional Family Systems

Few childhoods are more painful than those of kids who are mistreated while their siblings are praised and upheld. Preferential treatment is unfortunately common in dysfunctional family systems. These parents lack the ability to view their children as individuals. Instead, they see their kids as extensions of themselves and subconsciously project predetermined roles onto them. A golden child who can do no wrong is chosen as a reflection of the parents' best qualities, perhaps because they are docile or remind the parent of themselves. A scapegoat is also chosen as a target for everything the parent rejects about themselves. When Dad yells at Mom and Mom can't set boundaries due to fear, she instead finds the scapegoat and yells at the child for inciting Dad's rage. Scapegoating in family systems is also known as Cinderella Syndrome or target-child selection, in which one child is singled out for abuse or neglect.

If you're an adult child of a dysfunctional family, the role(s) subconsciously assigned to you by your parents may be impacting your life today. Scapegoated children are more likely to struggle with complex PTSD, abusive relationships, and emotional volatility. Golden children are at risk of becoming avoidant, narcissistic, or depressed because their true sense of self was never encouraged to flourish behind the mask of the designated favorite. You could also be the lost child, who tends to live in isolation and immerse themselves in fantasy. You could be the caretaker who stepped in to act as the agent of responsibility when your parents were unable to fulfill their duties. You could also be the mascot, who relies on humor and immature jokes to lighten the mood when Mom and Dad seem angry. All of these roles can arise in response to the inability of one or both parents to put the emotional needs of their children first.

Growing up with an abusive, emotionally absent, or detached parent is often the source of the deepest wounds that make up the core of our trauma. Some refer to these internal centers of pain as the "mother wound" and "father wound" to differentiate the specific issues involved in these connections. In Western culture, we associate mothers with abundant love and unconditional acceptance. They're viewed as a place of refuge from the cruel external world. Fathers, by contrast, are associated with protecting and providing. Dads help the child move out of the nest and into the world. The ways in which we feel let down by our masculine or feminine parent differ from each other, causing them to manifest in specific ways.

The bond between a mother and child begins in utero. When the safety of this connection begins to unravel, it can have a pro-foundly negative impact, putting kids at risk for low self-esteem, codependency, relationship challenges, and an inability to self-regulate emotions. Some daughters grow up not only disliking themselves but disliking other women, too, lashing out due to their mother wounds and perpetuating the cycle. A mother with internalized misogyny may believe girls who are quiet and submissive are more valuable, causing her to be cold toward an expressive daughter. She may also turn her child—usually a son—into a replacement husband if her emotional needs aren't being met within her marriage, giving them adult responsibilities as the man of the house. While not universal, these patterns show how mother-child wounds can shape identity and emotional cycles across generations.

The father wound is also caused by absenteeism, emotional neglect, abuse, or an unattuned caregiver, but the impact hits differently due to society's associations with masculinity. Sons and daughters with father wounds tend to feel unworthy, needing approval from others, especially other men. Studies often find that women with father wounds may find themselves in relationships with emotionally unavailable men. Father wounds are typically found in those of us with dads who were belittling, demeaning, and focused on exercising dominance.

It takes time to identify these wounds, how they're manifesting in our present-day lives, and why our parents' behavior was harmful. As difficult as it is, we must find the courage to connect with the pain of our inner child so we can acknowledge, grieve, and release it. Guilt, shame, and anger can arise when we confront the truth of our past, but processing these emotions allows us to eventually shift our perspective. It can be intensely empowering to awaken to the realization that there was never anything wrong with you and what you experienced wasn't your fault. All children deserve to feel safe during childhood and have their emotional needs met. By reconnecting with our deepest pain, we can finally come home to ourselves and release the burdens we should never have had to carry in the first place.

How Trauma Impacts the Brain and Body

An unpleasant experience becomes traumatic when the mind and body are overwhelmed by terrifying, inescapable fear and unable to properly process it afterward. A toddler who's blasted with anger by a parent but not comforted afterward, for instance, can't make sense of how to handle the fear in their body. Should they relax or stay vigilant around the parent once trust is broken? What if it happens again, or frequently? As a result, the fear associated with the experience remains in the subconscious mind, triggered later by various stimuli. The nervous system is permanently put on high alert, priming the child for hypersensitivity in their fight, flight, freeze, or fawn reactions. They believe something is wrong with them and enter a status quo of anxiety, depression, confusion, and despair.

After decades of living with trauma stored in the mind and body, our health and relationships can be adversely impacted to the point of disintegration. Diseases related to stress, autoimmune functioning, and wear and tear on the immune system are more likely to arise when we ignore our emotional wounds. We can find ourselves isolated, suffering in silence because close connections feel so triggering for us. The good news is that there is hope. If we're willing to confront the pain underlying our behaviors (the feminine behind the masculine), we can shine a light on the shadows keeping us stuck below sea level. We don't have to hit rock bottom. There are integrated people in the world who have done the healing that lies ahead of us. Help is available the moment we're ready to reach out for it.

With awareness of the energetic template passed down by our parents, we can consciously make changes to how we balance our masculine and feminine energy, allowing us to rise to a more integrated place. By working through our personal trauma, we can break the curse of intergenerational trauma running through our bloodline so future generations can find more peace at home than we did.

After family, our friendships provide the next template for how we handle our energy. This adds another layer to our perception of the world and our place within it. In the next chapter, we'll explore how our experiences with friendship influence the masculine and feminine within us.

Key Takeaways

- Our family provides us with our original energetic template. If there's an imbalance between the masculine and feminine forces of our household, we're likely to internalize it.

- Trauma is passed from elders to younger generations through the behavioral and psychological patterns they model at home. Research suggests trauma can be inherited genetically as well—explored in a new field of study known as epigenetics.

- In dysfunctional families, parents subconsciously project predetermined roles onto their children, resulting in vastly different childhood experiences between siblings.

- Children can develop mother wounds and father wounds that adversely impact their relationships with men and women in the future.

- Trauma is residual fear that becomes trapped in the body and mind after a terrifying experience we lack the inner resources to process.

- We can work toward integration by shining a light on the traumatic or dysfunctional patterns we inherited, working to rewire them in our minds and bodies, and creating a healthier balance between our feminine and masculine energies.

Reflections

- What was the dynamic between your caregivers like?

- In what way was there an imbalance of masculine and feminine energy in your home?

Friendship Through the Masculine and Feminine Lens

PEAK INTEGRATION

Ride-or-die friendships that last through thick and thin
Communities that inspire and enrich our being and purpose
Friends who can have difficult and honest conversations

*TRUSTING FRIENDS, RESPECTING FRIENDS,
SUPPORTING FRIENDS, NURTURING FRIENDS*

INTEGRATED FEMININE *LOVE-BASED FEELING*	INTEGRATED MASCULINE *LOVE-BASED ACTION*
• Valuing meaningful connections based on love and support • Upholding loyalty in friendships • Feeling we have someone in our corner • Having an openness to being held accountable • Feeling that we can be ourselves	• Showing up for a friend in need • Holding friends accountable to their higher selves • Supporting friends without judgment • Encouraging friends and their success • Maintaining quality > quantity in friendships
DISINTEGRATED FEMININE *FEAR-BASED FEELING*	**DISINTEGRATED MASCULINE** *FEAR-BASED ACTION*
• Feeling a lack of support from our friends • Assuming friends are talking behind our back • Feeling pressured to participate in things we don't want to do • Thinking we can't tell friends the truth • Wanting our friends to be stuck or unhappy	• Stabbing a friend in the back, gossiping, or intentionally hurting their feelings • Staying in an unsupportive friend group • Engaging in one-sided friendships • Being a "yes-man" who never holds friends accountable • Maintaining quantity > quality in friendships

CHAPTER 6

Friendship

"A friend is someone who knows the song in your heart
and sings it back to you when you forget the words."

—UNKNOWN

While growing up within the structure offered by our family and education system, we begin making peer connections that become friendships. With whom we choose to surround ourselves as kids reflects some of our first expressions of personal agency and our energy. Our friends impact our personality, confidence, goals, desires, dreams, morals, values, and sense of safety. They can help us float above sea level or pull us down into the depths of disintegration.

A 2010 meta-analysis of more than 308,000 people by psychologist Julianne Holt-Lunstad showed that people with no friends or high-quality friendships are twice as likely to die prematurely—a risk factor even greater than the effects of smoking twenty cigarettes per day.[1] We *need* strong, integrated friendships to thrive, and the quality of those connections hinges on the energy of all parties.

Friendship on the Axis

The energy of our friendships provides a reflection of where we find ourselves on the chart in the context of these close connections. They can pull us down or help us rise, deeply influencing our interests, views, and how we perceive our place in the world. When we wonder what kind of person we are and the value we bring to the table, one of the first places we look is at our friendships, especially when we're young.

Friendships rooted in disintegrated masculine energy are low-vibe connections that often thrive on gossip or putting someone down. We can also find ourselves in one-sided friendships where one person gives more than the other or where one person takes more control. Manipulation and ulterior motives may be present, along with a lack of accountability. It's easy to feel used in these relationships, as people stuck in the disintegrated masculine are often looking to dominate or exploit others to serve their own interests in some way. This energy can also be present when one or both people act like "yes-men" within the friendship, unwilling to tell each other when one of them is doing something wrong. It can also be an energy of "quantity over quality" in friendships when we collect superficial connections rather than those that provide deep mutual support.

In the bottom-left quadrant, we have examples of disintegrated feminine energy in friendships. These are the fear-based feelings we experience when there's gossip or a lack of support coming from those we consider friends. We can feel unheard or lonely in our friendships, or like we have no true friends at all. We can feel peer pressure from our friends or fear losing them when the connection becomes distant or strained. We can also feel deep, lasting shame or guilt after we've hurt a friend, especially when they leave us. All these experiences in connection to friendship have the power to pull us down energetically.

In the top-left quadrant is the integrated feminine frame of friendship. Here we have meaningful connections based in love and support. Both parties are trustworthy, loyal, and willing to listen to each other. There's an openness toward accountability alongside safety for everyone to be themselves. Honesty, authenticity, and encouragement of one another provide the deep feelings of connection we need to thrive together as a social species.

The love-based feelings of the integrated feminine in friendship fuel the love-based actions we see in the top-right quadrant. This can include checking in with our friends to see how they're doing or showing up for them when they're in need. This is where we support our friends without judgment and encourage them in their quest for success. When we act from our integrated masculine energy, we become more concerned with the quality rather than quantity of our friendships, seeking depth with a few close confidantes.

Peak integration in our friendships looks like supporting one another through thick and thin. In these connections, everyone can rest assured that the desire to boost one another's well-being is mutual. It can also look like having a community of friends that both inspires and enriches your purpose as you go through life. These groups gear us toward our best selves. Peak integration in friendships also looks like the ability to have difficult but honest conversations. Within these types of close-knit networks, we can enjoy the optimal quality of connection we're made for.

In the Emotion-Belief-Choice-Pursuit energy pipeline, our integrated feminine energy allows us to show up consistently in our friendships in pursuit of mutual engagement. When everyone participates in the village we all need, everyone benefits from the fruits of its labor.

My Story: A Crashing Friendship

As was the case in many areas of my life, I had to figure out the disintegration I brought into my friendships the hard way. The most obvious example of how this played out was when my longest-running friendship crashed and burned before my eyes in a highly visible manner. Before I found my voice later in life, I was the quiet kid who was too shy to approach others. The friendships that stuck were the ones I made with kids who liked to take charge. This was the case with Quincy, my best friend since kindergarten, and our connection would go on to influence the trajectory of my life.

Quincy's dad, Leo, was a famous R&B singer back in the '90s when fame actually meant something. He would create incredible experiences for us, from basketball camp to concerts to Disneyland to Vegas to rides on private jets. My young friends and I would get competitive, vying for Quincy's attention so he'd choose us to come along for the fun. Those of us who weren't chosen were subjected to major FOMO, which created animosity at times.

Naturally, Quincy was spoiled by this situation and would act like a bit of a brat on a power trip, bossing everyone around as the ringleader of our group. His attitude was: "Today we're gonna be the Blues Brothers. I'll be John Belushi and you all be the other guys."

Quincy's dad provided me with an entirely different template for fatherhood than I was used to at home. My dad was in and out of my life, only getting involved when it suited him. Leo picked him up from school every day despite his busy schedule of making albums and music videos. He gave his full presence to everyone he spoke with, including me, which made me feel seen in a way I wasn't used to. He would tell me he loved me at times, making me feel like a second son to him.

Quincy's personality softened into a caring, thoughtful, down-to-earth demeanor as we grew older. He was like a brother to me, wholesome in all the ways I wasn't. He would have given me the shirt off his back to help me if I'd asked him to. Neither of us had ever fit smoothly into other social groups, and the fact that we were different always brought us together. Through our alienation, we found fun and common ground, and that home base of familiarity served us well throughout the rest of high school.

Quincy and I ended up attending different colleges and didn't speak as much during those years. After graduation, I moved back to LA, and we started hanging out again. This is when I met his girlfriend, a professional influencer named Tanya. Right from the beginning, she gave me lots of attention, which massaged my ego and the insecurities I still held at the time. She was conscientious, attuned to all the fine energetic details between people, and could go over the top to make others feel special when she wanted to. She was also a lot like Quincy used to be when he was a kid, acting as the ringleader who brought our group of friends together and keeping a bossy hold on those in her orbit. Over time, I grew attracted to how she moved in the world—despite being in a relationship with Anna, my girlfriend at the time.

Tanya and I had similar personalities. We networked easily and felt comfortable starting conversations with strangers. We were also both highly disintegrated in our energy at the time, and our below-sea-level perspectives on life aligned smoothly. Our friendship, while enticing, lacked boundaries and became flirty. We tried to play it off as if we were simply close friends, but we both knew it was more than that.

Eventually, Quincy and Tanya got engaged, and I was Quincy's best man at their wedding. Soon after they tied the knot, Quincy left town on a trip and Tanya reached out to invite me over to their place. That night, she and I crossed the forbidden line and embarked on an extended affair, unbeknownst to either of our partners.

While I felt guilty over our deception at the time, cheating and shadiness were so woven into my paradigm that I couldn't feel the magnitude of the potential harm I was creating. Disintegrated masculine energy had normalized deception as standard male behavior in my mind. I'd been forced to spend my childhood lying for my dad, acting like none of the women buzzing around him existed. I'd had a double life at school and kept all my friends at arm's length so I could hide the dysfunction at home surrounding sex and porn. I had cheated on ex-girlfriends before but had always gotten away with it, telling myself I would stop before ever getting caught. *Really, this is the last time.* It wasn't the last time, though. I didn't stop. The high of the thrill was too intoxicating to quit.

Tanya started scheming over time about how we might make our dirty secret legitimate someday, and I followed her lead. One night, she playfully asked Quincy how he would feel about the possibility of an open relationship and who he'd feel comfortable letting her date. He responded with my name, and she had him repeat himself as she secretly recorded him on camera. She sent the video to my phone, and I watched my best friend proclaim he would hypothetically give me permission to mess around with his wife, unaware I had already been doing so for quite some time. Tanya also got Quincy to admit he was attracted to my girlfriend, and she'd bring her name up while they had sex, planting seeds of non-monogamy in his mind.

"Tell me what you like about her," she'd say.

Quincy sat me down soon after to let me know how he felt about Anna, floating the idea that we could swap partners occasionally if the ladies were up for it. Playing dumb and acting surprised, I admitted my own interest in Tanya, and he gave me his blessing to go for it. She and I then continued our affair without shame, figuring she had handled it all like a pro and we'd be sailing smoothly from then on out. Unfortunately for Quincy, and as I figured, Anna was weirded out by the idea. He didn't get anywhere with her, and she was still unaware of how Tanya and I were betraying her.

As the situation went on, Quincy, his father, Leo, and I began briefly collaborating on a creative project that didn't go well and led to the beginning of the fallout between us. That was the last time I ever talked to Leo. As my friendship with Quincy fell apart, Tanya started getting antsy about the possibility of our connection ending, both as a friendship group and our infidelity. She wanted me to apologize to Quincy and smooth things over, but I wasn't willing to do it and got pissed off that she'd taken his side. Once that failed, she switched to focus on our romance, and I responded coldly.

"What about us?" she asked.

"There is no more us," I responded.

Eight months went by with no word from either of them. I focused on my career and my relationship with Anna, still living below sea level, hustling but lost. Quincy then got in touch out of the blue one day, asking to meet up.

When we did, he called me out on my shit. "I know about everything that was happening between you and Tanya."

Immediately, my heart sank. *Shit*. Tanya had always told me never to let word of our affair get out. I'd been living a double life for so long that complying with her request for silence had been easy for me. In the end, however, she was the one to tell him, ready for revenge after how I'd treated her when we ended it.

"Yeah, it seemed like you two really cared about each other," he went on, calm and respectful as he spoke. "Anyway, man, I think it's best that we stay out of each other's lives from now on."

Shame flooded my being and consumed me as he left. What the fuck had I done? *Why* had I done it? How could any of it have been worth losing my best friend since kindergarten?

In one fell swoop, everyone I cared about heard through the grapevine that I was a lying asshole with zero integrity. A bright spotlight of judgment lit up every angle of my shadow for all to see. While the urge to blame others was there, I knew I had no one to blame but myself.

The pain of the situation was unfathomable, but I figured I would handle it in my own way as always, grinding to the other side through willpower and avoidance, appearing to take it in stride. I kept thinking about how everything had gone too far. The cheating. The porn. The constant deception. A long string of memories passed through my thoughts, reaching all the way back to those first days at home with my dad. Who would I be without the mask he'd given me? Where was the little boy who belted out love songs about his crushes in elementary school and dreamed of getting married to the love of his life? Why did I feel so far away from who I knew I was at my core?

I don't have many regrets in life, but what happened with Quincy and his wife is one of them. At the same time, I might never have been pushed to take my healing seriously if I hadn't hit that rock-bottom moment. I might still be lost below sea level, drowning in my own hedonistic confusion without the clarity I formed around the choices I want to make in life. For those painful yet transformational lessons, I am grateful.

The Choices We Make Around Friendship

Once we see how our choices are impacting the big picture of our life, our decisions around friendship start holding more weight. Motivational speaker Jim Rohn is attributed as saying we are the average of the five people we spend the most time with. We absorb their energy and begin taking on their traits without noticing it. Staying in friendships that clash with our needs, beliefs, and values can lead to major issues in our personal lives. Our "chosen family" will never align with us perfectly, and that's good in its own way, but it's important to be mindful of what friendship means to us. What kinds of friends should we choose to surround ourselves with? What boundaries should we hold with them? What traits and habits will tell us we've found one of our people? How will hanging out with them impact us over time?

For most of my life, I've had issues around self-expression in friendships with other men. From the outside looking in, it seems women have stronger dynamics around expressing their inner worlds with one another. From having deep, emotional conversations to trying on clothes together, there's an element of shared exploration of the self. I rarely experience this with guy friends. Our social imbalance toward the disintegrated masculine encourages us to shut one another down when vulnerability is expressed.

When I was twelve, I remember telling Quincy my parents were getting divorced.

"Yeah?" he said. "Mine have been divorced for years. Big deal."

I had always wanted us to be able to support each other in a meaningful way, but I felt I couldn't go to him for connection over deep topics, so I stopped trying. We never developed the ability to be raw and unfiltered with each other in the midst of discomfort. As men, most of us fear emotional intimacy with other men and instead seek it out solely from women. The older I get, the more it seems like we guys need excuses to get together. We need sports to bond over. Activities to do. Games to play. Clubs to visit. Rarely do we get together to catch up and talk about our inner worlds, even when we're suffering deeply. Many of us feel so divorced from our emotions that we lack confidence in understanding or describing them. Without safe emotional harbors, we're far more likely to get sucked below sea level by the entropy of disintegration.

Part of choosing the friends we need is knowing which ones to stay away from or avoid opening up to. We're not going to be a good fit for everyone, and not everyone will be a good fit for us. There's no ideal situation in which we'll get along perfectly with all the people we interact with, but this is a good thing. The theory of Dunbar's number holds that the human brain can only really maintain about 150 personal connections at once anyway.[2] Creating the quality connections we desire can take time and some discomfort, but truly supportive relationships can end up lasting a lifetime. Even when they don't, we can grow in different directions without beating ourselves or anyone else up about it. Every connection we make has lessons to offer us, even if that connection is temporary.

While living in North Dakota, I had a basketball teammate from Australia, whom I nicknamed Aussie, and he was the first person to show me what emotional intimacy could be like with a guy friend. We were able to talk about everything together, even my dad's suicide, which I'd never opened up to anyone else about until then. We embarked on a whirlwind bromance, open about our love for each other because he normalized it for me. When I told him about my rock-bottom moment after everything that happened with Quincy, he cried, wishing he could have been there to help me through it.

Aussie has always cared enough to make me feel loved in those dark, honest moments. There's no judgment or shame. I've come to realize I need the full spectrum of masculine and feminine energy in my personal relationships, not just the bottom-right quadrant. I used to think Aussie was an outlier and I'd never be able to find other guy friends like him, but as I've shifted my internal landscape, the external world has brought me connections with more like-minded people. He's no longer an outlier because my standard for connection is people who own their shit—people who can talk openly about the realities of life. Those who can't do that can't offer me the friendships I need in order to grow and create fulfillment.

The friendships we choose throughout life offer us continuous opportunities to try on different ways of thinking and living. Through the ups and downs of these relationships, our inner world is reflected back to us, delivering clarity about who we are and what we want for ourselves. Our time in life is limited, and this realization causes most of us to transition from quantity to quality with our friends as we age. More than anything, it's crucial to ensure the people we choose to surround ourselves with align with the ways we want to grow.

The Give-and-Take of Friendship

Before we do the work of creating integration in our lives, the boundaries around our friendships can be hazy. How should our friends show up for us, and how should we show up for them? When disintegration—imbalance of the masculine with the feminine—is our status quo, we tend to operate from ego, which can lead to using or taking advantage of others. We can also end up on the other end of the spectrum, falling prey to bullying, codependency, or ongoing states of victimization. The common thread is one of craving validation from an unhealthy place. Without energetic give-and-take based on mutual respect and support, we can be left asking ourselves, "Is this person using me, or is our bond genuine?"

I once watched an interview with billionaire businessman Mark Cuban. He was asked whether he was afraid his friends might be using him so they could be close to his money and status. "It doesn't cross my mind," he said, explaining that when he and his friends hang out, there's a clear separation between his career and his personal life. He doesn't need to be surrounded by people who praise him for his success. Time and experience have proven that those chosen friends care about more than his wealth or accolades.

There's a fine line between transactional relationships and ones that are mutually supportive, making it difficult at times to distinguish between the two. Everyone has needs, and our connections with those we care about can fall out of balance unless we're all benefiting relatively equally.

How can you know if you're being used? Clairvoyance around this question has to do with sensing whether the other person is consciously manipulating you. Do they truly have your best interests at heart, aligned with your authentic wants and needs, or will they say whatever they have to say to get what they want from you? As we know, healing and integration hinge on honesty, truth, and the desire to illuminate what's hidden beneath the surface. Some people (like myself) are simply opportunistic, looking out for potential collaborators and allies in their quest to achieve their purpose, but upfront about their intentions and seeking mutual benefit. Shady "friends" stuck below sea level are those who leave out important information that impacts you or use their words to twist reality so you don't get wise to their tactics.

A big issue that comes into play when we're giving and taking in friendships is social pressure. We may feel pushed to give too much by doing things we don't want to do, effectively abandoning ourselves and breaking our own boundaries when we acquiesce. This is especially difficult to resist for those who are raised to be people-pleasers. Situations involving peer pressure, teasing, bullying, or other forms of abuse can become a recurring theme in such cases. Many of our most unpleasant experiences as kids end up being traumatic because they happen in front of our friends, causing potent humiliation that burns itself into our psyche. It's important as we heal to fully claim our power over our own actions. Anyone pushing you to give more than you wish to give or to join them in activities that make you uncomfortable is asking too much. Tell them no.

Case Study: Cyd
I Stopped Trying to Make Things Right

I like to think I'm constantly evolving as a person. One of the biggest lessons I've learned came from showing up for a friend who never showed up for me. This person offered me an opportunity to work together at a startup, and I loved the idea, envisioning camaraderie and a purpose-driven career. There were promises of a high salary, bonuses, and other perks—none of which I received, even after exceeding my goals.

As I watched others receive those same perks I was promised, I began to feel like my friend wanted to keep me stagnant. Later, I was presented with an ultimatum: Accept additional responsibilities without additional pay or quit. I walked away and never looked back.

Fifteen years later, I ran into this person in a parking lot, of all places, and we had a brief chat. I felt we had both grown and been given another chance to make things right, so we picked up where we left off. They had recently suffered a loss and needed help—my help—to get through this difficult period. Again, I jumped in to assist, and they dangled the carrot once more, making promises that were never fulfilled. Maturity helped me realize they weren't going to change. When the same issues resurfaced, I stopped trying to make things right. Whether or not this person ever learns their lesson, I walked away for good because I had learned mine.

Cyd embodied the integrated principles of feminine compassion and masculine support. Her friend, by contrast, operated from a self-centered place of disintegration. This imbalance helped Cyd prioritize her own well-being. Through the self-love of the integrated feminine, she took the integrated masculine action of self-protection. By walking away, Cyd remained above sea level.

Be a Balloon

The people we choose to have in our lives are reflective of which quadrant of the energy chart we currently inhabit. If our friends are trapped in their disintegrated feminine, feeling hopeless and depressed, chances are we share that energy. If they're habitually driven by their disintegrated masculine, we likely are too.

It's nearly impossible to become integrated when we spend a large percentage of our time with disintegrated people. Energy is contagious, and when we allow low vibes into our sphere of being, we block ourselves from getting where we want to be.

I will always honor Quincy's choice to remove himself from me and my disintegrated behavior. As Nana regularly told me, "Love is do right," and I hadn't done right by him, even after everything we'd been through together.

Our friends can serve either as weights or balloons in how they impact our energy. They can pull us down or lift us up. Leaving me behind enabled Quincy to cut off the weight I was bringing into his life. The move also meant he could be a balloon for me by refusing to enable my addictions and harmful coping mechanisms. I could no longer afford to live a double life from that point on. His departure forced me to get my shit together—and for that, I will always be grateful.

Through self-awareness and energetic fluency, we can try our best to be the balloon our loved ones need without abandoning our own spiritual sovereignty. The soul family we develop while working toward integration will be caring and respectful toward our energetic boundaries.

Great friendships help us become and remain integrated. If your friendships are pulling you down or keeping you low somehow, you might consider distancing yourself and being more mindful about the friends you keep. Breaking longtime bonds can be painful, but it makes room for the chosen gems we find true resonance with.

Our chosen family, apart from our friends, often includes our significant others. In the next chapter, we'll explore integration and disintegration of the feminine and masculine through the lens of love.

Key Takeaways

- Our friendships have the power to pull us above or below sea level. We need integrated friendships to thrive, and the quality of those connections hinges on the energy of everyone involved.

- If we want healthy, integrated friendships, we must choose integrated, supportive friends whose values align with our own.

- Healthy friendships hinge on an equal give-and-take. It can be difficult to tell when we're being manipulated, and we must learn never to abandon ourselves nor lose sight of our humility.

Reflections

- Do you feel like your friends lift you up or pull you down?

- What impact do you think your energy has on them?

Romance Through the Masculine and Feminine Lens

PEAK INTEGRATION

Bliss in emotional intimacy
Feeling and maintaining connection
Surrendering to love

*TRUSTING PARTNER, RESPECTING PARTNER,
SUPPORTING PARTNER, NURTURING PARTNER*

INTEGRATED FEMININE
LOVE-BASED FEELING

- Fostering reciprocal understanding, connection, and validation
- Knowing your boundaries and values in the relationship
- Loving your partner as they are
- Maintaining loyalty
- Feeling intense love and connection

INTEGRATED MASCULINE
LOVE-BASED ACTION

- Providing safety to communicate
- Setting healthy boundaries
- Creating time for your partner
- Committing to work through hard moments
- Owning a wrong/mistake
- Leaving a relationship that is no longer serving you or your partner

DISINTEGRATED FEMININE
FEAR-BASED FEELING

- Tolerating being unseen, unheard, used, or disrespected in your relationship
- Declining to communicate an issue due to fear of a partner's reaction
- Listening to react, not connect
- Feeling deserving of mistreatment
- Wanting your partner to be someone else

DISINTEGRATED MASCULINE
FEAR-BASED ACTION

- Cheating
- Using people
- Ghosting or abandoning someone
- Shutting down or getting back at your partner for hurting you
- Having unhealthy boundaries around privacy (too rigid or overly fluid)
- Hiding your true self from your partner; people-pleasing

CHAPTER 7

Romance

"To give the most fragile parts of you to a person who was once a stranger is the bravest act a human could do, which is why falling in love is scary as hell."

—MICHAEL TAVON[1]

Our romantic relationships offer some of our most profound and rewarding opportunities for integration. Finding balance in how we manage our masculine and feminine energies goes a long way in determining the health of our connection with our partner. The people we love are mirrors, reflecting the energy we emit. As we open our hearts and let them walk through our minds, they unintentionally take out flashlights and illuminate the dark corners we've hidden and disowned. Our deepest wounds are triggered in those vulnerable moments, and we lose sight of love, both for ourselves and others. Through inner work, we learn to get back to love, returning to the home within ourselves where it resides, and our significant others shine the light that shows us the way. In this chapter, we'll look at romantic love through the lens of the feminine and masculine inside us.

When I was a kid, navigating feelings of love felt straightforward. My attraction to the opposite sex was informed by simple considerations. Did I enjoy being with them? Were they fun and kind? Did they like me too? Over time, this clarity was obscured by layers of conditioning passed on by the media and men like my father. My ideas about how women should look and behave in the world were twisted by the template of the disintegrated masculine. Soon, I lost sight of the line between where my authentic choices around romance might end and where choices based on that template began. The weight of society's impressions on my psyche had me ignoring the warm fundamentals of love and making choices to service my ego, much like Dad always had. Those of us from disintegrated families swear up and down, "I'll never become my parents," but we are fated to reproduce their template until we learn healthy strategies for finding and sustaining the integrated love we seek.

We all want love in our lives, but we tend to lack the knowledge and self-awareness we need to understand our patterns around romantic intimacy. Without the insight gleaned from dedicated inner work, the whole thing can feel like a roller coaster, sending us all over the four quadrants of the energy chart. How can we protect our hearts while seeking partners? Why are we attracted to the people we like? Why do we run into the same issues over and over again? Why is there always so much drama involved? Confused, fearful, and frustrated, we go online looking for answers. Influencers offer up endless content meant as guidance for navigating relationships, but many of them are just as unhealed and disintegrated as we are. Rarely do we get relationship advice from long-term couples who consistently model healthy partnership. Over time, our lack of success connecting in intimacy pulls us deeper below sea level, robbing us of one of life's greatest joys.

Romance on the Axis

The energy of our romantic relationships offers a reflection of where we are on the chart in terms of how our hearts relate to those who attract us. We can behave as healthy, supportive partners who enhance the lives of others or end up traumatizing them through heartbreak or disintegrated dynamics.

Disintegrated masculine energy can show up in romantic relationships as cheating, ghosting, yelling, punishing, controlling, stonewalling, violating privacy, and any of the other toxic behaviors described in this chapter. It can also involve tolerating hurtful behavior from partners, staying with someone for the wrong reasons, or losing our sense of self in an attempt to enmesh with our partner. All of these destructive choices are rooted in fear.

Disintegrated feminine energy in romance revolves around feelings of being unseen, unheard, unappreciated, disrespected, used, or abandoned. It can also involve feeling afraid of our partners or unable to be ourselves for various reasons. To be stuck here is to languish in fearful feelings.

The integrated feminine shows up in relationships as love-based feelings of connection. It's about knowing we are seen, heard, and loved. It's about being curious about our partners and loving them as they are. It can also involve confidence in our boundaries within relationships and a clear understanding of our own values around connection.

The integrated masculine can be expressed in relationships through various actions. It can also involve apologizing, setting healthy boundaries, or creating safety for your partner to communicate even when they're feeling emotionally messy. As Nana always said, "Love is do right."

Peak integration in relationships involves experiencing bliss in emotional intimacy, feeling and maintaining connection, having equal give-and-take, and surrendering to love. The journey to this state is a marathon, not a sprint, and takes considerable time to build. Once you get there, it won't be forever, as entropy gears us toward disintegration. To elevate from the weight of disintegrated energy together, we must make it a habit to do the inner work it takes to get there.

My Story: Making Mountains out of Molehills

Until I got into therapy after the Quincy debacle and started looking in the mirror—*really* looking—my romantic relationships reflected the disintegration within me, but I couldn't see my own toxicity. It wasn't just about my cheating and all the deception that came with it, but also the way I handled conflict when triggered. Girlfriends would inevitably do something that hurt me, usually unintentionally, and I would react as if they had committed a mortal sin for failing to anticipate my reaction. "Why didn't you think about that beforehand?" My tone implied they were stupid for their lack of telepathy. I felt I could read minds, so why couldn't they?

As delusional as that sounds, I would go on to learn my self-proclaimed telepathy made some sense at the subconscious level. The hypervigilance I developed in response to my childhood made me keenly attentive to other people's feelings. I learned to track their energy according to every subtle shift in their voice, body language, and facial expressions, always reading between the lines, to the point that anticipating emotional needs became second nature. My brain is now loaded with stories about what people's behaviors mean, which is advantageous until the moment I get it wrong.

Before the start of my healing process, I couldn't imagine, entertain, or accept any interpretation of reality aside from the one my mind concocted. If my partner wasn't agreeing with my story, I assumed they must be lying, throwing false versions of reality my way to distort the truth and escape my judgment. I not only needed to be right, but I also needed to rub their nose in how utterly wrong they were so I could move forward with my ego intact. I chose the harshest words possible during arguments and, like my father, used emotional distance to assert my power. "I'm not talking to you until you take the time to think about what you did. Use your head."

While my authoritarian efforts only ever resulted in heartbreak and more conflict, I genuinely had no idea how difficult I was in relationships. From my end, little issues felt huge. Every molehill looked like a mountain. Naturally, my partners would start walking on eggshells in response to my behavior, fearful of setting me off, and the whole connection would eventually feel unsafe. The bad feelings between us would get so intense that disconnection felt like my only option. I was constantly running from emotional accountability, unaware of the "why" behind my feelings. During conflicts, why was I so hell-bent on vilifying and punishing the people I loved? Did I fear abandonment? Was it really all my partners' fault or were my expectations unreasonable? I had no clue. What I did know was that many of the women I dated left with the impression that I was a fucking asshole, as evidenced by the texts they'd send after we'd parted ways:

"You are scum and I hope you're aware of that. A predator would be the least anyone could label you. There are no words for men like you, and I could say that I hope you find peace with your demons, but I'm

sure they are just as disgusted with you as half of the people you come
into contact with."

Looking back, there's no denying the part I played in creating that
picture of myself. For a while, especially during my Tinder phase, I
dated from a place of shallowness, feeding the worse of the two wolves
inside me. The walls around my heart were well fortified then, causing
me to feel nothing for any of the women I spent time with. I didn't want
to open up and *give* because vulnerability was unbearable. I wanted to
take to whatever extent I could get away with. Anything I gave in return
would purely be in service to my ego. Getting a woman off ten times,
while pleasurable for her, was still all about me and how I wanted to see
myself. My attention was never consistent and always revolved around
getting women comfortable enough to fuck me. Getting to know them
and who they were was never my priority. While I was aware of all
this, the programming behind it was invisible to me. I figured I was a
bad person, but what do you even do about that?

What I now know is that I was afraid of the very thing I craved most:
to finally feel *seen* for who I really was. Deep down, I felt flawed due to
how I'd been conditioned as a kid, figuring that if I showed someone
all sides of me, they would leave or reject me like my dad did. I think
of the parts of myself as hotel elevators divided into sections of floors.
I used to show partners floors 1–30 or 60–90, but never every floor. I
desperately wanted that though, seeking the same attentiveness and
attunement I offered to those I truly cared for. The first time I actually
received that deep care was from my first therapist. He wanted to know
me, not judge me.

These days, I think of fulfilling relationships as those where I can
show my partner all my floors. They don't necessarily have to get off
the elevator to explore for themselves, but they should know each floor
exists so they can know what they're signing up for (including the
floor where my shame lives). The best relationships lead us to discover

floors we didn't even know existed, helping us expand and explore the magic of life in greater depth. To form and maintain these connections, learning to understand and manage our energy is essential. One way I've come to better understand my own disorganized push-pull patterns in relationships is by learning about attachment.

Attachment Theory and the Masculine/Feminine

Our disintegrated feelings around love most often stem from primal, subconscious fears we hold around our own survival, particularly in relation to close connection and abandonment. Parents (or other primary caregivers) who habitually frighten, judge, reject, belittle, dismiss, or hurt us can considerably harm our development by gearing our nervous system toward fear. Fear can also become hardwired in children whose parents behave inconsistently—like those who are kind when they're sober but mean when they're drunk—leading to confusion and a lack of trust. Unable to contextualize or process the unnerving behavior of our seemingly all-powerful parents, we adapt by taking on the coping mechanisms that work best for us, whether that means clinging to our caregiver or avoiding closeness with them.

While these coping mechanisms are the best options available to us when we're kids, they cement themselves into our subconscious mind as the invisible patterns of behavior that go on to plague our intimate relationships later in life. Researchers have observed and studied these developmental phenomena through what's commonly known as "attachment theory," an area of psychology that gets at the heart of how love works.

Attachment theory suggests roughly 50 percent of children end up "securely attached" to their caregivers. They enjoy safe emotional connection at home, become comfortable with both closeness and independence, and are equipped to maintain healthy relationships as adults. They operate above sea level in intimacy, able to function from a relatively integrated standpoint the majority of the time. The other half of the population, made up of those of us who grow up feeling fearful, becomes "insecurely attached." To survive the existential terror that comes with our shaky connection to our distant, disintegrated, or inconsistent parents, we take one of three main routes:

- anxiously cling to them

- avoid too much closeness with them

- oscillate between a combination of the two by first seeking closeness, then pushing (or frantically shoving) it away

As we grow, these strategies follow us into adulthood, and we revert to them while navigating closeness with others.[2]

"Anxiously attached" people are the ones in our dating pools who text all day every day and want commitment after two weeks. They fear we don't actually like them and crave constant reassurance that their presence in our lives is indeed wanted. "Avoidantly attached" individuals make us wait to hear back from them and dodge conversations around commitment, keeping us at arm's length. Those with the third style—"disorganized attachment"—may go all in with us initially only to abruptly cut and run from the relationship, much to our shock and dismay. The common factor in insecurely attached adults is an association between deep-seated fear and close connection.

While insecure attachment styles are destructive to emotional intimacy, they also come with certain benefits that keep us hooked. The roller coaster of emotion that accompanies "toxic" relationships is often interpreted by our brains as excitement or passion, and the media reinforces this view. Dynamic, drama-filled love stories sell better than those rooted in domestic bliss. As a result, securely attached people can seem boring to those who were neglected or traumatized as children. The highs and lows of disintegration are addictive and create what can feel like intense emotional depth. For this reason, disintegrated relationships feel familiar and comfortable to people whose minds run primarily on fear. Integration feels foreign and even threatening in some ways. "How could I ever get serious with one of those emotionally stable people? They've got it all together and will never understand me. I'm too fucked up for them."

Additionally, each of the three insecure attachment styles comes with superpowers that can work well for us in our adult lives. Anxiously attached people advocate for connection and are more open to doing relational work than those who give up easily. They're loyal, devoted, forgiving, nurturing, reliable, and supportive of their partners. Avoidantly attached people often come off as charismatic and cool-headed, electing to avoid conflict whenever possible. They're able to jump in and handle challenges from a logical standpoint, unphased by situations that cause emotional upset in most people.

Disorganized types tend to offer rich inner worlds, always caught up in excitement or intensity that rubs off on those around them. They are passionate, offering high highs and low lows, and emotionally attentive at a level others only see in movies. These superpowers, originally rooted in disintegration, can result in some of our most admirable traits.

While anyone can gravitate toward any of the four attachment styles, patterns arise based on how we're socialized.[3] Core masculines, especially those raised in the tight confines of patriarchal influence, tend to lean avoidant in relationships, opting to steer clear of intense displays of emotion during conflict. They often end up stuck in the bottom-right quadrant of fear-based action, not wanting to confront the root of the problem. Core feminines, who are often raised to people-please, tend to lean anxious and get stuck in the bottom-left quadrant of fear-based emotion. This can prevent them from taking the action needed to go from problem to solution. These labels lie at the end of fluid spectrums, however. We've all come across anxious core masculines and avoidant core feminines at points in our lives.

Insecure attachment is the basis of disintegration in the lives of most people. Our attachment style holds great sway over our worldview, determining our fundamental beliefs about ourselves and others. Securely attached people are generally at ease, feeling safe both in solitude and intimate relationships. Their core belief is "I'm okay; you're okay." Anxiously attached people feel uncomfortable alone, only able to find emotional safety when they're intimate with others, but they spend that time worrying their partner will leave them. They believe "I'm not okay; you are okay."

Avoidantly attached people feel safe by themselves, but not in close relationships, and are typically put off by other people's emotional "stuff." Their core belief is "I'm okay; you're not okay." Those with disorganized attachment feel uncomfortable alone *and* with others. Often, they believe they possess some fundamental flaw that causes others to treat them badly, as their parents did in the past. They think, "I'm not okay, and you're not okay either."

One of the most difficult attachment-focused experiences for adults is what's known as the "anxious-avoidant dance."[4] Often, we're initially attracted to our romantic interests partly because they possess traits we feel unable to access within ourselves. For this reason, anxious attachers find themselves drawn to the bold confidence and stoicism of avoidants. Avoidants, on the other hand, find the emotional availability of anxious types intriguing and comforting. (Disorganized attachers find themselves at different points along the anxious-avoidant spectrum based on the energy their partners are giving them. With avoidant partners, they'll cling, then swing avoidant in connections with more anxious people.)

Unfortunately, unhealed avoidants are unequipped to provide the very thing anxious attachers seek: a stable, two-way street of affection and support. Many end up in break-up–make-up cycles that last months or even years, attempting to find a comfortable balance between independence for the avoidant and emotional closeness for the anxious person. The disintegrated ego that forms after trauma tells each person, "Look! It's the missing piece to your puzzle! Your soulmate!" But this is an illusion; the core wounds within both parties make harmonious love impossible to sustain. The avoidant creates distance, the anxious pursues them, confused and hurt, and resentment between the two runs deeper over time.

The good news is that insecurely attached people can "earn" secure attachment through inner work and relational support. Anxious people can work on their self-esteem deficits and fear of abandonment. Avoidants can work on their fear of vulnerability and resistance to closeness. Disorganized individuals can do work in both areas. This not only improves the quality of our intimate relationships but our lives as a whole. If you find yourself struggling to set boundaries, people-pleasing, or pushing away those closest to you once intimacy is established, it's worth looking into the role your attachment style may be playing.

Through attachment theory, we can better understand our own *why* and those of others, allowing us to integrate our masculine actions with our feminine energy. None of the ways partners treated us in the past were personal. Their behavior was simply a reflection of what happened at home when they were a child. It becomes much easier to leave judgment out of the equation when we're able to see the big picture of cause and effect around attachment.

Case Study: Shannon
Feeling My Own Emotions Again

I'd just spent yet another sleepless night on the couch sobbing in complete despair. My husband of a decade walked into the room, looked at me with disgust and disdain, and asked what I was doing.

"I can't stop crying. You're openly having an affair and throwing it in my face every day. What am I supposed to do?"

His response before leaving the room: "Stop being so dramatic."

My abusive marriage had taken its toll, and I was frozen in inaction. I didn't know how to process, much less identify, all the emotions I was feeling. After starting sessions with a trauma therapist, I allowed myself to take a week away from my husband, which made space for me to feel my own emotions again. This was the first step toward the process of unfreezing so I could start taking action again.

I asked my husband once again to stop seeing his mistress and join me in the hard work of fixing our marriage. Once again, he said no. Rather than crying, this time I told him, "You've made a decision for both of us, and it's time to separate. I need you to leave." This moment of alignment between my feelings and actions felt empowering and, without me knowing it, was the moment my true self began to heal.

Shannon was frozen in the bottom-left quadrant of the chart, stuck below sea level in disintegrated feminine energy. With the help of a therapist, she honed her masculine energy toward action and made space to heal her heart. After taking another shot at reunion with her husband, she chose herself by integrating her feminine and masculine energies, finding empowerment through aligned authenticity.

Seeking Ourselves in Each Other

When it comes to love, core feminines and core masculines tend to desire partners who are in touch with the energy they're less comfortable embodying. I've often heard heterosexual women say they want partners who aren't necessarily feminine, but who are in touch with their feminine side. I've also heard their male counterparts in the dating scene say they want to be with women who don't allow their emotions to get in the way of taking action toward solutions to problems. The feminine wants to talk about the *why*, while the masculine wants to skip ahead to the *how*. Peak integration in relationships is about both—co-processing the *why* behind our feelings in order to get through the *how* together.

Men stuck in disintegrated masculine energy insist they want partners with no attachment to their own masculine energy. They seek out unhealed women who coddle them, act like doormats, and tell them whatever they want to hear regardless of how they behave. Dating gurus and influencers often reinforce this destructive desire, urging women to reject their own masculine energy so they can be chosen. Those who support patriarchy are drawn to this messaging, but such imbalances are never sustainable. The idea that one can fully control the emotional experience within a relationship is an illusion. Integrated men are attracted to integrated women with their own voice, interests, and purpose. Ones who won't sacrifice their sovereignty for anyone or anything existing outside themselves, who are independent in how they move through the world.

In healthy relationships, both partners get their needs met. Figuring out ways to make that happen will always involve continuous communication. At our jobs, we have systems of compensation and procedures to ensure fairness, but we hesitate to bring the same level of organization to our love lives. We sail the waters of romance without a map and then act surprised when our impulsive strategies for conflict fail to get us to our desired destination.

It can be helpful to approach conflict together with some sort of structure or procedure in mind, a bit like we do in business meetings. We're all looking for a way to express our emotional, feminine side safely, and creating a masculine container can provide that space.

It's now clear to me that we should be checking in with our partners on a consistent basis, not just when conflict arises. Having regular conversations about how both people are feeling, with the goal of mutual understanding and resolution, can be a way of normalizing communication around relationship satisfaction.

Freedom and Security

The modern normalization of open relationships, polyamory, and other forms of consensual non-monogamy highlights our existential pull between freedom and the security commitment provides. Some people point to non-monogamy and call it "natural," highlighting the harems that exist in the animal kingdom. In my case, what felt natural to me ended up being highly destructive and was based in disintegrated positioning. I would never push anyone to choose monogamy if non-monogamy worked for them.

In response to the immense challenges that can come with marriage and long-term relationships, our society has increasingly opted for "commitment lite." We want the benefits of romantic intimacy without any of its potentially harmful effects. We claim to want friends with benefits or casual sex because we lack examples of happy, committed couples. The media has flooded our minds with unrealistic expectations of constant joy in relationships. Porn has us convinced healthy couples never fight and fuck at least twice a day without fail. We look around and, surprise, none of that is happening for anyone.

Our demands are unfulfillable, but we subconsciously cling to the idealistic fantasies underlying them. Energetically, this means we have one foot out the door with everyone we're intimate with rather than experiencing the full enrichment we could be creating together. Choosing to engage in these patterns with multiple people can bring deep stress and emotional chaos that destroys our chances for peace.

True commitment is the choice to be responsible and accountable to our partners. Our ability to stick to this choice is often a direct reflection of how we commit to ourselves. To keep our internal promises to ourselves—that we will eat well, exercise, get enough sleep, or hit our financial goals—requires immense self-discipline, if we're honest. The effort it takes just to get through the day can be overwhelming, especially before we put in the work to heal our patterns around disintegrated thinking. We can't properly take care of others until we learn to take care of ourselves. To access the benefits that come with commitment in love, commitment to ourselves must become our status quo.

We protect ourselves from fears of feeling trapped or engulfed by love by opting for freedom, but a lack of direction and companionship in our lives can lead to decay of the soul. Life is hard at times, and we need to be able to find a comfortable balance between freedom and structure if we're to enjoy stable relationships. We're all trying to crack the code to establishing this balance, trying to dogmatize the rules of intimacy, but the energy of human connection is fluid. Only the long-term work of getting to know our partners through give-and-take can unveil this sweet spot for both people.

The Four Pillars of Relationships

For a while, people in the dating scene would talk about the five "love languages" outlined by author Gary Chapman, which are physical touch, words of affirmation, quality time, acts of service, and receiving gifts.[5] In truth, everyone needs all five of these things to various degrees in intimate relationships, and all five can be expressed in both integrated and disintegrated ways. In my mind the true pillars of relationships are trust, respect, comprehension, and intimacy. If one of them is fractured, all of them will fall, and it's up to us to figure out where those cracks are showing up so we can fill them in.

Mending the cracks in the pillars of our relationship is ultimately what will help keep us together. Rather than trying to be right when conflict arises, we can focus on what needs to be mended. Has someone's trust been shaken? Does someone feel disrespected? Is there a lack of comprehension somewhere? Is there something standing in the way of intimacy? With communication around these considerations, we can protect our energy and that of our partners.

Our romantic relationships are meant to trigger and shine a light on the disintegrated parts of us. Who we're drawn to at eighteen is likely to differ from who we want in our lives at thirty-five. We often look for someone to complete us when we're young but realize as we mature that the path to integration is about getting back to our wholeness and finding a partner who can be whole beside us. Mastering how we handle our feminine and masculine energies can help us bridge the gap between our feelings and actions in the context of intimate connection.

No discussion of masculine and feminine energy in relationships would be complete without an examination of sexual dynamics. In the next chapter, we'll look at how these energies show up and play out in our sexual lives, both below and above sea level.

Key Takeaways

- Our intimate relationships offer some of our most profound opportunities for integration.

- People living below sea level in romance usually struggle with issues related to attachment. Through healing and integration, we can "earn" secure attachment.

- We subconsciously look for the self-rejected parts of ourselves in each other.

- We feel an existential pull between freedom and the security commitment provides. We must learn to work with our partners to create a sustainable balance of togetherness and separateness, independence and interdependence.

- The four pillars of a relationship are trust, respect, comprehension, and intimacy. Mending any cracks in those pillars can help couples stay together.

- The path to integration is about returning to our wholeness and finding a partner who can be whole (or healing) beside us.

Reflections

- Which attachment style do you identify with most and why?

Sex Through the Masculine and Feminine Lens

PEAK INTEGRATION

Union of masculine and feminine energy as a pleasurable exchange
Spiritual and soul expansion that occurs with the right person
Comfort with switching the energetic dynamic of the bond
Safety in vulnerability

TENDER OPENNESS, MUTUAL SATISFACTION,
CONSCIOUS CONSENT, SACRED EXCHANGE

INTEGRATED FEMININE *LOVE-BASED FEELING*	**INTEGRATED MASCULINE** *LOVE-BASED ACTION*
• Having sexual confidence and enthusiasm • Communicating clear boundaries and asking questions • Feeling empowered and worthy of pleasure • Desiring to please and be pleased • Dialoguing with your partner	• Providing a safe environment for sensual expression • Being attentive to your partner's verbal and nonverbal communication • Pleasuring your partner • Controlling urges according to relationship boundaries and expectations
DISINTEGRATED FEMININE *FEAR-BASED FEELING*	**DISINTEGRATED MASCULINE** *FEAR-BASED ACTION*
• Holding discomfort; "putting up with it" to please a partner • Lacking clarity about one's desires • Having shame around sexuality • Leaning into a narrative of unworthiness, unattractiveness, or lack of sexuality • Viewing sex as validation of worth	• Engaging in sexual violence, addiction, and degradation of sex partners • Holding misogyny or misandry • Prioritizing one partner's needs • Attaching sex to an outcome • Using sexuality to numb feelings instead of awaken connection

CHAPTER 8

Sex

"We are all born sexual creatures, thank God, but it's a pity
so many people despise and crush this natural gift."

—MARILYN MONROE[1]

Few aspects of life are louder in our culture than sex, and the reasons
for this are easy to see. Greatly informed by how we were raised,
our sexual tendencies reflect back to us the most vulnerable parts
of our psyche. Our true self shows up when we're intimate with our
partners, who learn the full scope of our personalities. Together
in the bedroom, we play a primordial game of the body and mind,
where giving and taking has the potential to result in new life. This
is ground zero for the integration of masculine and feminine energy,
the divine playground where we open the portal to creation. Here,
the stakes are high. Do we feel safe there with our partner? Do they
feel safe there with us? There's much we can learn about ourselves,
love, humanity, and our spiritual essence through these intimate
meetings of the flesh.

Despite the immense importance our relationship to our sexuality plays in our life, almost none of us grow up feeling confident about it. For most of us, our first experiences with sex start in the quadrant of the disintegrated feminine; we don't know what to do and feel fearful in response. This is all part of the process of growing up, but it can keep us stuck in a miserable state of confusion unless we find functional ways to integrate via our sexuality.

In many ways, our culture fails to honor the feminine in sex. Mainstream pornography serves up an eternal buffet to feed the disintegrated masculine, while soft sex imbued with loving emotion seems more taboo than ever. We've come to a dark place. If our world is to reintegrate and move toward greater collective harmony, we must bring health and balance to the influence of our polar energies in the area of sex.

Sex on the Axis

The energy of our sex lives reflects our relationship to sex on the energy chart. Above sea level, we can reach the transcendent heights we hear when people rave about the incredible sex they're having. Below, we can experience some of the most terrible hits possible to our confidence and mental health. Our connection to sex greatly informs how we feel about ourselves and those we get intimate with.

Disintegrated masculine energy can show up in our sex lives as the degrading energy we see in mainstream porn or the prioritization of one person's needs over another's. It can also show up when we're pushing boundaries without asking, using others for pleasure, or indulging addictions related to orgasm or power in the bedroom. This is the most dangerous of the quadrants, where traumatic sexual experiences occur and go on to haunt us.

Disintegrated feminine energy in the area of sex can look like putting up with sex in order to please a partner or feeling afraid to communicate our own desires. We may feel shame around certain sexual activities and desires or view ourselves as unattractive and unworthy of pleasure. To be stuck here is to be limited by fear and feelings of hopelessness around sexual intimacy.

The integrated feminine shows up in sex as the confidence and enthusiasm that makes great sex fun. Feelings of safety, worthiness, and true desire are free to come out and play in this space. Communication, expression, and conversations around consent flow freely. We all desire to be in this space with our sexual partners, where we can be ourselves and show our feelings without judgment.

The integrated masculine can be expressed in sex by providing safety to our partners and honoring the value of our intimate connection with them. We put effort into paying keen attention to their energetic and physical signals, reading between the lines to track where they're at. We take the time to pleasure our partners without a goal or agenda in mind. To provide this for our partners allows them to let their guard down and enjoy the ride.

Peak integration in sex involves the union of our polar energies, when the feminine and masculine collaborate in ecstasy. Vulnerability becomes safe and enriching, leading to the secure intimacy we've always searched for. Activities around power exchange result in greater closeness rather than feeling that someone has gotten away with something. The souls of both participants become free to expand.

My Story: Not Sure What "Normal" Sex Was

I remember seeing my friends grimace and yell, "Eeew!" at the idea of sex when we were kids. Those moments produced a clash of cognitive dissonance in my inner world, highlighting the strangeness of my upbringing. Sex never seemed gross to me because it had been everywhere from the start—my dad's cheating and the women who came into our lives as a result, along with all the ways I was used to lure them in. The sex tapes they made together, carelessly left out for me to find. The *Playboys*. The objectifying, misogynistic jokes. The double life I had to live to survive my childhood. All of this had me feeling powerless over the influence of sexual energy in my own life. It was everywhere, all the time, and the man I looked up to prioritized it above nearly everything else.

At around the age of eleven, I got into porn, and the internet pulled me down a rabbit hole of increasingly harder content. My trauma around sex and the powerlessness I felt over its constant presence had programmed me with a predilection for dominance. Eventually, I found chat rooms where I could ask questions and talk about my explicit interests with real people. I would push boundaries, disrespectful and dehumanizing in my approach, caring nothing about the humanity of the person on the other end. I couldn't see their faces or feel their disgust or pain.

In person with women, I was far more respectful but still explicit in how I talked about my sexual interests and asked questions about theirs. Women didn't talk about sex with the braggadocio that boys and men around me did, which I liked because I personally had no desire to brag in front of the guys. I was years ahead of them anyway, fully experienced long before any of them lost their virginity. It was clear, however, that talking so openly about sex wasn't normal for most people. Armed with my father's ability to get others to open up, I would get women to tell me things they'd never shared with anyone about their desires and experiences. "I've never talked about this before." The feeling of specialness those words inspired had me drunk with pride. Many of those women wanted a relationship with me, however, or at least a continuing friendship. Too often I failed to sustain those connections, and the women got angry, saying they regretted ever telling me such personal information. They felt used and objectified.

While experimenting with different women, it became clear that my most pleasurable experiences involved people with high levels of childhood trauma. From where I stood, healthy, "vanilla" women seemed boring, and I felt they could never understand me. The "crazy" ones were more comfortable with their sexuality and understanding of what I wanted to do with them. They didn't want to hide their bodies or fuck with the lights off and were game to indulge how I reenacted my own trauma through my kinks. Sex tapes. Degradation. All of it was on the table when I met the right people.

The patriarchal messaging in movies, hip hop, and advertisements further solidified the impression that degrading women sexually was just something men did. Men who didn't treat women that way weren't men, the messaging said, and I didn't want to fall into that camp. This all went against the values I was taught at my Southern Baptist elementary school, where even Disney was said to represent sin. I had wanted true love as a child, to meet a woman I could devote myself to and marry young, but Dad did everything he could to burn that vision down. "Don't get married 'til you're forty," he told me. "Play the field."

Other male role models in my life seemed to echo my dad's sentiments around womanizing to some degree. Even Leo, Quincy's celebrity father, cheated from time to time when the opportunity presented itself. The only male role model I had with a healthy approach to sex was my uncle. When I was around twenty-five, years before he confronted me and got me into recovery over the Tanya debacle, I asked him, "When did you stop cheating on your wife?"

He was taken aback, wondering where I got the idea he ever would do such a thing to my aunt. "I've never cheated on her, Pierce. Not once."

It was the first time a man I looked up to showed me there was another way. If my uncle was at a party and the opportunity to cheat arose, his motto was simple: "Just go home."

My own addiction to cheating began in the context of my longest relationship. My girlfriend Anna was shy and liked it soft-core, preventing me from playing out the fantasies in my head. Resentment built, and I eventually got those needs met elsewhere, but I still tried to get her to open up to my desires. I would ask her to watch porn and study up on all the taboo activities she knew nothing about, never communicating what I wanted directly because I didn't want to catch any judgment. I wanted her to want the things I wanted without having to talk about any of it. I wanted her to read me without having to make myself vulnerable. *Do the work for me. Work for my love.* None of this was successful, of course, because people can't read minds, and that devoted woman finally left me when my affair with Tanya came to light.

The corrosive hold of the disintegrated masculine on my sex life had me swimming in shame and loneliness. As an adult, I had no reference for how to connect with women emotionally through sex, but I also lacked the ability to connect emotionally outside of it. All my friendships with women were laced with sexual attraction, resulting in messiness around boundaries and ruined opportunities for safety around platonic interactions. Eventually, the act of sex itself stopped being fun, as my addiction to porn wired my body with increasing levels of pathology. I could be in bed with a beautiful woman, having what should be an incredible experience, but lack the ability to get hard unless she did and said every little thing I wanted. My brain and body needed a precise cocktail of a specific series of stimuli, one after the other, for me to stay sexually engaged. The first time I couldn't stay hard, I felt embarrassed. When it became a regular thing, I knew something needed to change.

The double standard of patriarchy in our society tells us shallow, strings-free sex will poorly impact women but never men. We're supposed to think of women with a "high body count" as shallow, dirty, and awful, while men with notch-filled bedposts are seen as studs, pimps, and players. I've never judged promiscuous women, but speaking for myself as a man, casual sex, porn, and the influence of hookup culture had me circling the drain of an ever-deeper sickness of the soul. The ability to suppress my vulnerable feelings, manipulate women into my bed with false dreams, and subsequently abandon them was corrupting everything good about who I was. In my heart, I yearned for what all people want: secure, interdependent attachment. I wanted a ride-or-die partner who would be there for me no matter what was happening in life, someone I never had to worry about losing.

Imbalanced, disintegrated masculine energy can have us goal-oriented and obsessed with outward appearances, trapping us in the adrenaline rush of a superficial sex life lacking in substance. If you're a core masculine who can't climax anymore because you're too caught up in the fantasy you've built around your ego, it's time to start leaning back into the feminine energy you've suppressed and tried to disown. We all have a need for softness, support, intimacy, and meaning in our relationships. For me, it took the profound shame and isolation that resulted from hurting people to get me to look at myself and finally ask, "Who am I?" Until that point, the toxic lies of sex-soaked patriarchy had obscured the very question from my mind.

Treating Addiction

Sex addiction is different from addictions like drinking because no one can tell when you're acting out. Someone aiming for sobriety can be caught drinking more easily than a man like me can be caught glancing at women's asses or dissociating into harmful fantasies. For me, alcoholism or drug addiction never felt like threats. Substances never raised my mood or empowered my confidence in the same way. Irresponsible expressions of sex were always new, fresh, interesting, and in alignment with how I wanted to view myself, even while all of it was hurting me at my core.

When you get into therapy, whether it's for sex addiction or other dysfunctional patterns, you begin to see how your disintegrated strategies around that problem bleed into everything else. The avoidance, lies, and self-deception aren't left in the bedroom. They follow us around, setting fire to all our relationships and our inherent potential in life. What you're seeking seeks you back, and if you're seeking shallow pleasure, eventually you'll find your life is void of depth entirely. Those who truly cared for you at some point were all forced to leave. Part of the challenge for core masculines struggling to break out of this inner prison is realizing that although recovery seems like a lonely road to take, it's far less lonely than the path they're currently on.

Adults with unprocessed childhood trauma are often terrified that changing the choices they make will mean losing everything that's been keeping them alive. They fear they'll have to become someone they're not rather than returning to the authentic self they've pushed away. As someone who chose to change course, I found that the moment I committed to healing, I began to attract the very people I'd been searching for. I didn't know where I was heading (at times, I still don't), but I knew I trusted my uncle and the therapist he connected me with. Beneath my masculine need for control was a feminine need for safety, something the world tells men they don't need.

Working through my issues around sex freed me from the conditioning behind my darkest inclinations. The idea of chasing a thrill by cheating on a partner just doesn't seem worth it anymore. I'm far more focused now on getting to know the women in my life for who they are and how they feel, as well as the joys of platonic friendship. Healing has also opened the door to the feminine energy I had disowned within myself. I reacquainted myself with my need for commitment, trust, transparency, and stability. To live an integrated life above sea level, we must find this path back to our authentic selves.

How Disintegrated Programming Influences What We Like

What we're into often stems from our childhood conditioning. We may create fantasies around traumatic experiences involving our parents—like mine with my dad and his cheating—in an effort to "reenact" the memory stored in our subconscious while striving for a different outcome. In my fantasies around domination, I could finally be the man in control rather than the confused little boy watching his dad exploit women on tape. To scratch these sexual itches around familiarity gives us a primal feeling of rightness, satisfying the imprint on our minds and hearts. We seek out partners who affirm this subconscious self-concept, trapping us in cycles of unhealthy relationship dynamics that cause us pain. While most sexual activities can be enjoyed safely and consensually, healthy relating can only be achieved when we break out of mindsets that lead to self-hatred.

For a clear picture of how your desires work, ask yourself: What did you have to tell yourself about your parents to keep your attachment to them as a child? What traits of theirs did you have to normalize or even idealize in order to survive your childhood? How are those traits showing up in your sex life?

Kids from dysfunctional families often escape into in-depth fantasies for comfort, particularly ones about escaping or being rescued from their emotional circumstances in some way. They may eventually end up turning to porn, video games, or drugs, but the essence of this escapism all ties back to unprocessed trauma. Through their attachment-related daydreaming, they begin to craft their sexuality around what's known in psychology as "the healing fantasy," which reflects the needs of their repressed authentic self.[2] They create deep-seated core beliefs around what others should be and do in order to love them properly.

For instance, I wanted to be seen from a place of deep, holistic understanding. I wanted my partner to take the time and effort to study me from all angles, to the extent that I would never need to communicate my own needs. I had so much shame around what I wanted and why that I couldn't do the work of examining *myself* to the same degree and instead projected that work onto my partner. *YOU need to do this for me.* How could anyone ever get to know me so clearly when I didn't even know myself yet? What I wanted was impossible.

Your Turn: Examine Your Expectations

What subconscious expectations might you be bringing into your sexual relationships? How might your healing fantasy be informing what you're seeking? To find your answers to these questions, complete the following sentences:

I wish other people _____

_____.

Why is it so hard for people to _____

_____?

For a change, I would like for someone to _____

_____.

Maybe one of these days, I'll find someone who _____

_____.

In an ideal world with good people, other people would _____

_____.

What commonalities do you notice? For me, all my answers had to do with being deeply seen and understood in the way my dad had never made me feel. He hadn't been interested in who I was in my heart or what I'd wanted for my life. I was his little player-in-training, the future NBA star. When I found myself in relationships with women who didn't do the work of looking closely at who I authentically was, in spite of all my intense efforts to evade the vulnerability that would come with showing them that person, I felt triggered and insisted they should change.

If your fantasies are driving your sex life, you're bound to hit a crisis at some point. Real intimacy is never built when we're on the hunt for dopamine hits and ego gratification. Trapping ourselves in a cage of impossible ideas that can never exist in the real world keeps us far away from the fulfilling love we all want most. These out-of-date programs have to go if we're to make room for mature relationships where we can have connected sex that makes us feel seen and valued for who we are. While I'd never tell someone to quit porn, drugs, video games, or intense sexual fantasizing, these forms of escapism do no favors to users who overindulge and end up missing out on what matters.

Hypersexuality in Traumatized Kids and Adults

Studies have shown that survivors of sexual abuse can exhibit symptoms of hypersexuality as a result of their traumatic experiences. This phenomenon is characterized by an obsessive fixation on fantasies, urges, or risky behaviors. It can lead to a high number of sexual partners, sex addiction, involvement in sexually abusive relationships, and difficulty enjoying true intimacy, among other effects. Certain demographics are more prone to experiencing hypersexuality as a result of trauma, including survivors of childhood sexual abuse, people with complex PTSD, and individuals with insecure attachment styles.

If an experience involving sexuality is indeed so traumatic to a child, why would they go on to seek more of it? The answers can be both physiological and psychological. During a traumatic experience, our bodies release hormones like cortisol and adrenaline, which can impact the normal functioning of our brain's reward system. This can lead to an increased drive to seek sexual pleasure as a way to cope with the emotional distress caused by the trauma itself. Some survivors feel that using their sexual power allows them to reclaim a sense of control over their bodies. They may also grapple with intense emotional turmoil and seek connection through physical intimacy, inadvertently utilizing hypersexual behavior as a substitute for genuine intimacy.

It took me years to understand that exposure to my dad's lifestyle had indeed been traumatic. The kids around me didn't have their innocence leveraged, as I did, as a way to attract sexual partners to their parents. Those kids didn't stumble across porn or videos of their parents having sex with various people. I see now how all of this led to hypersexuality in my own life. There were no boundaries in my dad's home, and sex was central to everything. Focusing on my fantasies and attempting to become like my father felt like a means of relating to him. I simply wanted connection that felt gratifying and validating, but I missed out on the fact that sex was something to be handled with care—something private and special rather than gratuitous.

The Empowerment of Sexual Confidence

We often hear people refer to sex as a "need," but unlike food, water, and sleep, it's not something we die without. Those carnal requirements tend to lie a bit further from how we think about ourselves. To feel sexy and desired—in touch with our "mojo"—has little to do with weight or height and everything to do with our confidence in our creative life force. To feel ugly or undesirable, by contrast, can polarize us right down to rock bottom, disconnected from our earthly vitality. To be in touch with this part of ourselves, whether we're single or in a relationship, communicates to others a knowing of the self. It's the masculine energy of security and stability that comes with the knowledge of what we want and how to handle ourselves intimately. People with this confidence don't give off the impression that they're needy, but rather grounded in what they want. When we have healing to do, accessing this confidence becomes impossible, so it's worth examining what our intimate challenges are.

Many of us meet resistance when it comes to the issue of communication around sex. We need to talk about what we like for things to go well, but it's a topic that makes us feel vulnerable. Core feminines, from what I hear, are often sick to death of being sexualized on a constant basis and would rather not talk about sex all the time. As a man, I want to make my partner feel sexy by communicating openly about my feelings, but I don't want to cross the line of making her feel creeped out or objectified. I don't want any more women feeling used by me, but I have frequently felt judged for voicing my desires within my committed relationships. Balance is needed for both parties to feel safe.

Researchers have found the disgust response tends to be higher in women than in men, particularly in the sexual domain, lending to the fact that we men can be into some pretty odd shit. When I think of some of the porn I've liked, I notice a lot of it was shocking, disturbing, or weird for the sake of being weird. I've always felt an ego-driven desire to make my partners feel safe enough to push boundaries in the bedroom, though always consensually. We men lack templates for what playfulness might look like rather than rough attempts at control. Why make love when we're unconvinced it will be pleasurable for us?

We're told we need to lead, not be present and play, which saddles us with an agenda or goal. We lose sight of our integrated feminine energy and cut ourselves off from our intuition, focused on *doing* rather than *feeling*. Through this mindset, we become selfish and controlling, making every interaction all about us. The reality is that we can't control exactly what happens in our partners' bodies and minds. All we can do is create safety, try to learn about them, and do our best to create the experience they're looking to have, provided we're up for it.

Case Study: Thomas
We Discovered an Infinite Variety of Ways to Enjoy Each Other Sensually

Following surgery for prostate cancer at the age of sixty-eight, I lost the ability to get erections. It was then necessary for me to redefine how to perform with my partner. I already knew, in theory, that I could still have a satisfying sex life without intercourse, but nevertheless I found myself in unfamiliar territory. Luckily, I was blessed with a loving, creative partner who welcomed exploration. I came to realize that I had relied much more than I needed to on a stereotypically traditional, predictably intrusive (so to speak) definition of good performance.

Years of practice accounting for and communicating my full range of emotions became an asset as we discovered an infinite variety of ways to enjoy each other sensually. The result of this "forced" learning was a new level of mutual pleasure so complete and distinctive that my partner, who calls herself a gender-reconciliation activist, repeatedly said, "We should take this on the road so you can teach other men how to satisfy their partners." I attribute my side of our shared evolution to my ability to accept and embrace the full range of my emotions. This helped us explore vulnerability in new and wonderful ways.

Thomas arrived at the disintegrated feminine quadrant of the chart after losing his ability to be intimate in ways that followed conventional scripts. Through vulnerability and acceptance, he was able to heal his feminine energy and move into aligned masculine energy, where he and his partner explored new strategies. Integration on his feminine side helped him account for his full range of emotions, while integration on his masculine side helped him communicate them clearly and openly.

Immersing ourselves in fantasy is a useful coping mechanism when we're young. When we lack control over our environment, choices, and lives as a whole, imagining ourselves in more empowered, pleasurable, or controllable circumstances can help us get through negative experiences with less pain. However, getting lost in our fantasies or lacking the ability to clearly separate them from reality leads to disintegrated behavior when we're adults. For the feminine and masculine to unite sexually from a place of integration, the starting point must be an equal playing field where both people meet in trust, empathy, and care for each other. From this status quo, we can travel anywhere on the map, trying on any role that suits us and indulging our playful side.

The yin-yang dynamics of masculine and feminine polarity are rooted in the soul, evidenced by how they've played out in spiritual arenas since the dawn of time. Next, we'll explore how these energies manifest in our relationship to the Divine.

Key Takeaways

- Sex is ground zero for the integration of masculine and feminine energy, but many of us struggle to feel confident or safe in this area.

- What we're into sexually stems directly from our childhood conditioning. Many of us adapt to abuse, neglect, or dysfunction by forming healing fantasies around the needs of our repressed, authentic self.

- Feeling sexy gives us a sense of confidence in our creative life force, but sex itself is a vulnerable topic that can cause friction or distance between core masculines and core feminines.

- Learning about our subconscious programming equips us to compartmentalize our fantasies from reality in healthy ways.

- Through integration, we can create the common ground necessary for a conscious and thrilling sex life.

Reflections

- How does the "you" in your fantasies differ from the "you" of your everyday life?

- How are your fantasy "self" and fantasy partner(s) providing comfort to your psyche?

Spirituality Through the Masculine and Feminine Lens

PEAK INTEGRATION

The experience of enlightenment
Personal, non-performative connection with a higher power
Unconditional connection and communication with the Divine
The ability to access the ultimate portal of love

EMOTION-BELIEF-CHOICE-PURSUIT

*HUMBLE SURRENDER, UNWAVERING FAITH,
EMBODIED JUSTICE, PURPOSEFUL DEVOTION*

INTEGRATED FEMININE *LOVE-BASED FEELING*	INTEGRATED MASCULINE *LOVE-BASED ACTION*
• Remaining open to other beliefs and practices • Connecting to the feminine and masculine energy of your higher power • Finding comfort and presence in your beliefs; connecting to an inner truth • Loving self and the external	• Keeping commitment and devotion to a spiritual practice • Practicing prayer and meditation • Engaging in a community of like-minded practitioners • Living in accordance with your spiritual beliefs • Treating others as you would want to be treated
DISINTEGRATED FEMININE *FEAR-BASED FEELING*	**DISINTEGRATED MASCULINE** *FEAR-BASED ACTION*
• Feeling shame for the way you are • Experiencing spiritual deprivation or emptiness • Believing that you are unworthy of God's love • Fearing God	• Resisting opposing beliefs; passing judgment • Proselytizing • Acting superior to others • Committing hateful acts in the name of God

CHAPTER 9

Spirituality

"Religion is for people who are afraid of going to hell;
spirituality is for those who have been there."

—VINE DELORIA JR.

When you think of your "higher power," whether that's Jesus, Allah, or a more generalized presence of universal oneness, what does your relationship to it entail? Is your concept of spirituality about being or doing? Love or action? Integrity or good works alone? In the realm of spirit, peak integration requires both, calling us to both be and do by uniting the feminine and masculine in reverence of the Divine.

We have the free will to choose what the term *higher power* means to us throughout life. Unfortunately, many of us have moved away from God entirely due to imbalances in the masculine and feminine energy of popular spiritual traditions. Organized religions have historically thrived on disintegrated masculine dynamics, seeking to control the masses through rigid moral principles. Spiritual practices rooted primarily in feminine energy and inner practices can feel too vague for some people to connect with. Our purpose in this book is to combine loving intention with order, allowing us to sustain a close connection with our higher power that serves our authentic self and our vision of who we wish to be in the world.

The 12-step tradition, which I've worked through, asks us to open ourselves up to the idea that a power greater than ourselves can restore us to sanity. This foundational act empowers us to surrender, letting go of all the heaviness we're unable to hold on our own. When we're caught in the shadow of disintegration, we're often trapped in our own personal dogma, insistent that we're in full control over ourselves, others, and our perception of how the universe works. By admitting it's all too big for any of us to carry on our own, we invite the possibility of greater clarity about the truth of who we are and how our lives are unfolding.

Spirituality on the Axis

Our spiritual beliefs are represented on the energy chart in relation to how we experience God and relate to the spiritual journeys of others. Below sea level, religion and spirituality tend to create immense conflict, shame, and even violence. Integrated attitudes toward God, by contrast, provide us with some of life's most sublime experiences.

Disintegrated masculine energy shows up in the spiritual sphere as any fear-based action we take in relation to God. This can look like dogmatic judgment, self-righteous behavior, or attempts to convert unwilling people to one's religion. It can look like committing violent or hateful acts in the name of God. Our modern imbalance toward disintegrated masculine energy in organized religion has resulted in less overall interest in religion throughout our culture.

Disintegrated feminine energy in the area of spirituality can look like deep shame or disconnection from God, or the sense that we're unworthy of God's blessings. We may fear God or find ourselves stuck in a spiritual scarcity mindset, believing we are limited rather than expansive in spirit.

In spirituality, the integrated feminine is felt as an openness toward all the universe has to offer, even when it comes to clashing beliefs and practices. It can also be felt as confidence that we're divinely protected, or a connection to God via our inner truth. This is where we feel love for ourselves and all beings, grateful for all that the energy of creation provides.

We see the integrated masculine in spirituality in the form of commitment to a spiritual practice such as prayer or meditation. It can also be seen in our actions around devotion, the search for spiritual truth, and engaging in communities of like-minded practitioners. Through divine masculine action, we bring our good works to the world.

Peak integration in spirituality can be likened to what Eastern traditions refer to as enlightenment. It is a deep, personal, non-performative connection with the higher power of our choice, allowing us to maintain an unconditional connection with the Divine. This enables us to remain in touch with our inner portal to the ultimate source of love.

My Story: Religion and Spirituality

I inherited my spiritual beliefs from my mom's side of the family. Her mother, my Nana, worked as a cook at a megachurch for forty years, serving cardinals, bishops, and other VIPs of the Catholic world. She went to Mass every day and passed her lifestyle down to my mom, who was into Catholicism but also open to more mystical energies. Mom got into tarot, Lenormand cards, and runes while incorporating Bible passages into her readings. I grew up watching her practice and integrate divination through Scripture, her cards, astrological charts, spirit guides, and angel guardians.

My mom's ability to see through the veil filled our house, culminating in a number of notable experiences. During high school, my deceased grandfather would come to her in dreams and tell her details about mischief I was getting up to with one of my more problematic girlfriends. After getting caught sneaking around a couple of times, I learned to trust Mom's mysticism.

Her ability to communicate with ghosts existed within me as a kid. When I was a toddler, Dad worked nights, and I slept in my parents' bed. There was a rocking chair in the room, and I told my mom I was "scared of the man in the chair," who would wave at me and call himself Ed. My grandfathers, who I never met, were named Edwin and Edward. No one could ever decide which of them I might be seeing. These experiences with intuition strengthened my connection with my feminine side and began informing how I handled my choices.

A turning point in my spiritual journey arrived when I released the traditional beliefs of my Catholic upbringing in favor of a more personalized spiritual path. I believed in God, but I didn't *feel* it inside me before that point. After my dad committed suicide when I was in high school, my heart started searching for answers, and I began exploring what God might actually feel like for me. I started doing yoga with a spiritual teacher and tried mushrooms to access different realms of consciousness. During my senior year of high school, I took a class about religion, where I learned about Buddhism, Hinduism, and more.

Eventually, I was able to integrate my authentic spiritual beliefs with my actions, harmonizing the energies of my spiritual framework. These days, I attend Agape, a trans-denominational spiritual center led by Michael Beckwith, who not only cites the Bible in his sermons but also the Quran, Torah, and other sacred texts. As a Catholic who's been discriminated against by other types of Christians, I've always sought integration between various schools of thought in my spiritual life.

This impacts my purpose even today, guiding my internal reflections and external acts of service.

When I first heard my dad had passed, my first thought was for the well-being of his soul. "I hope he's okay," I said, praying he hadn't ended up in Hell. These days I choose to think of God as a love-based being rather than the wrathful one I was taught about in Baptist school. It doesn't click with me that a supreme being would be ruled by ego, neediness, and everything that's wrong with humanity. Rather than Hell, I've come to believe in Karma and Eastern traditions around reincarnation. In a universe that runs on cycles through the duality of yin and yang, it makes sense to me that we would go through multiple lives, choosing which difficulties we'll take on in our current journey through consciousness.

What Is God?

It's understandable that atheists would reject the idea of an all-seeing, dogmatic old man keeping score in the sky. We can't deny the existence of spirituality as a whole, however, as the energy that fills and connects us and is felt by everyone at all times. Already, we have many ways of measuring invisible energies that affect us, like X-rays and ultraviolet light. There's no telling what else is out there waiting to be discovered.

The more we resist acknowledging the existence of the unseen both within and around us, the further we drift from our true nature. Many traditional interpretations of the Divine can feel too rigid, particularly those that emphasize disintegrated masculine traits. I find it challenging to reconcile the idea that God loves everyone equally but only offers salvation to those who believe in Jesus. Perhaps we're all tuned into a universal frequency of consciousness, capable of sensing, observing, and reflecting one another's energies.

There's an age-old question about whether the energy that powers our spirits, which many experience as God, is inherently benevolent. But what if God, as a supreme being, embodies the full spectrum of both the masculine and feminine, just like nature and everything else around us? To reach peak integration is to achieve harmony between the two. It takes a dedicated spiritual practice to arrive there and even more work to maintain our position. God is always available to us, but we're human and inevitably hit challenges throughout our journey, which is how learning happens. We lapse into periods below sea level, where the disintegrated feminine governs our emotions and the disintegrated masculine directs our actions. With a strong channel to God, we can access spiritual guidance and harmony more often and more quickly than without.

Many people who live their lives stuck below sea level believe something is inherently wrong with them. If that were true, we wouldn't be here today. The God that made us is fully invested in giving us the best possible chance at survival. Though most of our universe consists of freezing darkness, light and life continue to prevail. Every child is born into this world wanting that warmth, connection, and benevolence. That's the basis of who we all are. There is nothing wrong with you, me, or any of us. By finding access to our spiritual power, we can discover everything that's *right* about ourselves.

Case Study: Kevin
It's Not Their Orientation; It's Their Openness

Many years ago, I was a young priest in a parish, inexperienced but doing my best. One day I happened to overhear a conversation between two elderly gentlemen from the church. They had no idea I could hear them and spoke freely.

One asked, "Do you think the father is gay?"

"Of course he is," replied the other. "That's why he's the best priest we've ever had."

This conversation startled me. I would have expected them to be uncomfortable with homosexuality, coming from an older generation. Their words got me thinking about what it was they were noticing. What made them suspect the father was gay? I became more observant and thought a great deal about the human behavior I saw around me. I soon realized that what we observe in others isn't "gay" or "straight" behavior, but feminine and masculine energy. In our culture, gay men are often more comfortable with their feminine side than their straight counterparts. This is why certain professions attract those who are more in touch with the feminine side of caretaking or spirituality, regardless of whether they're male or female, straight or gay.

Reflecting on my own profession, I suddenly realized why so many of the most insightful priests have been the gay ones. Why, in so many cultures, gay men have been the shamans who served as the bridges between worlds. It's not their orientation; it's their openness to the feminine side that all of us are given but most of us fear. I'm grateful for that overheard conversation.

After overhearing this conversation, Kevin realized the nurturing behavior he saw in men was rooted in their connection to integrated feminine energy, not their sexual orientation. He learned that the feminine underlies our expressions of caring and mysticism, and that this energy is available to us all.

The Shift After Awakening

We spend the first stage of our lives living in our ego, making choices from behind the mask of the false self we show to the world. At some point, reality roughly brushes up against the story of our false self, and we experience cognitive dissonance. If this experience is impactful enough, we awaken to the fact that what we've been telling ourselves is inaccurate. This can shatter our sense of self and send us into a dark night of the soul, feeling as if we might be losing our mind. The shift that comes with aligning our perception more closely with the reality we share with others allows us to begin swimming toward the surface through the process of integration.

The awakening that followed my rock-bottom moment came to me through a sense of curiosity that had already been brewing within me, wondering how my life could be different. When we're at our lowest, we find ourselves in a place we've never been before, which encourages us to seek answers we've never looked for before. Asking new questions and laying new pathways of thought is critical to letting go of the patterns that lead us astray. We must plant our feet firmly in the ripe soil of change and embrace the unknown. From there, we can begin to explore in ways that feel safe to our soul.

Awakening, unfortunately, often causes us to lose people in our lives. Those who can't follow us into the future as we rebuild ourselves fall away. We take our power back by focusing deeply on the steps of the healing process. Our desperation for recovery from our suffering becomes so loud that we're willing to do whatever it takes to find the answers we need. In this focused place of self-reflection, we can zero in on the root of our issues and change our perception around how we're living. Embracing our authentic selves without shame allows us to integrate the new wisdom we've gathered. From there, we can begin to make better choices that align with our vision of who we want to be.

The Search for Truth

At the heart of spirituality is the search for the truth of the nature of our existence. There's something satisfying about hearing truth that resonates with the universal intelligence within us. It hits our inner knowing, and we feel a sense of rightness and peace. Unfortunately, this quest for truth can open us up to magical thinking, making us vulnerable to the predators of the earth. Many power-hungry figures have used spirituality to manipulate and abuse others, driven by their own agendas. The social hierarchies created by these people have no place in a world where we're all created equally by God. Energy is the great equalizer, and titles like *priest* have no bearing on karma. Many people have understandably rejected religion and spirituality altogether, feeling that believing in God will involve them in systems of exploitation and control run by lying, manipulative charlatans.

The top-down, authoritarian approach to spiritual practice is feeling increasingly antiquated now that the hearts of so many abusive religious leaders have been exposed. Modern-day spirituality leans more toward the idea that we can all take our personal power back by venturing within.

It takes great humility to find the truth we seek about ourselves and the world, particularly when it comes to the part we play in our pain. When we show up in life as if we have all the answers, we can't grow into our true power. Living in the lies of our own delusions remains our status quo until we're willing to admit we don't, in fact, know it all and need help moving through our journey. Without that openness to new knowledge, we never get deep enough within ourselves to find out what's going on with us. The ego operates based on what we feed it. It aligns with the values we build around our subconscious core beliefs. We can change the programming we feed the ego to manifest the goals of our authentic self.

The Imbalance of the Masculine

Religion thrives on masculine energy, striving to apply moral structure and rules to the chaotic nature of life. Spirituality is more anchored in feminine energy, having more to do with the unseen laws of nature and the workings of cause and effect. There's nothing inherently wrong with religion, but it often feels vapidly disconnected from the underlying frequency of *feeling*.

Much of the backlash to religion exists in response to the disintegrated masculine behind much of the suffering it creates. The feminine is attacked and targeted for control. Conversations about purpose, dreams, and creativity—the true substance living within us—are eschewed for sermons shaming believers for their alleged sins. The physical manifestation of this beatdown of the feminine shows up in how women are treated within several mainstream religions. They're told what to wear, say, do, and think. They're told God is male and women were created within a man's body (the rib of Adam) rather than the other way around. When misogyny is tied to systems of morality, the feminine suffers in other aspects of life.

The feminine represents rest, compassion, and countless other traits we all need to live healthy and fulfilling lives. By acting as if the feminine is beneath any of us, we block ourselves from the ability to feel or find love. When we live in the prison of a massive, fragile ego, we divorce ourselves from our connection to the source energy we call God, the great equalizer. No one is above anyone else on the spiritual plane.

Many ancient spiritual traditions have portrayed a balance between the divine masculine and feminine, leaning away from the imbalance of masculine energy we find in modern organized religion. Taoism emphasizes the interconnected, interdependent nature of yang and yin, with yin representing the cosmic feminine. This universal polarity is mirrored in Hindu stories of Shakti (feminine) and Shiva (masculine); Saraswati (feminine) and Brahma (masculine); Lakshmi (feminine) and Vishnu (masculine); and their avatars, Radha (feminine) and Krishna (masculine); and Sita (feminine) and Rama (masculine). We also see both gods and goddesses in the traditions of ancient Greece, Rome, and China. The divine feminine spirit has its place in the tales of creation.

New Takes on Religion

Research in the field of neurobiology shows that spiritual experiences likely occur in the prefrontal regions of the brain that handle our high-level cognitive processes.[1] When the mind senses a threat and the amygdala takes over, sparking a fight, flight, flee, or fawn response, the prefrontal cortex essentially goes offline, no longer in control of our executive function. This implies that when we're stuck in survival mode, powered by fear and other low-vibrational emotions, we inhibit ourselves from activating the part of the brain that allows us to connect to God. We remain blind to higher states of consciousness until our mind, body, and spirit can confidently feel safe and open to divine connection. For this reason, practices like meditation can provide paths toward experiences involving spiritual enlightenment. As the nervous system learns to relax, the amygdala can do the same, allowing the prefrontal cortex to take the wheel.

The power of faith has been well documented in its ability to bring us through the hardest of challenges. In Viktor Frankl's book *Man's Search for Meaning*, he theorized that the people who survived the Holocaust alongside him, who had some degree of agency over their lives, were those who anchored themselves in a spiritual foundation of hope.[2] The same can be said for my Black ancestors who survived the era of slavery in America, who had no reason to believe things could ever get better for them but rooted themselves in faith regardless. Though we're limited from viewing the broader picture in survival mode, we still have access to our connection to God.

Death comes when we remove our ability to choose by accepting that there's nothing we can do for ourselves. Our main challenge in life is to not get stuck below sea level in a state of despair. Through integration, we keep our spirits alive. We always have a choice, even if that choice is to hold on to our sense of faith.

The psychedelics movement has also gained steam as a legitimate means of spiritual healing. Our collective craving to go inward and explore our feminine energy can be jump-started by plant medicine like mushrooms or ayahuasca. Controlled use of psilocybin has been shown to improve symptoms related to depression, anxiety, PTSD, and other conditions rooted in our subconscious programming. Though the safety of these substances is often disputed, the future holds promise for greater choice in how we treat sickness stored in the soul as trauma.

We might also think of therapy as a new form of church, as it invites everyone to have a seat at the table of healing and engage in acknowledgment for who they are. We're all looking for avenues where we can express ourselves without being judged, along with communities that acknowledge all parts of us. With a good therapist, emotions like anger or loneliness are welcome. They don't make us demonic or pathetic, only human. When we're tuned into our feelings, we can find balance between our masculine behavior in the world and the feminine *why* beneath the surface.

For many of us, music has a place in our spiritual experience. It's the one tool that can instantly unite us all on the same energetic frequency, creating powerful emotions in the brain and body. This applies to all genres of music—we can connect with others over hip hop, R&B, rock, or country while being fully ourselves. At concerts, crowds move as individual pieces, each unique yet flowing together in harmony. It's good to keep in mind how much the music we consume impacts our spiritual nature. When we primarily listen to dark, demeaning, low-vibe content, that energy becomes part of our vibrational makeup.

> *"Music, I believe, was put on earth to enlighten and empower us, and make us feel closer to our center."*
>
> **—PRINCE**[3]

For me, the true key to accessing peak integration through spirituality has been by linking emotion with my belief in the presence of God. Those who seek to convert us to their religion urge us to skip to belief, right over our feminine *why*, but embodiment is key to all effective healing practices. While heady intellectualizing about God can provide much moral inspiration, the body is where we personalize our connection with the Divine.

Individualism and Justice in Modern Spirituality

The Age of Enlightenment brought about a wave of rational thought that caused many to reject the dogmas of organized religion. What began as a necessary pushback against rigid patriarchal structures gradually shifted us into an era where reason and materialism took center stage. Today, we see the echoes of that shift in the rise of modern spirituality. It's no longer about submission to a higher authority but about cultivating personal growth, fulfillment, and balance. This sounds appealing on the surface, but there's an inherent risk in how we've come to practice spirituality in the Western world. Spirituality, for many, has become an inward, almost privatized journey. We seek mindfulness through yoga, self-discovery through meditation, and healing through energy work. These practices are valuable, but they're often framed as isolated, individual experiences. We talk about unity in the classroom, yet the moment we step outside, we return to our personal lives, and the sense of community dissolves.

In many ways, our spiritual practices reflect the same individualism that dominates Western culture—a culture that encourages us to improve ourselves but often at the expense of a broader, collective transformation. This focus on the self can even be commodified. Spirituality, like many things in the West, becomes another product to consume—a means of self-optimization. It's a cycle of self-care that doesn't always extend outward to the care of others. This self-centric approach can leave us disconnected, longing for deeper community yet unsure how to build it.

True spirituality, in its most powerful form, transcends the individual. It doesn't stop at inner peace. Instead, it calls us to turn that peace outward and build justice in the world around us. Throughout history, some of the most impactful spiritual leaders understood this deeply. Figures like Jesus, Martin Luther King Jr., Nelson Mandela, and Sojourner Truth didn't just pursue personal enlightenment or salvation—they were driven by the conviction that spirituality must create a more just, compassionate society. They recognized that real peace requires fairness, equity, and the courage to fight for the dignity of all people. Spirituality is not an escape from the world's problems—it's an invitation to engage with them. If we truly believe in interconnectedness, we must not limit that belief to yoga mats or meditation cushions.

In Buddhism, bodhisattvas are enlightened deities who have put off entering paradise in order to help others reach enlightenment as well. This reflects a key truth: Spiritual progress means little if it's not shared. In the Judeo-Christian tradition, the idea that all people are made in the image of God means every person is worthy of respect, care, and love. To act against another is to act against the divine spark within them. Spirituality is about awakening to this truth—not just in ourselves but in every person we encounter. It's about recognizing that the personal and the collective are intertwined, and that any meaningful spiritual practice must extend beyond our individual lives to bring healing and justice to the world.

An integrated spiritual practice includes both an internal, mystical relationship with the Divine and outward contribution to equality. This approach combines our feminine, internal experience of mysticism with masculine action. Our inclination toward justice is an expansion of our nurturing desire for inclusiveness, but the fight to get there is a masculine-energy affair.

Our relationship with God is both personal and sacred. It's our birth-right to choose a perspective of spirituality that aligns closely with our internal truth. Our spiritual endeavors are also communal. When we cultivate a strong, love-based connection to the Divine, we can expand by giving to others and delivering blessings into their lives. The oneness of God unfolds in the cycle of how we pour into one another.

Much of how we choose to live is rooted in our relationship to our purpose. When our connection to our higher power of choice is strong and clear, we can move in a consistent direction that serves our reason for being on this earth. Next, we'll explore the role of purpose in relation to the polar energies in our lives and how we can use them to drive our lives to our desired destination.

Key Takeaways

- To reach peak integration in the area of spirituality requires us to both "be" and "do" by uniting the feminine and masculine in reverence of the Divine.

- Many people have moved away from the concept of God due to imbalances between the feminine and the masculine across different religions and spiritual practices.

- We're all connected to divinity as conduits of the universal energy of consciousness. As products of this intelligence, we can believe God is working in our favor. We are one.

- Spiritual awakenings reveal the gap between our false and authentic selves, aligning our perception more closely with the collective's shared reality.

- At the heart of spirituality is the search for the truth of the nature of our existence. We can reclaim our personal power by venturing within to find the truth of ourselves.

- Spirituality runs on feminine energy, while religion thrives on masculine energy. The feminine is often targeted for control by men in religious traditions, but no one is above anyone else on the spiritual plane.

- The prefrontal cortex goes offline when we're disintegrated and stuck in survival mode. When we learn to regulate our nervous system, we open ourselves up to deeper spiritual experiences.

Reflections

How does your belief in a divine connection shape your understanding of self, your relationships with others, and your actions in the world?

Purpose through the Masculine and Feminine Lens

PEAK INTEGRATION

Being in the state of creation
10,000-hour mastery of one's trade
Living one's *ikigai* or *raison d'être*

EMOTION-BELIEF-CHOICE-PURSUIT

*INSPIRED DRIVE, CLEAR INTENTIONS,
MEANINGFUL IMPACT, COMMITMENT*

INTEGRATED FEMININE *LOVE-BASED FEELING*	INTEGRATED MASCULINE *LOVE-BASED ACTION*
• Feeling that you are positively contributing to a greater cause • Feeling inspired and motivated in what you do on a daily basis • Apprenticing (like residency as a doctor); being a sponge • Having integrity • Taking pride in your work • Embodying your purpose as an artform	• Committing to a sustainable and long-term pursuit; sticking with something consistently; being resilient • Embodying commitment and discipline to continuous growth • Being a leader • Preparing for the moment • Engaging in community culture
DISINTEGRATED FEMININE *FEAR-BASED FEELING*	DISINTEGRATED MASCULINE *FEAR-BASED ACTION*
• Operating from a mentality of scarcity • Avoiding conflict at the expense of your own well-being • Approaching work without purpose or joy	• Micromanaging • When leading, putting all responsibility on team members without support • Continuing to participate in a system you don't believe in without any strategy or plan for change • Hustling for your worth

CHAPTER 10

Purpose

"In your life, at any given moment, the strongest
dream of that moment wins that moment."
—DAVE CHAPPELLE

Western cultures are obsessed with hero stories starring people who rise from rock bottom to a place of peak integration. We watch movies like *Batman Begins*, rooting for the protagonist to master the lessons delivered by the wounding of their tragic past. This "started from the bottom," rags-to-riches mentality is the basis of the American Dream. Our entertainment industry sells us the message that we can get rich doing whatever we want while making an unforgettable impact, along with the hope that comes with that dream. With the power of the internet and widespread availability of in-depth knowledge, this promise of personal prosperity seems more attainable than ever. We can learn to code for free, sell our art to millions online, or host our own podcast, all from the comfort of our homes.

In spite of the availability of avenues for fulfilling our potential, many of us still feel lost and hopeless. For millennials like myself, life is like a restaurant with too many choices on the menu. The sheer number of possibilities overwhelms us into apathy. We watched our parents work themselves to the bone and swore we would have more fun, stunting our ambition in the areas of self-discipline and sacrifice. "Wait your turn," we were told, but our turn didn't arrive. The rich got richer as the middle class disappeared, along with our dreams of buying homes and starting families of our own.

After observing this turn of events, Gen Z declared, "Fuck that; my turn is now." While they possess unparalleled access to opportunity and knowledge, they have grown up immersed in a culture of superficial visuals, where success and fulfillment seem easily attainable. Their social validation often stems not from in-person interactions but from clicks, views, likes, and comments. This digital-first upbringing can lead to identity deficits, as real-world connection and attunement are critical during formative years. The resulting disintegration is evident in rising global rates of depression and anxiety, creating barriers to discovering our purpose—the central path to meaning and fulfillment in our lives.

Our purpose comprises the *why* behind our feminine energy, which determines the direction of our masculine-rooted actions. Capitalism and social media push us to focus on the external, but achieving fulfillment requires us to divide our attention between our inner and outer worlds, forming an energetic channel. We can't discover the unique fingerprint of who we are without ease of access to our deepest internal states. We can't operate from our authentic self while the neurosis of our ego is perpetually in the driver's seat. The dopamine rush of a thousand likes is fleeting, but sustainable, long-term fulfillment is powerful enough to carry us through the most dreadful of life's challenges.

Our purpose sustains us, remaining constant regardless of which energetic quadrant we're currently in. It is imbued with rich meaning that goes above and beyond the thrill of pleasure, and this meaning is always connected to our sense of being part of something bigger than ourselves. Through our purpose, we establish a solid place in the world from which to unite with our chosen family.

It's easy to get stuck in disintegration when we lack purpose or feel hazy about what it is. Our feminine energy holds the secret to understanding what we specifically are here for. It's not enough to intellectualize; we must embody our purpose, feeling it down to our bones, for our masculine energy to follow. Peak integration looks like mastery of our vocation, full alignment with our purpose, and achievement of our personal definition of success. Working with the energy chart can aid us in getting unstuck from what holds us back from this state when we're feeling like cogs in a machine, doomed to slog through life.

Purpose on the Axis

As we work toward integration in the area of purpose, we remove blockages in our Emotion-Belief-Choice-Pursuit pipeline, allowing us to move easily through the four quadrants of the chart. Below sea level, we tend to lose touch with our purpose or feel confusion about how to pursue it. When we rise into the integrated feminine and masculine quadrants, clarity of thought reveals our purpose, and we empower ourselves to take action in order to achieve it.

Disintegrated masculine energy shows up in our purpose in the form of bad work ethics that bring ourselves and others down. If we're leaders, we may find ourselves micromanaging others or putting responsibilities on our team without providing them with proper training or support. As employees, we might find ourselves "quiet quitting," only clocking in for a paycheck and doing the bare minimum. We might hustle for our worth or avoid self-exploration, deciding instead to settle for a job we hate. All of these disintegrated actions create harm for ourselves and others.

Disintegrated feminine energy shows up in our purpose as fear that we won't be able to survive, better our lives, or make an impact through our work. We can feel emotionally drained in this place, disconnected from ourselves and others due to our lack of hope. We might fear trying new things and failing at them because we personalize failure and make it about us. To get out of this energy, we must do the work of rewriting our subconscious stories around our abilities and our *why*.

The integrated feminine is felt through our purpose as the joy of living in alignment with our authentic self. In this space, we feel inspired, motivated, and fulfilled. We take pride in the work we do and deeply believe in our mission. We learn to embody our purpose as an art form, confident that what we create will help those who resonate with its energy.

The integrated masculine energy that comes with living our purpose looks like consistency, resilience in the face of failures, delayed gratification, and an overall adeptness at self-discipline. Leaders who operate from this space are able to delegate work responsibly, providing training and support to their team. They know how to push others in productive ways that challenge them to grow. In this space, we stay connected to our purpose and help others do the same.

Finding peak integration through our purpose is about accessing the "god state" of creation, highlighting the moments when feelings for our highest good align fully with our actions. Here, we reach the level of mastery described by Malcolm Gladwell as the 10,000-hour rule.[1] This is where we embody what the Japanese call *ikigai* or what's referred to in French as one's *raison d'être*. Here, we live our reason for being.

My Story: Vanishing Hoop Dreams

Many of us end up figuring out our purpose through our careers. By now, you know I thought I had my purpose figured out from a young age. The external world had me convinced I'd be a basketball superstar, but I didn't practice the right skills or give my all to the game. I was destined to play in the NBA and wouldn't need a normal job like the other kids at school, I assumed, so why take education seriously? By the time my sophomore year of college was over, I knew that dream would never materialize; after that rock-bottom moment, I underwent a death of the ego.

In theory, I could have trained harder to keep my dream alive, but the emotional pain I was feeling prevented me from finding anything stable to grasp for resilience. But beyond my grief stood an uncomfortable truth, which was that my work just wasn't in alignment with that of a pro basketball player. Growing up, I played alongside pros like James Harden, Brandon Jennings, and DeMar DeRozan, but the game meant something different for them. Basketball was their ticket out of poverty, and they had been conditioned to work their asses off to make those dreams their reality.

I never got that messaging as a kid. People took one look at my height and told me I'd be in the NBA no matter what, and during the early years of my education, they were right. As a kid, I was dominating with minimal effort. But when I saw my peers surpassing me in high school and college, driven by the solidity they had built around their work ethic, I came to realize that I had never applied myself that much in any area of life. The amount of work I would have to put in to catch up was insurmountable.

From there, I had to come up with another plan. While this was painful at the time, I'd do it all over again. I had been looking externally for validation and direction, allowing my ego to convince me all I had to do was show up while everyone else put in the work. The slap of humility forced me to look inward at who *I* was. What did *I* want to do with my life?

In search of a completely different life, I moved to a small town in North Dakota to attend Dickinson State University for my junior and senior year. While I continued to play basketball there, I let go of all the NBA stress I'd been holding, and no one there treated me like some disposable player, as prior coaches had done. The people there saw me for who I was—and for the first time in my life, I knew what that felt like. I had lived my whole life striving to live up to dreams other people had created for me, which led me to a place of total isolation. I found myself out in the boonies of Midwestern America, freezing my ass off in the snow each day. Despite the darkness of that period, a lightness began to shine through, slowly lifting my spirit out of the rock-bottom prison I'd created for it. All the shit from my past was suddenly out of sight, out of mind. Everyone hitting me up about those heavy things had gone silent.

Say what you like about North Dakota, but the place gave me hope for a second chance at life. I was able to relax into my feminine energy and open myself up to new types of knowledge, no longer surrounded and pushed by disintegrated masculine paradigms. I started to feel ambitious about creating community around myself and working toward dreams that actually belonged to me, not to someone else.

The biggest shift toward integration for me during my time at DSU happened when I met Dr. Grabowsky, my communications professor. He and his colleague Professor Marcusen masterfully fostered an environment for supportive discussions and debates about interpersonal communication. I was so energized by the class that I would hang out with Dr. Grabowsky during lunch in the cafeteria to chat with him about politics, international business, and whatnot. We built a personal relationship in that way, and I opened up to him about my education journey, along with the challenges I'd struggled with. He cared enough to listen, which few people had done for me before that point. Those conversations elevated how I thought about learning. I could fill my mind with knowledge that would empower me to engage with and impact the world in ways that went beyond sports. Yes, even *me*, the 2.0 student from the San Fernando Valley who had spent all of elementary school rocking up to class without paper or a pencil.

I later became part of the DSU multicultural committee, which gave me the chance to broaden my horizons and earn the encouragement I craved. I've always over-relied on external validation as someone with core masculine energy, but it was the fuel I needed at that time to let go of my disappointment in myself and finally taste freedom. It didn't matter that I had nothing lined up for my future. I felt relief, along with faith that I would find my purpose somehow.

As graduation approached, the university president recognized my public speaking skills during my presentations and invited me to become the first student ever to deliver a commencement speech. I accepted his offer, and the experience lit me up, opening my eyes to how electric it could feel to stand before an audience and bring everyone there together around ideas I was passionate about. I set my sights on developing a career that would allow me to build connections around the common issues that unite us.

I came into the professional world looking to make an impact and found my first real job at an energy drink company that hired me as a marketing coordinator at $33K per year. There, I made a habit of talking with everyone I could, building relationships across different departments, and my salary was eventually bumped up to $44K. In 2018, I got a job offer from a cannabis company that had heard of my marketing work at the energy drink company. They asked me what kind of salary I was shooting for. Nervous and unsure of my worth, I asked for $60K and was granted $65K immediately. Over the course of several months, I was so successful in the role that I bumped up to six figures, and I was finally able to breathe financially. I loved traveling for work and the opportunity to meet new people regularly. I was excited to make connections. The company itself was also incredibly diverse, employing women and people of color at the highest levels of leadership. This experience ignited a passion in me to foster deeper connections within communities of color and inspired me to pursue a purpose-driven path that aligned with my values.

Reflecting on the experience and thrill of delivering my commencement speech, I joined Toastmasters International during my cannabis marketing days, eager to refine my public speaking skills. Soon after, I landed my first TEDx talk in November 2019, where I shared the story of my failed basketball journey in a speech titled "Playing the Game of Social Pressure." It was cathartic to open up about my hidden fears and wounds and express vulnerability for the first time. Afterward, I was approached by various representatives who invited me to speak at their events and companies. This moment marked a turning point in my life, especially considering that just thirty days before stepping onto that stage, Quincy had sat me down to confront the situation between Tanya and me.

Torn between the excitement of the TEDx opportunity and the weight of my shame, I seriously considered backing out. But with encouragement from my family and my therapist, I moved forward. From that moment on, I was hooked on public speaking, realizing it could be my platform for connecting communities through open conversations about big ideas.

After COVID-19, I got laid off from my latest cannabis marketing job, but by then I didn't care. I had figured out what I wanted to do with my life. I then landed a second TEDx talk and gave a speech titled "Finding Meaning in Madness," where I spoke about my experiences with addiction and loss. I was determined to bring people together through mastery of the inner struggles that plague us all. I poured my whole self into public speaking in a way I never had in basketball, fully embodying the work through daily practice and dedication. Finally, I felt inspired and knew I was inspiring others at the same time.

As I became more fluid in the mastery of my own feminine and masculine energy, an urge to share my personal experiences around the topic grew. The disintegration felt pervasively throughout society wasn't just affecting my life but also the lives of everyone I knew, and I made it my mission to help others become aware of and activate their most integrated selves.

Having grown up the way I did, being told I'd be famous and growing up around famous people, my associations with success were larger than life. I had wanted to be seen, known, and discussed, but this yearning for fame faded the more I aligned myself with my purpose. The *why* became more important, allowing me to zero in on a vocation I'll never tire of. We all need to fulfill the masculine energy requirements of securing our lifestyles, but we want to do so through work that gives us life rather than sapping it from us. This takes consistent dedication and sacrifice, regardless of where we land on life's chessboard, and it can be challenging to work our feminine energy into such paradigms. Through integration, our purpose can be both discovered and sustained.

Purpose Is About Meaning

In spiritual communities, there's a sense that we're all here for a reason. Our unique experiences, skills, and insights prime us to take on certain roles from a place of authentic truth. You are meant to create impact in the world in some way, helping people in ways you needed to be helped but weren't in the past. Once you figure out where your purpose lies, you must then get others to *feel* the truth within you. All of this can be frightening when you've attached meaning to your identity that's based in disintegration:

- "I'm a bad person."
- "No one will ever accept the real me."
- "I have nothing to offer."

Limiting beliefs like these will blind you from your purpose and convince you that your dreams are impossible before you've even begun to work toward them. You might be stuck in depression, unaware that joy is the natural state underlying your trauma-based feelings, and feel strongly that your misery must be your truth. "Why look on the bright side when everything feels so bad?" To create meaning in our lives that serves our highest good, we must explore our disintegrated feminine energy and reframe the beliefs blocking our authentic *why*.

Gain clarity around your feelings and perspective of the world. Are you a bad person or simply a human being who's made mistakes due to disintegrated conditioning? Will no one ever accept the real you, or have you simply not met those who will yet? Do you really have nothing to offer, or is your audience out there waiting to hear your specific wisdom? When we examine the evidence underlying our beliefs, we can begin to search for proof of new beliefs instead.

"Everything you think is true."

—PRINCE[2]

Finding Our Purpose Takes Time and Failure

No one is born with an understanding of what they're here to do. We're often beaten down as kids, forced into the paradigms of other people until we get fed up and decide to try doing things our own way. We have to experiment, make (sometimes huge!) mistakes, and develop emotional maturity through trial and error. It's crucial to maintain a big-picture perspective throughout this process because once we gain enough experience, we'll be able to look back with gratitude for the bullshit we endured in the beginning. We learn what *not* to do. What *bad* leadership looks like. How disintegrated energies feel and the harm they cause. Getting to the other side of these struggles gives us a general idea of what the world is like and how it might be different. It helps us realize we can make our own mark and do it our own way.

With enough experience under our belts, we begin to understand that the grass truly is greenest where we water it. Remaining stuck below sea level, pulled below the surface by our traumas and formative wounding, causes us to mismanage our energy. Over time, we can learn to refocus the attention we've been putting on our fears, limitations, and resentments. When we're no longer exhausting ourselves with thoughts that make being in our bodies a miserable experience, we can get into our masculine energy and begin to take action that brings balance to our mind-body feedback loop, allowing us to rise to a more integrated place over time.

Money Is a Relationship

Many of us grow up forming an unpleasant relationship to money. We may fear there will never be enough of it, that we're unworthy of it, or that we lack the intelligence or qualifications to make the money we want. This often happens in families where parents experience financial insecurity or make their children believe, whether subtly or directly, that they will always need their parents' money to survive. Your subconscious beliefs about money are likely to have a direct and powerful influence on your ability to align your life with your purpose. You can't work your magic out in the world if you're unable to support yourself. Analyzing your money mindset and rewriting your personal stories around money can remove the invisible barriers holding you back from building the wealth you want to enjoy. Instead, you can tell yourself:

- "Money comes to me easily."
- "Financial abundance is my birthright."
- "There's more than enough money to go around."

Running these thoughts through your head will allow you to rewire your mind's money story, even if you don't believe them at first. Once you've opened your mind to the true possibilities around you, you'll be able to earn as much money as you want. You'll feel confident in your worth and have no need to compromise from a place of fear.

You might think, *No client will ever pay me the rate I want to make.* Is that true, or have you simply not connected with the people who will see your value for what it is? Never allow self-imposed intimidation to kill your dreams. Provided you don't quit on your purpose, you're bound to make progress.

This is not to imply we should strive to get rich while bypassing pain. The reality of life is that we always have to sacrifice something while pursuing what we want. Achieving financial freedom requires immense sacrifices of time and effort for most people. Having a family requires us to step away from our work and focus fully on our loved ones. Creating a loving romantic relationship requires compromising on what we want in order to balance our needs with those of our partner. This is not a sign of failure. Everything worth doing requires some amount of difficulty. If our biggest dreams were easy to achieve, everyone would be doing them. The struggles we choose to work through mark what makes us special.

Limiting Beliefs in Different Areas of Life

Because our limiting beliefs are often subconscious, it can be difficult to identify what they are and how they're currently affecting us. One helpful tool is to write down our dominant beliefs relating to different areas of our lives. Consider what goes through your head when you think about these categories:

- Spirituality; soul
- Physical health; body
- Finances; money
- Purpose; career
- Emotions; mind
- Family; childhood
- Friends; community
- Relationships; love

Try writing down a number of statements that reflect how you feel about these aspects of your life and your competence in those areas. Here are some examples:

- "I'm a lazy person; I'll never be in shape."
- "I'm too stupid to make good money."
- "Marriages always fail."

When you pull back and look at the big picture your answers provide, you'll likely find that you feel more integrated in certain areas than others. You might, for instance, feel confident about your physical appearance and health but clueless or fearful when it comes to love and connection. The problems in your areas of deficit are likely to reflect your limiting beliefs rather than actual flaws. In these cases, you can begin to rewrite the stories you've been telling yourself.

- "I'm not a lazy *person*; I just *feel* lazy right now. I can get in shape by changing my mindset and working hard."
- "Anyone with the right mindset, skills, and opportunities can make good money, including me."
- "Many marriages fail, but mine doesn't have to, and even if it does, that won't mean my partner and I are failures. We'll get through whatever happens between us."

The trick during this process of reframing is to tap into the voice of your higher self. The ego—the voice that's usually running the show—is both rooted in fear and focused on survival. It has no interest in hearing whether the thoughts it heeds are realistic or not. If the ego believes you're a loser, it's not going to latch on to thoughts about your potential. It will kill you where you stand instead, inhibiting your growth. If it believes you're "too much" for everyone, that fear will permeate all of your interactions and rub off on others.

Listen instead to your higher self, the voice that answers when all else inside you is quiet. The higher self has no fear. It knows you're not a horrible person. This quiet center of wisdom holds the answers to all your questions, provided you're willing to make time and space to hear them. Ask it which frames align best with your purpose as you rewrite your limiting beliefs. What was true for you in the past but isn't anymore? What meaning have you attached to the pain behind your limiting beliefs? Realize that none of the scripts you've written about yourself are objectively true and you can tweak any of them anytime you want to.

The pursuit of manifestation, often referred to as the Law of Attraction, revolves around the fact that the energy we put into the world determines the energy that will come to us. Too many people get caught up in the hope that asking the universe for what we want will be enough. There's merit to the premise of manifestation. When we shift our energy toward money, people, or situations, we change the ingredients we're using to create our personal experience, resulting in a different reality. It's essential, however, to move into our masculine energy and take action if we're to materialize the energy of the feminine in our world. We can visualize and clarify our intentions to a T, but none of it will unfold until we get off the couch and participate in our fate.

Before making it big as an actor, Jim Carrey wrote himself a check for $10 million and dated it Thanksgiving 1995. Allegedly, he kept it in his wallet, and just before his self-imposed deadline rolled around, he found out he'd be making $10 million for *Dumb and Dumber*. If Jim Carrey had written that check and sat in his room playing video games, he would never have become the world-class actor we know and love. He was specific in asking the universe for what he wanted, then took action around the self-discipline and work ethic he had attached to his vision.

If you're looking to manifest a specific dream, it's also helpful to visualize the challenges that will come with it in addition to the benefits. This is not to discourage or stress you out but rather to guide you deeper into the realities of the goals you seek. There's a shadow side to everything, and connecting holistically to all aspects of your vision gives more power to the energy you will use to attract it.

Case Study: Steve
Who I Am Is Unchanged

In 2024, I was let go from a company I'd been working for since 2016, where I had worked my way up from a part-time support agent to a full-time department head. I'd been a longtime fan of the company's products—music creation software tools—before I

continued

was hired. When I got the job, having already made the brand a big part of my own sound and musical identity, it was a dream come true. During my time on the leadership team, I was a fierce advocate for our customers. Supporting them was all about repairing damaged relationships with our brand, which required a lot of empathy and communication.

When the CEO told me my role was being cut, I lost a huge part of myself, but the skills and experience I gained, along with the confidence I developed, remain a strong part of me. Having so much of my purpose wrapped up in my career could have been disastrous for my self-esteem, but I've remained optimistic. I now structure my time in ways that allow me to keep growing.

At his job, Steve was able to unite his feminine and masculine sides by serving his customers with empathy. He used integrated masculine energy to offer leadership that communicated feminine energy support. Though he eventually lost his job, he was able to remain aligned with his purpose by carrying the confidence he gained with him.

The union of masculine and feminine energy within us determines the quality of our purpose, when and how we discover it, and our ability to align with it more closely as we grow. Through the inner work of rewriting our subconscious scripts about ourselves and our lives, we can heal the emotional wound impacting our feminine energy, allowing us to heal our *why* and move into love-based action. From here, true change begins.

Our purpose is intricately connected with the quality and state of our mental health. Next, we'll examine the different angles of wellness and how the topic feeds into the reality we create for ourselves.

Key Takeaways

- The status quo of disintegration keeps us from discovering the importance of our purpose, the path to creating fulfillment in our lives. Our feminine energy holds the secret to embodying our purpose so our masculine energy can manifest it.

- To discover where our purpose lies, we must create meaning in our lives that serves our highest good by reframing any limiting beliefs blocking our authentic *why*.

- It takes time and failure to figure out our purpose, as we must first learn what *not* to do. Over time, we learn to refocus the attention we've been putting on our fears, limitations, and resentments.

- Our subconscious beliefs about money have a powerful influence on our ability to align our life with our purpose. Rewiring our limiting beliefs about money can help us feel confident in our worth.

- We feel dissatisfied in life when our basic human needs go unmet. Taking action to fill those gaps can help us align with our purpose.

- Limiting beliefs can keep us disintegrated or stuck in certain areas of life. We can reframe them by tapping into our contrasting experiences and the voice of our higher self.

- The pursuit of manifestation requires us to first shift our feminine energy, then leverage our masculine energy to create our desires through action.

Reflections

- How do you define your personal mission or calling?

- What steps are you taking to align your life with that vision?

Healing through the Masculine and Feminine Lens

PEAK INTEGRATION

Loving what is
Forgiveness and surrender
Living in post-traumatic growth

EMOTION-BELIEF-CHOICE-PURSUIT

HOPE, RESILIENCE, COMMUNITY, PERSONAL RECOVERY

INTEGRATED FEMININE
LOVE-BASED FEELING

- Having compassion for your own experience
- Having gratitude for the lessons you've learned
- Demonstrating acceptance
- Facing your fears
- Feeling there's something *right* with you

INTEGRATED MASCULINE
LOVE-BASED ACTION

- Asking for help; going to therapy
- Setting boundaries
- Communicating authentically about how you feel
- Addressing the sources of your trauma
- Engaging in community
- Reframing your disintegrated or limiting beliefs

DISINTEGRATED FEMININE
FEAR-BASED FEELING

- Experiencing emotional paralysis; feeling frozen
- Intentionally feeding behaviors that negatively impact your well-being
- Being deluded
- Focusing on worst-case scenarios
- Believing there's something wrong with you; shame

DISINTEGRATED MASCULINE
FEAR-BASED ACTION

- Reenacting trauma reenactment; repeating destructive cycles
- Avoiding negative feelings and problems that need to be handled
- Allowing isolation, concealment, deception
- Hurting others to feel better
- Falling into addiction
- Expressing toxic positivity

CHAPTER 11

Healing

"We learn geology the morning after the earthquake."
—RALPH WALDO EMERSON

As the world enjoys steady access to more psychological education than ever before, we're collectively coming to realize just how many of us are operating under the spell of our traumas. These emotional curses have the potential to stunt our growth, imprisoning us behind the invisible bars of our subconscious mind. We doom ourselves (and those close to us) to cycles of reenactment based in ancient inner wounding. To experience integration, we must first regain autonomous control of our thoughts, emotions, and energy. Mental wellness is the key to unlocking the answers we need to rise above sea level rather than continuing to drown while grasping at anyone who might save us, pulling them under in the process.

As Bessel A. van der Kolk says:

> We have learned that trauma is not just an event that took
> place sometime in the past; it is also the imprint left by

that experience on mind, brain, and body. This imprint
has ongoing consequences for how the human organism
manages to survive in the present. Trauma results in a
fundamental reorganization of the way mind and brain
manage perceptions. It changes not only how we think and
what we think about, but also our very capacity to think.[1]

When we're unable to process dire states of overwhelm, negative
emotion is stored in the body rather than released. We hold on to the
feelings associated with the experience so we can somehow "solve" it
by ensuring it will never happen again. The coping mechanisms we
subconsciously develop as a result, often immature and maladaptive
in nature, continue to impact our perception of ourselves and the
world from behind the scenes until we're willing and able to take on
the hard work of healing. Rewiring our inner world by learning to free
ourselves of our more warped, upsetting perceptions may be the most
important thing we ever do for ourselves. The benefits of releasing
the load we've been carrying while developing new, more effective
coping mechanisms ripple out into every area of our lives. To heal is
to choose freedom.

When we repress and run from the deepest issues keeping us below
sea level, we believe we're avoiding pain. This, unfortunately, is an illusion
that keeps us from embarking on the healing process in a sincere way.
We can avoid *awareness* of our pain, but it's still trapped within us,
growing and festering over time. Rather than avoiding it, we carry and
walk with it. We drag it behind us like a ghost that speaks to us through
our subconscious. By the time we're adults, we believe this pain is a
part of who we are. Unable to connect with our authentic self, we block
ourselves from connecting authentically with others. Our external world
forever remains a reflection of what's happening for us internally; we
are co-creators of our reality. The only way out is through.

Healing on the Axis

We can use the energy chart to identify where we're at in our healing process. Before we begin the journey upward from rock bottom, we're stuck in disintegration the majority of the time, only occasionally getting our head above water to take a breath. Once we've made it above the surface, we can work toward integrated feeling, thinking, and doing.

Disintegrated masculine energy shows up in our mental health as harmful behaviors like blame, judgment, avoidance, lying, or complaining. From this space, we might hurt others in order to make ourselves feel better about our pain. We might reenact our trauma, creating the same problems over and over by way of our subconscious programming. We may actively avoid dealing with our negative feelings, effectively neglecting the problems in our lives that need to be dealt with. These actions destroy our connection to ourselves and those around us.

Disintegrated feminine energy shows up in our mental health as the fear-based feelings that keep us stuck in powerlessness. This can involve denial, depression, delusion, and devastation. It can feel like emotional paralysis or a feeling of internal shock that keeps us frozen, hindering our ability to take action that will better our life. This space is characterized by the deep subconscious belief that something is wrong with us.

The integrated feminine shows up in our mental health as compassion, patience, acceptance, gratitude, relief, and a holistic perspective of our trauma that allows us to maintain a more objective view of our life. Here, we can enjoy the peace of emotional safety and have faith in the belief that something is *right* with us.

The integrated masculine shows up in our mental health as the work of bettering our lives through actions that aid our healing. This can involve journaling, asking for help, going to therapy, setting boundaries, communicating from a place of authenticity, and reframing the limiting beliefs standing in our way. These actions are the ones that move us forward and create a better future for ourselves and those in our lives.

Peak integration in the area of mental health is about loving what *is* as opposed to what *should* be. It's an energy of both forgiveness and surrender that unites the love-based feminine and masculine within us. We feel triggered less and less often in this place, able to target our energy toward post-traumatic growth instead. We can embody the wisdom of the good we've experienced, release the pain, and step into full fulfillment in presence and gratitude. It's my hope that we'll all get here someday.

My Story: Dad's Suicide

We all experience a mixture of macro and micro traumas throughout our lives. As you know by now, most of my macro traumas involved my dad, whose ego could be felt by everyone in our family. We had to be on guard when he was home, constantly evaluating his moods and how to appease them. Despite the fact that everyone feared my dad, I identified with him and thought of him as a hero. He marched to the beat of his own drum—something I was never able to do in his presence, though I wished I could.

I never thought of the double life my dad had forced on me as trauma. The overexposure to sex, porn, cheating, and endless girlfriends felt like the way of the world to me. Wasn't everyone like that? After my parents' divorce, the disintegration in my family became clearer as the amount of supervision in my life plummeted. There were no boundaries at Dad's house like there were at Mom's, which started to bring more comfort as my life went sideways. He worked nights, meaning I could explore all the darker aspects of my attraction to women when I was alone at his place. I wanted to escape into pleasure like he did. That's what women were for anyway, right? Pop culture seemed to agree.

My basketball failures had always driven a wedge between Dad and me, but his cruelty became more brutal the older I got. He began walking out of my games in high school when I didn't play well, crushing my confidence and self-worth. My sense of isolation bled into my life at school, causing disconnection between my classmates and me. As my playing got worse, my coach began devaluing me too. Eventually, I transferred to a different high school, and Dad called me a pussy for running away from my problems. He would write me angry emails tearing me down with harshness and lashing out at me as his target of disappointment.

There were times when Dad would play ball with me at the park, along with a group of other guys, trying to help me practice and improve my game. My opponents would get brutal about it, and Dad never once had my back, always telling me to toughen up. One day in the car on the way home, he was trying to give me a pep talk and offered me a water bottle to drink from. I turned it down, and he punched me in the jaw before kicking me out of his car. Eventually he picked me up and dropped me off at Mom's for two weeks. He then showed up, and life went on as if nothing had happened.

During my junior year, Dad and I had a falling out over a bounced check. My girlfriend at the time told me she had found a check for $1,000 on the ground. Rather than tearing it up or trying to find its owner, she asked me if she could cash it out via my bank account. Not understanding how money worked at the time, I told her yes, figuring finding a check on the ground was the same as finding cash. My dad had set up my bank account in connection to my brother's. When she cashed the check, $500 was taken out of both of our accounts. Dad, figuring there was no way I could possibly be that stupid, went with the assumption I had committed fraud intentionally. Ashamed of me and my fuckups, he declared he wouldn't be talking to me for two full years.

I knew Dad had a habit of teaching people lessons by cutting them off. Still, the pain of abandonment by my childhood hero was profound. We didn't talk at all my senior year, and he didn't come to my high school graduation. In college at the University of San Francisco, I got into a fight with my teammate over our TV remote, of all things. I got knocked out, and the whole event had to be kept under wraps by my coach and teammates. None of my family or friends had heard anything of it, as far as I knew. Later, I drunk-dialed my dad one night, wanting to talk.

"I told you two years," he said playfully, as if the whole thing were a game to him. "Oh, and Pierce? Next time, give him the remote."

How he knew about the fight with my roommate, I'll never know, but his taunting had finally pushed me too far. I went off on him, calling him a shitty father. "Quincy's dad, Leo, was more of a dad than you ever were." A short time later, he and I ended up at the same basketball game. I saw him from afar but said nothing, not knowing it was the last time I would see him before he died. I was nineteen.

Dad had been planning his suicide for eight months before the night he took his life, we would later find out. He'd been through a long process of getting rid of things and settling his finances. As I was growing up, he always told me he wouldn't be around that long—that I should be prepared to be on my own without him. I never thought he'd end up shooting himself in the head, but it makes sense now, looking back. He'd been isolated, untethered and lacking purpose as he grew older.

Men with young souls rarely picture themselves slowing down. Women were the only pursuit that kept him grounded, but a womanizer's success with the ladies tends to wane as he loses influence and power. Disintegrated masculine energy was all he'd ever known, and his allegiance to it meant it was all he had in the end. While he had always been a source of comfort for those who knew him outside our family, telling them everything would be okay when times were hard, he never learned to turn that light back on himself.

I was wide awake at three in the morning the night he did it. Mom walked into my room suddenly to ask if I was okay.

"I'm thinking about death," I told her. "Not my death, just . . . death in general."

"I have a weird feeling too," she replied, "like something's not right."

In the morning, Dad's car was parked outside her house, filled with luggage. All his stuff was inside. We tried to get ahold of him but learned his phone had been disconnected. My brother searched the car and found all of Dad's belongings—his clothes, photos, even his gun—along with a suicide note containing a piece of dark encouragement: "Try not to shoot your brother." Later, we learned Dad's body had been found near a restaurant overlooking the ocean in Malibu.

My family and I processed our shock and grief in our own ways after that day. Dad's possessions and finances were divided according to the will he'd left behind—$60K for my brother, $30K for my half-brother, $17K for my mom, and memories for me. Beneath the surface, resentment brewed, stirred by our family dynamic and the tangled details of our past. Outwardly, I appeared fine, keeping my emotions tightly locked away. My struggles were quiet, subtle, and easy to overlook.

Lost in grief, my mom booked me a session with celebrity medium Tim Braun a year after Dad's death. When we met, he began to sense a younger version of my dad in the room with us, standing behind me. I was skeptical of his claim but kept listening.

"Your dad's got a sense of humor," Tim said. "He's flexing behind you now. Says you have to work for your muscles, but his are natural."

Crying, I remembered all the times Dad had done that exact thing at home. He would walk up behind me while I was looking in the mirror and flex his muscles while teasing me. Tim went on to say Dad was apologizing and could see clearly now. He was sorry for how he'd hurt me. I felt light and exuberant after the session, walking out with less weight on my shoulders, but I continued to feel skeptical. As a result, I spilled my pain into my relationships.

It wasn't until my fallout with Quincy and Tanya that I finally got into therapy. My uncle was the one to sit me down and shine a light on the shadow I was trying to avoid looking at.

"Your mom called me and told me everything that's been happening with you and Quincy. She's upset. What's going on, Pierce?"

The scrutiny of his gaze was mortifying. I felt like a drug addict who had just walked into an intervention. There I'd been, thinking I'd somehow persuade everyone to shrug my actions off like I did and forget about them over time. Now that my *family* understood the extent to which I was hurting people, willing to risk my connections with my closest friends, there was no going back. The mask would never benefit me again. I had no other choice but to confront who I had become and rebuild everyone's faith in me from the ground up, including my own. From rock bottom.

I broke down in tears and told my uncle about everything I'd been struggling with internally. He listened, asked questions to get a clear understanding of what had been happening, and told me I needed to start seeing a counselor. I knew he was right and agreed with him; fortunately, he and my mom stayed on me about it after I left. Had they not done so, I'd probably still be stuck. It's easy to choose disintegration and continue running away from ourselves when there's nothing holding us accountable. My uncle was compassionate but firm, insisting I find a practitioner who shared our Christian faith. I did as he asked, and finally at the age of thirty, my healing journey began.

After explaining everything to my new counselor during our first session, he told me he wouldn't help me unless I simultaneously worked a 12-step program for sex addicts. I began attending Sexaholics Anonymous (SA). In SA, *sobriety* meant no sex outside of marriage, no porn, and no masturbation. I felt I needed those parameters in order to change my habits and zero in on the root of my issues. At the meetings, I was pretty much always the youngest person in the room by thirty years and the only person of color.

Some of the members seemed envious that I had gotten in there to work on myself at such a young age, wishing they could turn back time and do the same. One guy, a father of two, had gotten away with cheating on his wife for twenty-two years. He'd finally gotten caught one day when he sent a dick pic to his daughter by mistake, intending to send it to his mistress. An emergency family meeting was called, and he confessed everything right there and then. His entire life was ruined that day, all because he'd never confronted the problem I was there to deal with. He said, "Pierce, you don't want to end up like me."

I had always known my actions around cheating were wrong, but I viewed them like an on-off switch I had full control over. I figured someday I would simply wake up and decide to flip that switch off forever. No effort required. My time in SA showed me my patterns weren't a switch. Not with my upbringing and well-ingrained history of deception. Not with the rabbit hole of violent porn I'd gotten sucked into online. Through the 12-step framework, I learned that healing from the trauma underlying any addiction hinged on honesty.

Until we can be truthful with ourselves and others about the harmful impacts of our dysfunctional programming, progress is impossible. We fuck ourselves over building the walls of our own lies around us in an attempt to shield ourselves from the pain of reality. Support groups like SA give us a masculine-energy container for us to express our feminine. Through open conversation, we model the strength of vulnerability for one another, shining light on the shadows keeping us lost in our own personal hell.

The first step of the 12-step program in SA read as follows:

We admitted that we were powerless over lust—that our lives had become unmanageable.

Working through this process of admitting my powerlessness involved writing out every experience I could remember in relation to sex. My life had been saturated by it, and seeing it all down on paper brought clarity around just how much I had prioritized it to the detriment of all else.

The second step followed:

We came to believe that a Power greater than ourselves could restore us to sanity.

The practice of surrendering through my spiritual channel with the unseen, asking God for help because I couldn't heal by myself, became a potent means of releasing my own resistance. My problem wasn't the cheating itself at all, but rather my inability to process the fundamental feelings we all struggle with in relation to desire, self-awareness, emotional regulation, and needs around intimacy. I didn't have the knowledge, tools, habits, or communication skills I needed to navigate my relationships. I wasn't taught boundaries around ethics and morals that were conducive to healthy connecting. Once I began seeing all this in myself, I could see it all around me as well. From there, I formed clarity around the kinds of people—friends and lovers alike—I wanted to associate with. It wasn't about judging the disintegrated ones I chose to stay away from, but simply about understanding that some people looked at life in a way that's not aligned with where I wanted to be heading. I didn't want the eventual consequences that come with living from behind the mask and making choices that hurt people. None of it had been worth it.

Once I was in recovery, everything about my family poured out of me. Everything I'd avoided had to be confronted and dealt with in therapy. The memories of affairs, porn, deception, and suicide.

The broken dreams and betrayals. Processing the feelings that were poisoning my body and relationships helped me begin to understand what integration might look and feel like.

The example my uncle had set was particularly impactful. I could begin to rewire the belief that all men cheat and dismantle the Madonna-whore complex poisoning my desires. Healthy relationships were possible for me. Self-love and harmony were possible for me. I wasn't evil or broken, just lost and wounded. Since then, my journey has centered on walking the path home to myself. To the passionate little boy who wanted to marry young and never had a need to lie to anyone. I've learned to confront my pain, no matter how much it hurts, and tell the truth when it's right to do so, no matter how much it sucks. I've also made some mistakes with this new practice.

In 2020, I wrote a blog post called "The Spectrum of Black Fatherhood" and published it on Father's Day. In it, I compared my dad to my uncle, who had always been a devoted father and faithful husband. The post was well-received by readers outside my family, but it infuriated my mom. She felt deeply betrayed and humiliated by my mention of Dad's unfaithfulness. From that point on, we didn't speak, and I no longer felt welcome at her house, even though I lived just down the street. My brother shared her resentment, and for the next several years, they both refused to talk to me.

A few years before publishing that blog post, I had booked a session with another medium, this one recommended by my aunt. I hadn't shared anything about my past or my first experience with Tim Braun. During the session, the medium said, "Your dad is here with us, but he told me he said everything he needed to say last time. He just wants you to know he's here." After the fallout from the blog post, feeling hurt and disconnected from my mom, I returned to see the same medium. This time, my dad's message was different. As soon as the session began, she said, "Your dad is here, and he says, 'Tell him he has my permission to share my story.'" At that moment, all the remaining weight I carried about my dad lifted from my shoulders. I was able to put it all down and write this book with what I felt was the freedom of his blessing.

This past Christmas was the first I spent with my mom in four years. Trapped by my anger and resentment, I had buried deep the pain I felt while separated from my mom. I had blamed her for the space between us, unwilling to look at my own contributions to the situation. In my work, I had said things about our family she hadn't been comfortable with me sharing at the time. She was caught off guard and felt disrespected. And I now understand how wrong I was for my approach.

Writing this book has been a process of healing not only for me, but for our relationship. Every weekend while writing this manuscript, I would meet with Mom to share the draft and work through the tools of the energy chart. For the first time, we talked through everything—all the pain and pieces we needed to shine a light on in order to reconnect. At one point she told me, "I love you, and I understand." I said the same in return. That was the turning point for us to finally see each other for who we were, not just as mother and son, but two human beings healing together. In some ways, we're closer than ever. And while my brother and I have never hashed out our feelings, we're at a point where we can be cordial. He knows my door is open.

And if you're reading this, Dad, I want you to know it's through your lesson that I know the depths of emotion. Pain, fear, anger, shame, forgiveness, and unconditional love—I integrate all these emotions in my love for you. I still love you hard, still grieve you hard, and still carry you with me wherever I go.

I ran from myself for so many years that I didn't even know what I was running from anymore. All I knew was I was terrified of stopping to look at the truth inside me. I couldn't let anyone get too close lest they see who I was. It all had to fall apart for me to start taking my own life seriously. I had to go all the way back to the beginning, to my earliest memories, to make sense of the road I had traveled. Once I got there, I realized looking wasn't all that scary after all. I had simply been under a spell, hijacked from within by a distorted image of myself, the world, and what it meant to love and be loved. The good, vulnerable person I'd hidden and abandoned was still there waiting for me, ready to forge ahead by my side.

Fear of the Unknown Keeps Us from Healing

When we're caught below sea level, living from a disintegrated place, the pressure to heal our trauma can feel like the scariest thing in the world. We're terrified of the unknown, unsure of what we'll find in the depths of our shadow. What if we *are* weak, terrible, pathetic, or unlovable? Who would we be if we learned to drop our defenses in order to see ourselves and others more clearly? Would shining a light on our true selves cause us to fall apart forever?

One of the most comforting aspects of beginning healing work is realizing that the shadow isn't a place of destruction but of discovery—what we fear most is simply the parts of ourselves longing to be understood. We've often been unaware of the true nature of ourselves and others, blind to how our childhood programming subconsciously guides us to reenact our traumas. For my wounded inner child, safety meant using deception around sex, a pattern that played out in all my romantic relationships. Looking at this objectively in therapy brought me great relief as I recognized that none of that programming reflected my true self. I could begin to release my urges around cheating, knowing my initial associations around it had been false. They had benefitted my dad and his story, not me, and that exploitative situation had long since ended. This kind of self-analysis brings layer after layer of repressed pain to the surface, but as we process it, we empower ourselves to shift our perspective.

You might worry that you *have* to be the person you've been until now, whether that involves anger, defensiveness, depression, anxiousness, lying, or passive-aggression. Many people feel like the world is falling apart around us these days and that they have to build walls around their hearts in order to survive. Some raise their kids from this space, like my parents did, insisting that softness will only lead to struggle down the road. In reality, you're bound to feel better once you've started the long climb back to the surface from rock bottom. The chaos within and around you will dissipate. The fog of confusion will clear, and the right path forward will reveal itself. I've never met one person who regrets doing their healing work, only those who wish they'd started sooner. To heal completely changes how we view and experience reality. Looking back, you'll be shocked at how much you suffered.

Most People Have to Hit Rock Bottom First

We all know integration takes work and the disintegrated life takes less effort. Avoiding self-improvement brings endless immediate gratification (though more pain and disappointment in the long run). Additionally, the system we live in doesn't seem to want us to heal. We're surrounded on all sides by stress, temptation, and threats to our peace. The powers that be want us addicted to social media, consuming products we don't need, and endlessly outraged at those they claim are against us. Healing is, in a way, the most revolutionary and subversive thing we can do in the face of oppression, but the rewards of disintegration feel more immediate. Most of us resist dealing with our mental health in a sincere way until we're absolutely desperate to change our reality, knowing we can't go back the way we came.

Rock bottom is where we finally find ourselves and, confronted with unprecedented pain, commit to treating ourselves better. Usually, this happens against our will, brought on by external circumstances.

We're all heading down a path, and if yours is pulling you into disintegration, there's only one way that can go until you decide to turn it around. You do not have to follow society to be loved, wealthy, successful, or comfortable with who you are. Just because you're surrounded by porn, cheating, objectification, cruelty, or dishonesty doesn't mean you have to take part. Just because the world seems like it's going to shit doesn't mean your life has to along with it.

Once you've awakened to your power and tasted the mind-expanding blessing of pure consciousness, it's difficult to go back. Soon after, you begin seeking role models and mentors who embody elevated values, living in ways that inspire you. You can follow their radiant example of love and adopt new mindsets that allow you to move forward in ways you can be proud of. You can rewire our associations with your vices and drop your outdated ideas about what they symbolize. Once you hit rock bottom and decide you've had enough of your own shit, life is bound to get better.

Case Study: Fariba
I Speak My Fears and Ask for Help

When I was fourteen, I lost my mother, father, younger sister, and grandmother in a car accident. The only survivor, I sustained serious injuries and was hospitalized for three months. This deprived me of the loving parental structure I needed to help me through adolescence and young adulthood. Though I was surrounded by love from friends and family, I lacked wisdom and guidance. These circumstances placed me in a box of fear, anxiety, and doubt, locking me into a "safe" approach to life. I refused to ask for help and never

continued

showed weakness. I masked my vulnerability to avoid pity. On the outside, I looked independent. Internally, I was shaky. I existed in this excess of passive energy for decades.

When I was sixty, I completed a life coaching certification program. The second day of the training, my teacher asked a question that brought on a personal breakthrough: "What's one old rule that governs the way you live today?" As I was writing my answer to his question, something shattered in my heart. I realized I'd been seeking answers from my deceased parents throughout my life, an expectation that put shackles around my ankles. I wanted them to tell me what was right and wrong, and I failed to take advantage of the opportunities in front of me. In that instant, I freed myself. I no longer shy away from challenges; I speak at my weekly Toastmasters meeting and lift heavy weights with my trainer. I speak my fears and ask for help when I need it.

Fariba was caught in disintegrated feminine energy in the years following the loss of her family members, keeping her passive. Upon realizing she had been looking to her deceased parents for guidance, she was able to heal her feminine side, rise above sea level, and use integrated masculine energy to take on challenges and seek support.

Support, Forgiveness, and Surrender

Many of us believe we can heal our mental health on our own, without the help or knowledge of anyone else. This isn't realistic for most people, unfortunately. Usually, our childhood traumas happen relationally and must be worked through in the context of our relationships as well. We must learn to trust that others can love and accept us for who we really are, then practice vulnerability with those safe people. These kind, supportive people can serve as witnesses to our pain as we work through the grief that brought us to the point of desperation. We can finally find the attunement we've always craved as we show them the painful, confusing things we've been hiding inside ourselves.

> **"Trauma is not what happens to us, but what we hold inside in the absence of an empathetic witness."**
>
> **—PETER LEVINE**

Support groups like Sexaholics Anonymous that follow the 12-step tradition are designed to provide this type of safe, supportive environment where anyone seeking healing can share confidentially, feel welcome, and meet like-minded people free of charge. In these groups, members are on parallel paths, helping one another rise. They are no longer stubbornly clinging to defensive delusions about themselves and the painful aspects of their pasts. These meetings can be great forums for making friends on the road to a more integrated life. You can also connect with a sponsor for one-on-one support as you go through the ups and downs of your journey. Healing is a long-term process that's more of an upward spiral than a ladder leading above sea level. There will be self-doubt, mistakes, relapses, questions, and endless awakenings as you integrate the parts of yourself that were exiled. Having a support network to rely on during this process is a great way to stay motivated and learn to co-regulate emotions with the help of others.

When we go through life collecting resentment formed through our negative experiences, it eventually culminates into an overall energy of bitterness we carry everywhere we go. Other people can feel this, sensing we're on edge, ready to be disappointed by the world yet again. They lack patience and compassion, assuming the worst of everyone they come across. It's impossible to live a free and happy life when we're stuck in this state. Joy and bitterness are mutually exclusive.

When I went through the 12-step program, I was guided to write down a list of all the resentments and fears I'd ever had, as these were the two biggest factors influencing me to act outside of my integrity. Resentments against people, institutions, expectations, *everything*. I had something to write down about practically every person I'd ever gotten close to in life. My parents, my exes, the Catholic Church, religion in general. By the time I'd finished, it was ridiculous how much I'd written down. It was a stark, visual, and quantifiable representation of all the poisonous shit I'd been holding on to. Whenever I thought I was done, more fears and resentments would jump into my awareness. More to add to the list. I'd had no idea just how much of a burden I'd been carrying.

Once we're open to the idea of finally setting down our baggage and letting our higher power handle it, we can release all the weight burdening our being. We can be lighter, more present, and energetically autonomous. The ghosts of the past lose power over us and can eventually stop haunting us altogether.

The concept of forgiveness can be a loaded one, especially when it comes to the heartbreaking reality of how we were treated as kids. Having been raised Catholic, I've always held on to the idea of honoring my father and mother. To honor them, for me, is to see them fully, acknowledge their flaws, and love them unconditionally for who they really are. Another way I honor them is to do the inner work they weren't able to do themselves, knowing they didn't have at their disposal the same resources I have today. I do what I can to understand their pasts and the choices they made, choosing to believe they did their best with what they had.

Our parents are gods to us when we're little. We love and admire them with all our hearts and want them to love us back. We make excuses for their disintegrated behavior, blaming ourselves and others instead, because to think they're not perfect is far too threatening to our young psyche. It's essential that we learn to take them off the pedestal we created for them so we can see them as imperfect people like us, helpless against many of life's challenges and equally confused in all the ways we have been. We don't know what we don't know. We can't. Neither could they.

If forgiving your parents feels impossible, I empathize. The anger we hold for them can seem endless. It takes time, space, and perspective to let go of everything creating the rage inside us. Know that if you continue to do the work, you *will* hit a point when forgiveness may seem possible. This doesn't need to involve psychic mediums, direct conversations, or resolution of any kind. Forgiveness is for you, so you can free yourself from the bonds of the bitterness standing in the way of your peace. It comes with the realization that none of what happened to you was personal. You weren't defective or unlovable. In reality, the people who hurt us are nearly always lost in the fog of trauma and hurting themselves. Like a drowning person in the ocean, they flailed and latched on to you, pulling you under so they could try to stay afloat. It wasn't your fault. It had nothing to do with the person you are, no matter what they told you, and none of it should stop you from fulfilling your purpose in this life.

Our willingness to forgive doesn't imply we're willing to play doormat for the people who hurt us. It's not an admission of defeat or invitation for others to treat us however they want. Clarifying and expressing our boundaries is an essential part of the healing process, with anger serving as the motivating fuel that drives this work. We can reframe our relationship to concepts like forgiveness and surrender in ways that make them work for us, without us having to lose anything. We can keep all our boundaries while setting ourselves free of other people's energetic waste. We can protect ourselves by acknowledging that nothing other people do is personal. It's about them, not us.

No one deserves to take up so much real estate in our mind that they rob us of our joy and kill our potential where it stands. We are worthy of living in a way that acknowledges these emotions, using them as catalysts for integrated choices, rather than letting them control our lives or diminish our potential.

Halting Our Projections

As we heal our mental health, we gain awareness of our subconscious programming through mindfulness of our emotions and the triggers that set off our fear. Many of the biggest triggers programmed into us in childhood are set off in the context of our intimate relationships. We associate something about our partner with repressed traumatic memories and project our angry, hurt, or anxious feelings onto them. Those feelings seem gargantuan and urgent, like threats to our survival that must be handled immediately. This is because our core beliefs about love were formed while we were small, defenseless, and entirely dependent on those we were most intimately bonded with. To see our partners for who they are, we must scrutinize our beliefs and expectations about love, along with our triggers and what those triggers say about *us*.

When I was a kid, my dad had women who knew he was married and others he lied to. I never blamed the latter for what they didn't know. There was no way they could have known how much they were indirectly hurting our family by being part of my dad's affairs. The women who knew he was cheating, however, sparked strong resentment within me. They were nothing like the principled, comforting women in charge of raising me—my mom, aunt, and grandma. They lacked morals and boundaries, and I came to hate them, unable to put the blame on the father I idolized. Siding with him against them felt like he and I were bonding in a way, and I was desperate for any sort of connection with him. Growing up, I was soon able to spot those types of women—the ones willing to do things like fuck married men—and began directing the darker aspects of my sexuality their way. I wanted to dominate them in bed. Disrespect them. Teach them a lesson. My anger and confusion were fully displaced.

Forming and sustaining healthy connections requires us to take full responsibility for our own shit. We have to open our baggage, sort through each piece one at a time, and own the stories we carry with us. It's on us to self-reflect on the things that set us off and get a clear sense of how we're contributing to the issue rather than dumping the onus on our partner. What expectation has been violated? Is that expectation fair? In my case, I was laying judgment on every woman I met, making assumptions about her value based on certain factors. Once I had placed them in the boxes where my brain thought they belonged, it was very hard for any of them to change my mind. This was destructive, unfair, and entirely my problem. By getting a hold on our patterns around projection, we can learn to leave these behaviors behind.

Part of moving forward as we heal is about learning to make discernments rather than judgments in our dealings with others. We learn we *must* protect ourselves by enforcing boundaries rooted in our authentic feelings. We can't attach ourselves to everything because a lot of it isn't good for us. Likewise, at the other end of the spectrum, we can't let ourselves idle in isolation, attaching ourselves to nothing at all due to fear of being hurt or hurting others again. We must learn what safe attachment actually means and looks like so we can form a code of conduct within ourselves. Those who deserve our attachment and those who don't will quickly make themselves known once we're clear on those boundaries. Only those who see us can earn access to our feminine energy.

Most of us who have been through trauma become experts at judging others as a form of defensiveness. We look out at the external world and think, *That's not for me. That behavior is wrong. This person is evil, etc.* True integration involves acknowledgment and acceptance of the dark and light energies we're all capable of in this world. We should judge not lest we be judged, for our self-righteousness will always look like hypocrisy at some point. Our truth is only true in the context of our subjective experience. This habit of judgment often blinds us from being able to see and consider alternative perspectives, imprisoning us in our own ignorance. We assume we know what there is to know when in reality we may have no clue.

Above and beyond judgment, we benefit from seeking *discernment*, a skill that allows us more objectivity and the ability to process nuance. We no longer have to split people into categories of good and evil based on how they make us feel. Instead, we can listen to the energy they create in our bodies and use that information to decide whether they're right for us or not. We do not have to judge or fix them. It's not up to us to decide their worth in the world, for we're all created equal as children of this universe. We can simply discern whether they belong in our world, and if the answer is no, keep our distance. Our approval of others is ours to manage but arbitrary in any case.

Much of our ability to stop judging others hinges on our ability to stop judging ourselves. If our autopilot setting is to search for flaws in others, we're almost certainly wired to do the same internally, lambasting ourselves for every perceived mistake or imperfection. We must honor our own experience and learn to love ourselves without reservation, declaring with compassion that we're finally, immovably on our own side. When we're able to give credence to the goodness within ourselves, we unlock the ability to extend the same compassion to others, even when we don't want them in our life. We can see they're acting erratically, and rather than calling them crazy, we can acknowledge the likelihood that they've been through terrible pain we'll one day have to bear on our journey. When we let go of our trauma-based urge to judge someone morally, we retain our ability to think logically from a place of empathic understanding.

In modern psychology, post-traumatic growth (PTG) is described as a positive psychological change that occurs after trauma has occurred. The idea is that we can find benefits in the work we do to heal our inner wounds. We can embrace the parts of our maladaptive coping mechanisms that function as relative superpowers while discarding self-limiting beliefs about ourselves. Children who grew up needing to be hypervigilant, for instance, are more likely to be especially empathic as adults, able to read the subtle cues of energy in others. Kids who grew up avoiding conflict, by contrast, tend to respond more effectively during times of crisis and are able to keep a tighter lid on their fear and panic than others.

We all had to develop certain strategies to survive our childhoods and can make the most of the skills we learned today. We can use them in our careers, helping others by virtue of our unique perspective. We can even become healers ourselves, serving as a bright light for those still lost in the darkness of the shadows that once consumed us. All of these steps are built on our ability to embrace the good in ourselves by reframing the painful memories of our past.

How we navigate and make use of our feminine and masculine energies determines the quality of our mental health. The mind is where everything begins for us, and the energy we cultivate drives the direction of our life's journey. By healing the trauma trapped in our shadow, we are able to transmute pain into love for ourselves and others. The joyful, compassionate, big-picture perspective that follows our healing primes us to live as leaders in the world. We can change the world simply by setting an integrated example for others, touching lives in ways we'll never fully understand. These are the building blocks of connection we're all going to need if we're to take on the future together. My healing is your healing. Your healing can save the world.

Key Takeaways

- Mental wellness is key to unlocking the answers we need for integration to take place. We can rewire our inner world by learning to free ourselves from our warped perceptions. We can't avoid pain in reality, only our awareness of it.

- Fear of the unknown discourages us from healing our trauma, but we empower ourselves by bringing the reality of our situations to light.

- Disintegration offers instant gratification in many cases, and most of us have to hit rock bottom to take our healing seriously. This is usually sparked by external events beyond our control.

- We believe we can heal our trauma alone, but this isn't realistic for most people. Support groups offer interconnected environments for healing relational wounds.

- Processing our resentments can help us release the burdens we've been carrying, allowing us to become lighter and more present.

- Forgiving those who have hurt us can release us from their energetic waste, freeing up valuable real estate in our hearts and minds.

- We often project our past trauma onto innocent people in the present without realizing it. It's our responsibility to own our baggage so we can stop projecting.

- It helps to practice discernment over judgment, as this allows us more objectivity and nuance. It's not our responsibility to judge or fix people.

- Embracing post-traumatic growth gives us a means of identifying our superpowers and using them to create the future we desire.

Reflections

- In what ways have you transformed or grown from the trauma you've experienced?

- What aspects of healing are still challenging for you?

PART III

How to Live Above Sea Level

Mastering the Feminine and Masculine

Once we've formed awareness around our
why, it is time to dive into our *how*.
Connecting with our true self, we can move into love-based action.
Uniting our feminine with our masculine, we hit peak integration,
embodying energetic mastery and full autonomy of spirit.

CHAPTER 12

Rising from Disintegration

"Everything—including love, hate, and suffering—needs food to continue.
If suffering continues, it's because we keep feeding our suffering. Every
time we speak without mindful awareness, we are feeding our suffering."

—THICH NHAT HANH, *THE ART OF COMMUNICATING*

By now, we've explored what masculine and feminine energy are, as well as how they show up in various areas of our lives. Here in part III, we'll discuss strategies for rising above sea level and sustaining an integrated state. In the final chapter, we'll focus on capturing Peak Integration, the main aim of this book. If you've been stuck in disintegration for a while, you might find it hard to imagine what living from a place of integration would be like. Just realizing and accepting that we're disintegrated in the first place can be a challenge when it's our status quo. Luckily for us, the human mind is highly adaptable to change. With self-knowledge, key strategies, and new habits, anyone can integrate.

You know by now that disintegration is the product of fear-based thinking that keeps our bodies and minds in survival mode. When we can't move out of this state, we lose strength in the part of the brain responsible for executive function and nervous system regulation, rendering us emotionally fragile. We become impulsive and unpleasant to be around, allowing minor setbacks to dim our shine. While getting stuck here can potentially pull us down to rock bottom, our negative energies are part of us, and it could therefore harm us to reject them outright. There are times when it's appropriate to take action based on our fears. We must develop the ability to discern when those moments arise and move back into integration once we've dealt with them. This requires us to face our fears and process our unpleasant feelings around them.

Disintegrated masculine energy is the most forceful and outwardly destructive of all the energies within us. In this quadrant of the energy chart, our attention is focused externally on whatever happens to be triggering us. By turning our focus internally, moving from doing to thinking, we enter the disintegrated feminine. Here, we can access the subconscious mind, where our ego works to protect us from our own psychological pain. We can reflect on our thoughts, feelings, and actions, analyze our belief systems, and begin to transform our perspectives. In this space of self-reflection, we can heal our nervous system, leading to seismic internal changes that produce a ripple effect that reaches every corner of our lives. In this chapter, we'll explore the pros and cons of disintegrated energy, the science behind it, how to know if we are stuck below sea level, and strategies for moving on from this stuckness.

The Pros and Cons of Disintegrated Energy

Because disintegrated energy exists to help us survive, we can use it to become aware of threats to our nervous system and protect ourselves from harm. Masculine energy puts us in fight mode, empowering us to push back when we're being mistreated. Feminine energy urges us to flee, freeze, or fawn so we can regroup and swim upward to sea level. Understanding the pros and cons of disintegrated energy can help us leverage its potential without allowing it to become a destructive force in our lives.

	DISINTEGRATED FEMININE	DISINTEGRATED MASCULINE
Pros	• A loud internal alarm • Potential for transformation • Creation of inner awareness • Space to reframe limiting beliefs • Catharsis • Leaps in wisdom and emotional maturity	• Immediate results/feedback • Pleasurable feelings of power; intoxication • Potential for drastic change • Protection from pain • Ego boost
Cons	• Anxiousness; worry • Insecurity; shame • Loneliness • Numbness • Impatience • Feelings of invisibleness • A scarcity mindset • Pessimism • Hopelessness	• Self-destructive tendencies; addiction; self-harm • Behavior that harms others; aggression • Loneliness; withdrawal; isolation • Ruined relationships • Legal or career problems • Physical illnesses

The disintegrated masculine garners us immediate results and feedback from our environment. While no one *wants* to go viral for losing their shit at Walmart, such behavior forces a reaction out of those around us. This gives us the impression that we're solving problems quickly and decisively. This can make us feel powerful, creating a surge of righteous intoxication that boosts our ego temporarily. We often utilize this energy with a desire to create drastic change. Without it, revolutions would never be fought and harmful behavior would go unchallenged. Remaining in this state is tempting, for it fills us with the illusion that hostility will protect us from pain, even when that's not the case.

The cons of disintegrated masculine energy are often extreme, which discourages us from acting upon it most of the time. The actions inspired by this energy can result in harm to ourselves and others in the form of violence, addiction, and pain. This can ruin relationships of all kinds, leaving us lonely and isolated in our misery. We can even run into legal issues resulting from illegal activity or divorce. The sheer intensity of the stress generated by the disintegrated masculine can ravage our immune system with cortisol, adrenaline, and other hormones designed to help us survive. Attempting to sustain this energy as our status quo can lead to physical illness in the form of diabetes, cancer, heart disease, and numerous other diseases that can be avoided through integrated lifestyle changes.

The disintegrated feminine comes with its own potent drawbacks, namely the intense emotional pain and fear behind our below-sea-level actions. This is where our anxiety and shame lie along with our loneliness, pessimism, hopelessness, and impatience. Here we feel invisible, numb, trapped in scarcity, and often angry or depressed. It can feel impossible to go on when we find ourselves in this place. Little do we know our darkest depths are the very places we can go to discover the keys to our energetic imprisonment.

The powerful advantages of the disintegrated feminine can be harnessed when we're ready to swim back up to sea level. This energy serves as a loud internal alarm that tells us something is not right in our world, bringing our attention to subconscious problems we may not have noticed or felt ready to confront. Without it, we would miss major threats and opportunities for the leaps in wisdom our darkest moments bring. In this space, we can create awareness around what's happening inside us and begin the process of reframing the limiting beliefs holding us back. This enables us to transform and achieve the catharsis we need to begin elevating. Through this hardship, we mature emotionally and try on new lenses through which to view life, leading to positive change.

The Science Behind Disintegration

We learned in chapter one that everything in nature flows from a state of order to disorder, and focused energy is required for order to be achieved again. This applies to our masculine and feminine energy as well; we are predisposed toward disintegration and must actively manage our energy to stay above sea level. Our brain and nervous system house the wiring behind this negative bias. As living beings, we're more likely to survive when our thoughts are geared toward detecting threats and our emotions are primed to respond to them, and our disintegrated energy exists for this purpose. If humans were geared toward positive thinking and relaxation, our predators in the natural world would have pounced on our laziness and wiped us out centuries ago.

It helps to understand a bit about how the brain and nervous system respond to threats during moments when our survival responses are activated. The human brain is organized in three sections:

- **The "reptilian" or "lizard" brain**, responsible for our autonomic functions and survival mechanisms, including fight, flight, freeze, and fawn

- **The limbic or "mammalian" brain**, responsible for our memories, emotions, habits, and attachments

- **The neocortex or "human" brain**, responsible for high-level reasoning, abstract thought, compassion, discernment, language, and logic

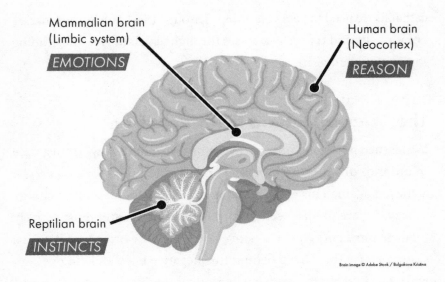

Mammalian brain
(Limbic system)
EMOTIONS

Human brain
(Neocortex)
REASON

Reptilian brain
INSTINCTS

Brain image © Adobe Stock / Bulgakova Kristina

The "reptilian" brain in humans operates all the neurological capabilities we see in reptiles. They run purely on instinct and don't spend any time attaching to their parents after birth. Once they hatch, they're thrust right out into the harshness of the world, vulnerable to attack. Evolution-wise, animals only began attaching to their parents once the "mammalian" brain developed. All mammals, humans included, have to attach to a caregiver for a certain period in order to survive. This is where our skills around unity and empathy come into play: Attachment to others is part of the evolutionary programming that has allowed us to thrive as a species. Ideally, humans would operate primarily from the neocortex, able to balance emotional regulation with the high-level reasoning that sets our species apart from others.

Trauma greatly hinders our brain's ability to keep the neocortex in the driver's seat. It traps the emotions we associate with past negative experiences (known as "post-traumatic stress") inside the body, keeping the nervous system on high alert. When disintegrated energy rules our lives due to this constant expectation of danger, our brain goes straight to its reptilian survival strategies when threats are perceived, knocking our neocortex and mammalian brain out of the driver's seat. It's therefore much harder to access our skills related to empathy and logic when the brain is intent on responding to attack. Until we psychosomatically process and learn to handle those negative emotions from the past, we remain stuck below sea level.

People born into families that provide a "mammalian" environment are primed for empathic attachment. During the crucial years in which their nervous systems develop, their blueprint for dealing with others sets them up for success when conflicts arise. Those of us born into more "reptilian" family environments, by contrast, enter the world focused on survival. We miss out on the foundation of healthy attachment needed for success in life because we don't know what it looks like or how much we need it. To get a handle on our triggers and protect our nervous system, we have to stop allowing the reptilian brain to take control of everyday situations that don't truly threaten our survival. To have a survival-sized reaction to small-potatoes problems not only wastes our energy but also ravages our health in the process.

When fear-based thoughts and emotions are our nervous system's template, love-based thoughts and emotions can feel threatening to our well-being. *I can't relax or feel too good about myself. Something bad will happen, just like in the past.* These thoughts are often subconscious, directing our behavior beneath the radar of our awareness. We reinforce the ingrained belief that nothing can get better for us and thereby block our own ability to feel better and take positive action. Love-based, neurologically "safe" thoughts and emotions can also seem boring. They lack the spiciness of the dangerous sensations we're accustomed to and fail to satisfy our addiction to those that trigger and excite us.

Limiting core beliefs stored in our subconscious underlie the fear-based thoughts and emotions that keep us disintegrated. These are cognitive distortions that prevent us from perceiving reality accurately. The familiar situations that cause us discomfort feel safe because we're used to the sensations they create, even when those situations are objectively hurting or holding us back. Our skewed perception also urges us to view the world and everyone in it in a negative light. Memories of fear and anger cloud our mental catalog of experiences, causing us to believe all people are fundamentally bad, selfish, or predatory. Even when someone is trustworthy, we may assume they'll betray us eventually.

Unable to hold all the complicated nuances of life in our minds simultaneously, we revert to black-and-white thinking, labeling people, things, and events as all good or all bad. The ambiguity of the gray area between good and bad or right and wrong feels intolerable to some. It feels far easier in these cases to cast judgment and catastrophize. If the world is terrible and we're all doomed, there's no point in fighting to improve anything. We can rest on the laurels of victimhood and remain in our comfort zone, regardless of how unhappy it keeps us.

Our nervous system does everything it can to protect us from pain, but the maladaptive coping mechanisms we learn as kids only end up prolonging and intensifying our pain as adults. Redefining what *safe* means for our nervous system involves reframing our perspective of ourselves and the world in ways that create empowerment, acceptance of difficult aspects of reality, comfort in the face of ambiguity, and more. We can then see ourselves and the world more clearly, without the shade of trauma darkening our perception, and build a life that supports our well-being. We can learn to let go of distorted thoughts and let in more positive feelings, enjoy the present moment, and practice receiving love.

Signs You're Stuck in the Disintegrated Quadrants

While we all experience disintegrated energy at times, there's a difference between passing through the lower quadrants of the chart and getting stuck there. Here are some signs that you might be stuck in disintegrated masculine energy:

- **You get angry easily.** It's both noticeable and disturbing to others.

- **You experience physical ailments.** This might include things like tightness, chest pain, and autoimmune symptoms.

- **You feel like everyone is doing things wrong.** You have all the answers and think everyone should listen.

- **Mistakes are unacceptable to you.** You can't tolerate flaws or errors on the part of yourself or others.

- **Competition is the only way to get you to do anything.** If there's not a way to win, you're not interested.

- **You don't care about anyone's feelings.** You're mean-spirited and recklessly insensitive. No one wants to collaborate with you.

- **You hold a false sense of justice.** You feel that if someone has done something wrong, it's your right to judge, belittle, and put them in their place.

- **Aggression is soothing to you.** You're addicted to the adrenaline high you get from feeling like you're in control.

- **You're constantly punishing others.** You feel a need to correct others and are quick to cut them out of your life if they upset you.

- **Your whole vibe says, "Don't fuck with me."** You want everyone around you to walk on eggshells so you can feel in control of your life.

We can also get stuck in the bottom-left quadrant of the energy chart. Here are some signs you may be trapped in disintegrated feminine energy:

- **You don't want to do anything.** Apathy and nihilism prevent you from wanting to take action.

- **You feel that no one understands you.** You convince yourself you're the only person in the world who thinks and feels like you.

- **You feel no support.** Rather than focusing on gratitude for what's available to you, you focus on what's not being offered.

- **You feel like you can't relax.** Potential external threats seem poised to attack you emotionally, financially, etc.

- **You're constantly looking for someone to vent to or commiserate with.** You use other low-vibe people as emotional outlets.

- **You hold on to a victim mentality.** For extended periods, you tell yourself you're not valued or cared for.

- **You don't trust anyone.** You're paranoid that everyone has it out for you.

- **You're too hard on yourself and others.** Your lack of tolerance for imperfection causes you to judge yourself and others for small mistakes.

- **You feel that no matter what you do, you aren't good enough.** You're always chasing new external accolades to validate your worth.

Tips and Tools for Rising Out of Disintegration

The disintegrated masculine robs us of connection by pushing others away while the disintegrated feminine can keep us caught in fear-based paradigms, creating a self-reinforcing feedback loop of destructive thoughts, feelings, and behaviors. The following strategies can be used, in no particular order, to free us from this loop and help us rise toward integration.

Observe and become mindful of your disintegrated energy.

When hostility, avoidance, and controlling behavior are our norm, we're often unaware of the anger, tension, and fear stuck in our bodies. We can even deny how out of control we are, insisting we're perfectly calm in the middle of a rage episode. To change our disintegrated patterns, we must learn to identify, name, and own what's happening in our body. When we practice observing these sensations, we can become aware of them more quickly, accept that they exist, and choose how to deal with them before they grow out of control.

Mindfulness exercises can help us create awareness around the energy in our bodies. They allow us to become more attuned to our internal and external, moment-to-moment experiences. These activities involve focusing on the feelings and sensations we experience without judging, interpreting, or assigning meaning to them. Dialectical Behavior Therapy (DBT), a structured form of psychotherapy for people who experience frequent emotional dysregulation, centers heavily on specific skills related to mindfulness, distress tolerance, and interpersonal effectiveness. Radical acceptance, in particular, is a distress-tolerance skill designed to help us accept situations that are outside of our control without judging them. Another useful tool for mindfulness is the Wheel of Emotions mentioned in chapter two, which can help us pinpoint and describe the sensations we're feeling. Over time, we can use this practice to train our awareness of what's happening inside us.

Create physical, mental, and emotional safety.

Inner healing is a vulnerable endeavor that requires time, effort, support, and the emotional bandwidth to process our thoughts and feelings. It's difficult to self-reflect or develop compassion for ourselves when we're in survival mode and relying on harmful coping techniques. We can't recover from drug addiction until we get sober. We can't heal the emotional wounds that keep us in abusive relationship cycles while actively in a relationship with someone who mistreats us. By leaving behind the people, habits, and situations that are harming our lives, we can start creating the safety we need to take the vulnerable plunge into the healing process. Once that safety has been established, we can begin the journey of rebuilding in integrated ways.

Going low or no contact can be an effective strategy for creating space for ourselves away from people whose behavior negatively impacts our well-being. Rehab centers and 12-step programs also serve as important tools for anyone looking to get sober or free themselves from other harmful addictions.

Get support from trustworthy people.
Connect and communicate.

Disintegrated energy backs us into a corner of isolation and avoidance like a wounded, frightened animal. We must learn to fight this if we're to integrate, which involves learning to lean into rather than away from discomfort. As much as we may want to solve our problems alone, we're less likely to succeed without support. We have to get back out into the world and reconnect with people we can relate to through authentic communication. This can feel daunting in our screen-addicted society where many of us would rather stay home than trouble ourselves with the effort of interacting in real life. It takes self-work to endure genuine vulnerability and learn to communicate about our emotions effectively, but our relationships are always better for it.

While the love of friends and family is always helpful, our most effective supporters are often those who have gotten to the other side of whatever problem we're struggling with. Alcoholics trying to get sober, for instance, tend to benefit more from support from ex-drinkers than from people who never drank in the first place. Therapy can also be an invaluable source of support, as most therapists are trained to spot patterns we can't recognize in ourselves and steer us in a more integrated direction.

Whether you choose to connect with a therapist, support group, or other source of help, the important thing is that they have your back as someone you can trust. Someone who cares for your best interests won't shame you for seeking help or take advantage of you while you're vulnerable.

Become present.

We often end up stuck in disintegrated energy when we're depressed or angry about the past. We can also live in fear of the future, burdening ourselves with anxiety. Ultimately, these emotions stem from our unpleasant memories or fantasies about what's to come. None of them reflect what's real and true in this moment. We can help ourselves move out of this energy by facing reality as it is right now, unobscured by the past or future. Through presence, we can respond to what's happening in our lives rather than reacting through displaced emotion or projection of what's happening inside us.

In addition to mindfulness and meditation, practices like martial arts can be excellent tools for sharpening our attention in the present.

Grounding techniques that help us feel embodied or put our attention on what's happening around us can also free us from dissociative patterns that keep us stuck in the future or past. Activities like tai chi, yoga, and dancing can also be useful tools for somatic healing. The Emotional Freedom Technique (EFT), also known as tapping, has also been shown to benefit the nervous system via acupressure. You may also consider massage, breathing exercises, and other relaxation techniques.

Learn to regulate your nervous system.

Because our brain can't function at its best when we're in survival mode, it's incredibly helpful to learn nervous system regulation techniques. To do this, we must come out of our fight, flight, freeze, and fawn responses and learn to relax. When we're safe and regulated, we feel calm, connected, settled, grounded, curious, open, compassionate, and mindful. This is the integrated expression of our highest potential. By making regulation our status quo, we learn to release tension and harmful, defensive emotions on a regular basis.

There are many effective tools we can use to regulate our nervous systems over time. I'm a big fan of breathwork, regular exercise, massage, and other relaxation techniques that help release tension. Research suggests mindfulness meditation also goes a long way in decreasing emotional reactivity, allowing us to stay in calm territory.[1] Journaling and therapy can help us identify our main emotional triggers so we can gain awareness of the people, places, and situations that throw us off track. When I'm feeling off, I often go journeying. I drive, walk, or run somewhere to remove myself from whatever environment is keeping my energy blocked. I put on my music and reconnect with myself, creating a change in perspective that recharges my batteries.

Reflect and take ownership.

The disintegrated masculine urges us to point fingers and cast blame upon ourselves and others. We may feel victimized, as if others are at fault for where we currently are, and while this may be true to an extent, we always have the agency to make empowered choices that can move us forward one step at a time.

Take some time to reflect on what happened in the past that brought you to where you are. Ask yourself, "How am I contributing to the parts of my life I'm not satisfied with? What perspectives and thought patterns contributed to the behavior that led me here? What core beliefs am I holding about myself and the world? Which experiences had the most impact on the trajectory I chose? What habits pulled or kept me below sea level over time?" Your answers to these questions can help you form the clarity you need to understand which parts of your life are in your control and therefore within your power to change.

Journaling on limiting beliefs is an excellent tool for reframing how we see the role we play in our own situations. Cognitive behavioral therapy (CBT) with a qualified practitioner can also offer a safe, supportive setting for exploring the vulnerable aspects of our shadow self we struggle to see. Twelve-step programs like Alcoholics Anonymous are another invaluable resource for anyone working to improve themselves, as accountability is inherent to the process.

When I'm stuck in disintegrated energy, I sit and try to make sense of my emotions, searching for dots to connect between what I'm feeling and the situation getting me down. I've developed a positive-thinking muscle anchored in meaning and purpose. It helps me analyze how my current experience is servicing a larger lesson that will make me stronger, wiser, or more connected. Sometimes this inner inventory audit wakes me up to how attached I've been to a particular outcome.

In the rare instance that I can't connect the dots, I practice gratitude, which eventually releases the disintegrated energy blocked inside me.

Connect with your higher power and surrender control.

We can't control anyone but ourselves, nor can we single-handedly solve the problems of the world. Trying to do so is exhausting, futile, and harmful to our health and relationships. Rather than seeking control over people and situations, we can focus instead on the aspects of ourselves we can control and change. Twelve-step programs guide participants to seek help with this from a higher power, like God or another conceptualization of the universal intelligence inherent in all things. This is the true source of our energy and can lead us back to our strength in times of crisis. During a quiet moment, allow any surface-level thoughts to dissipate and listen instead for the voice of your intuition. Surrender your desire for control to this voice with faith that the universe is handling the things you can't change on your own.

Spiritual practices of all kinds offer tools for strengthening our relationship with our higher power. Prayer, meditation, reading Scripture, and spending time in nature (known in Japan as "forest bathing") can also help us deepen our connection with the Divine. Cognitive behavioral therapy is also a useful tool for framing reality in a way that helps us focus on what we can control rather than what's out of our control. Radical acceptance, a practice that hones our ability to accept situations outside our control without judging them, can also help us prevent our pain from turning into the suffering that keeps us below sea level. Inner-child work can also be helpful for learning to release our controlling impulses. Often, our inner child seeks to control people and situations in order to prevent past pain from happening again.

Challenge and reframe distorted thinking.

Disintegrated thinking keeps us from perceiving ourselves and others in an accurate light. Our ego may tell us we're stupid, bad, unable to succeed in the world, or that people hate us. It may also try to convince us other people are untrustworthy, terrible, or uncaring. This type of black-and-white thinking is rarely entirely true. Challenge the limiting beliefs that brought you to where you are by looking for evidence that goes against them. When you find yourself thinking things like *I can never get anything right at work. I'm such an idiot*, think of instances when you did get things right and reflect on everything you have accomplished throughout your career.

The key to developing nuance relies on our ability to hold multiple ideas in our minds simultaneously. By doing this, we enable ourselves to release harmful generalizations. Once you've gotten into the habit of collecting evidence that contradicts the limiting beliefs holding you back, you can start reframing your thoughts in a more nuanced light. *Though I sometimes make mistakes at work, as all people do, I often do a good job. I bring value to this company.* These updated, more realistic perspectives can then be used as replacements for any distorted thoughts over time. It takes time, patience, and dedication to fully rewrite our internal scripts, but we're bound to create change over time if we're willing to keep at it.

Sometimes when I finally get an opportunity I've been working toward, I'll feel a sudden rush of fear and doubt. This can be paralyzing for me, preventing me from getting inspired or motivated. I grab a piece of paper and let it all out in a letter to myself. "Pierce, you've never done this before, you don't know if anyone will even listen to you . . ." Once I've gotten it all out, I reframe my thoughts with gratitude for the opportunity. "You've wanted this so much. God put you in this situation. You have the experience you need to connect with your audience." I then rip the paper to shreds. I once went through this ritual before sending a proposal for one of the biggest opportunities of my life. It worked like a charm, helping me wring out my energy blockages like a rag, and I've done it ever since.

Adopt integrated coping strategies.

Disintegration leads us to utilize unhealthy coping mechanisms during challenging times. We feel engulfed by unpleasant, overwhelming emotions and reach for the quick fixes available to us in order to feel better as soon as possible. Drugs. Porn. Shopping. Social media. These sources of dopamine make us feel better temporarily but create harm in our lives over time when we rely on them.

To rise above sea level, we can begin to choose ways of coping with our pain that help rather than harm our lives. Things like exercise, journaling, meditation, making art, and attending support groups require effort to implement as habits, but they can help us create connection, pull ourselves out of isolation, and shift our lifestyle over time.

Set boundaries early and uphold them.

When avoidant or aggressive coping mechanisms form, it often reflects a lack of fluency with boundaries. When we're comfortable setting boundaries with others, we're able to do so early and often, before we're so energetically dysregulated that we shift into survival mode. We must always remember we have more power than anyone else to change our life. We get to decide what we will or won't tolerate. We don't have to invest in people or situations that go against our needs. In fact, life gets better when we distance ourselves from influences that seek to anger and isolate us. Protect your personal sphere of energy and the quality of your mindset.

Therapy, mindfulness, and inner-child work are invaluable tools when we're working to clarify and strengthen our boundaries. Many of us struggle in this area after growing up in families where boundaries were ignored or nonexistent. Once your inner child learns they are entitled to their boundaries and can improve their relationships by expressing them, you'll be better equipped to set limits that reflect your true comfort levels before situations feel out of control.

Build self-esteem and compassion.

With safety, support, self-awareness, integrated perspectives, and fruitful coping mechanisms, we can begin to move into the energy of connection, compassion, and creativity. Disintegrated patterns keep us focused on the negative aspects of ourselves and others. We remain on the lookout for flaws in ourselves, other people, and the world. We treat ourselves with scorn and mirror this externally by criticizing others for not living up to our personal standards. When we begin to live an integrated life, love and compassion become our status quo.

Forgiving ourselves and others for our unpleasant past experiences, if possible, can help us get there. Positive self-talk each day can also change how we view ourselves. We can approach life with an understanding that we're all doing our best with what we have. Through loving ourselves in this way, we release judgment, perfectionism, and defensiveness.

Cultivate a mindset of abundance and hope.

The future is full of possibilities when we rise above sea level and begin to focus on the good in the world. With compassion for ourselves and others, we can believe in ourselves and our potential for greatness. We can also be on the lookout for others with an integrated mindset. These factors create abundance in our lives when we have faith that there is enough for everyone in this world. There's no limit to the amount of money we can make, the positive experiences we can have, or the great people we can meet during our lifetime. By the time we've completed the inner work needed to rise from the bottom-left quadrant of the chart, we're able to see the opportunities for expansion and prosperity around us. With time, we feel hope that the good life awaits us if we're willing to maintain an integrated paradigm.

I like to immerse myself in a constant diet of inspiration by watching how people express themselves. Athletes. Musicians. Writers. Hearing about what others are working on motivates me to work on myself. I'm fortunate in the sense that my work supports this. Listening to clients, supporting them, and holding space for their stories keeps me aligned with the purpose I've created for myself. When I face adversity, it helps me to talk with others who have been through the same challenges. These connections provide me with hope and continuous aha moments.

Making our way through these steps can feel as if we're pushing a boulder up a steep hill. It's a two-steps-forward, one-step-back process, but each integrated movement we make represents progress. With endurance, support, and faith, we can climb out of darkness to a baseline of functionality. This climb, while difficult, is our opportunity for lasting transformation. Reframing the stories we carry about ourselves, our traumas, and our fears rewires our brains and primes them for new possibilities of being. By learning to access joy again and let the light back into our lives, we reverse engineer our bias toward negativity.

Once we've risen above disintegrated waters, we find ourselves riding high on the life-giving winds of integrated energy. While integration offers whispers of eternal happiness and pleasure, we're likely to slip back below sea level unless we do the work of sustaining what we've worked for. Next, we'll talk about how we can stay above sea level long term and prime ourselves for periods of peak integration.

CHAPTER 13

Sustaining Integration

"I used to think I could antagonize myself into being a better me. It turns out, being hard on yourself doesn't motivate; it anchors you in place. It was when I decided to love myself without condition that I really began to grow."

—ERICA LAYNE

Integrated energy is highly coveted in our society. We are drawn to people with clear, centered minds and open hearts. We revere those who have achieved success and accomplishment through disciplined action. These are the most desirable states available to us, and they form the seeds of success. To sustain and make the most of our integrated energies, we must resist the pull of complacency. Integrated feminine energy can cause us to struggle to get into action. Once we feel relaxed, we want to stay that way, and making the leaps to bring our dreams to fruition can feel overwhelming. Integrated masculine energy can convince us we've learned all there is to know. Striving for achievement becomes our focus, and we lose our emotional connection to the world around us.

There is always more to learn and more work to do. The feedback loop between our confidence and competence runs on cyclical reinforcement—acting on our good thoughts and feelings creates more of the same. Ideally, life above sea level is an upward spiral. In this chapter, we'll explore the pros and cons of integrated energy, the science behind it, signs you're stuck in the top-left or top-right quadrants of the chart, and strategies for moving on from this so you can stay above sea level.

The Pros and Cons of Integrated Energy

The benefits of our integrated energy are often obvious. The integrated feminine underlies the most pleasurable thoughts and feelings available to us. The integrated masculine helps us bring our dreams to life and make progress in the world, which others are quick to celebrate. The drawbacks of these energies can be less obvious, however, and becoming aware of them can help us stay afloat when disintegrated habits threaten to pull us down.

	INTEGRATED FEMININE	INTEGRATED MASCULINE
Pros	• Compassionate • Secure • Trusting • Creative • Peaceful • Calm • Inspired • Confident • Fearless • Free • Ethereal • Enlightened • Logical	• Committed • Supportive • Structured • Disciplined • Consistent • Accomplishments • Leadership • Alchemy • Manifestation

Cons	<ul><li>Lazy</li><li>High on toxic positivity</li><li>Addicted to escapism</li><li>Stagnant</li><li>Stuck in denial</li><li>Comfortably numb</li><li>Analysis paralysis</li><li>Targeted for attack by the disintegrated masculine</li></ul>	<ul><li>Disregard for areas of life that don't revolve around achievement</li><li>Overinflated ego</li><li>Arrogance; overconfidence</li><li>Complacency</li><li>Inflexibility; rigidness</li><li>Aversion to change</li></ul>

The integrated feminine is where we all want to be. It's rare for most of us to access this energy on a regular basis due to the fact that there's always something to worry about or new problems popping up that demand our attention. For those who do make this energy their status quo, the glow that surrounds them is felt by all.

The drawbacks of the integrated feminine are characterized by a sense of frozenness. Feeling too good for too long can make us a bit lazy, stagnant, or comfortably numb. Why move into action when bathing in pleasure feels so great? We begin to resist our uncomfortable, fear-rooted feelings by clinging to toxic positivity or denial. We can get lost in pleasurable addictions to escapism or sacrifice our dreams to analysis paralysis. Our new business idea is genius, we insist, but it never seems to come together in the real world. We can also end up letting our guard down too much. The integrated feminine is the disintegrated masculine's main target for hatred, and while we never want to live constantly on guard, we must remain aware of the threats of the disintegrated world.

The benefits of the integrated masculine lead us to accomplish our goals and bring our dreams to life in the real world. It's a nurturing energy characterized by commitment, support, structure, discipline, and consistency. Here, we enjoy the process of working toward our accomplishments and moving into leadership roles. In this space, we alchemize and manifest the life we've been wanting. There's deep satisfaction to be found in the top-right quadrant of the chart.

The drawbacks of this energy revolve around the belief that we're the best of the best and therefore have nothing left to learn, study, or practice. We can struggle with arrogance, inflexibility, and an aversion to change that keeps us stuck in strategies from the past. We may also begin to ignore areas of life that don't revolve around our achievements, like our family members and friends. To practice unconscious competence—the ability to do great things without conscious thought—generates pride and security within us. Regardless, we need to be able to check ourselves if we're to stay in awareness, integrity, and alignment with our purpose.

The Science Behind Integration

Once we move above sea level into an integrated state, changing our energetic status quo becomes possible. We're still predisposed toward disintegration, mindful of the threats around us, but we're no longer on high alert in everyday situations. We're vigilant, but not hypervigilant. This opens us up to an entirely new way of experiencing life where we can function at our best and repair our relationships to ourselves and others.

When we're no longer in survival mode, our "reptilian" brain no longer needs to be in the driver's seat expending large amounts of energy. Small threats or issues no longer trigger our fight, flee, freeze, or fawn responses on a constant basis. The levels of hormones like cortisol and adrenaline in our body go down, enabling us to become calm, grounded, centered, and connected. Our parasympathetic nervous system, responsible for our physical responses related to restoration and healing, can come online, allowing the sympathetic nervous system in charge of our stress response to take a break. The inner and outer critics pointing fingers at ourselves and others quiet down.

Our "mammalian" brain can also relax when we begin practicing integrated ways of living. We become less aggressive and have more energy and trust for others, allowing us to move out of isolation and build supportive, authentic connections. Those who find themselves more anxiously attached no longer feel such an intense need to co-regulate their emotions with others. Instead, they give people enough space to support them without falling into codependent tendencies. Our need for healthy attachment and connection is satisfied more often, which frees up energy for the neocortex to take the lead.

Uninhibited by constant fear, we can drop any false roles we play and remain our authentic selves when we're with others. We become present and attuned to those we care about emotionally, allowing anxiety about the future or depression about past events to dissipate. When others tell us about their feelings and experiences, we can listen without judgment and respond with empathy. This safety of connection enables us to open up and talk about our own feelings in return. With enough practice operating above sea level, neuroplasticity ensues and our subconscious patterns begin to change. We develop nuanced perspectives rather than sticking to black-and-white thinking. We begin to see ourselves and others no longer as all good or bad, but as perfectly imperfect human beings doing our best with what we have.

When integration replaces disintegration as our status quo, our whole ethos changes from one of victimhood to empowerment. We replace learned helplessness with ambition and self-belief. Hopelessness is overshadowed with the knowledge that we're capable of great things. With restoration and safe relationships, our immune system strengthens. We sleep better and have more energy during the day, as we're no longer wasting valuable energy on disintegrated thoughts and situations. Our thinking, no longer clouded by pessimism, aligns more closely with objective reality. From that point, we just have to work to maintain the mastery we've developed over our energy.

It's possible to get stuck in our feminine and masculine energies above sea level. Getting stuck in the top-left quadrant of the chart, for instance, can keep us from taking the action steps necessary to bring our visions to life. This can reflect a lack of clarity; it's hard to move forward with confidence when we're unsure of exactly what we need to do. The term *analysis paralysis* describes the inability to make a decision due to overthinking or an abundance of choice. Research in psychology and neuroscience suggests overthinking holds us back by killing our creativity, destroying our willpower, and sapping our happiness.[1]

Getting stuck in the top-right quadrant can lead to a fear of change and hinder our desire to take risks. Once we've gotten good at something, we can feel pressure to stick to exactly what made us successful in the first place rather than evolving through continuous growth. We may resist the idea of reaching for higher goals, opting instead for contentment with where we're at. Our comfort zone becomes too comfortable to leave behind due to how celebrated we are.

The praise and encouragement we get just for showing up render us dopamine junkies. Somehow, we lose our ambition through the belief that everything will stay the same from here on out. *I've made it*, we think. *I can coast on what I've created so far*. This strategy can never serve us well in the long run. Change is always around the corner and our best bet for adapting is to aim for continuous growth. Without it, we sink back down below sea level and find ourselves disintegrated once more.

Signs You're Stuck in the Integrated Quadrants

Are you able to sustain integration above sea level, or is stuckness in one of those quadrants threatening to pull you back down? Here are some signs that you might be stuck in the top-left quadrant of the chart, unable to move from your integrated feminine energy into your integrated masculine energy:

- **You're in the same place you were three to six months ago.** The results you're producing aren't improving. (This isn't a cause for judgment or shame but a compassionate opportunity for exploration.)

- **You feel good about an idea but doubt whether you yourself could actually achieve it.** You tell yourself you need more money, support, or time to move into action. "As soon as I have _____, I can get started."

- **More things are being added to the to-do list, but nothing is being checked off.** You keep adding more requirements to your goals without taking action.

- **You have no energetic boundaries.** You lack awareness around the protection you need to sustain and support your integrated feminine.

Below are signs you may be stuck in the top-right quadrant, at risk of sinking into disintegration once more:

- **You're questioning why you do what you do.** You're extraordinarily accomplished but feel out of alignment with your purpose.

- **You don't feel emotionally connected to what you're doing anymore.** Feelings of fulfillment are elusive.

- **You feel like you can't rest.** You're physically tense from doing too much.

- **Your schedule is overbooked.** You create no opportunities for downtime.

- **You've lost or are losing interpersonal connection with loved ones.** You no longer know the day-to-day details about the lives of those close to you.

Tips and Tools for Sustaining Integration

The integrated feminine can keep us stuck in our positive thoughts and feelings, preventing us from taking action. The integrated masculine can cut us off from our purpose and have us so focused on achievement that we become strangers to those we care about. The following strategies can be used, in no particular order, to keep us from stagnating so we can continue doing the work necessary to stay above sea level:

Align your emotions and beliefs.

When we find ourselves stuck in the energy of the integrated feminine, there's misalignment happening between our emotions and beliefs. We feel good about ourselves and our ideas, but we lack belief in our ability to make them happen in reality. Our belief in ourselves and our purpose is everything when we're moving into action. Research about the placebo effect shows we can heal our bodies solely by believing in our ability to do so without doubt or question.[2] When you believe in your ability to bring your dreams to life, you'll find it much easier to take the necessary steps. Journaling about limiting beliefs, meditating, and using positive affirmations all can help us make these mental shifts.

When we're stuck in the disintegrated masculine quadrant, it's helpful to pause and revisit our core values. This creates space where we can evaluate how we're out of alignment with the direction we want to be heading. Sometimes our values change as we grow, and we find ourselves wanting to take a different path. We have to get vulnerable with ourselves and dwell internally so we can ground ourselves in the foundation we wish to build from. You can fill out a personal values assessment or consult the spiritual traditions of the world to narrow down and define the values that matter to you.

Focus.

Feminine energy is unfocused, characterized by its free and exploratory nature. Our ideas and feelings can be all over the place, making it difficult for us to move in a specific direction. Focus is necessary if we're to channel our integrated feminine energy into the masculine action required for success. Put your attention solely on what you need to do in this moment. Get into the frequency of manifestation so you can embody the energy of the person you're working to become. Zero in on what's important and leave the rest on the brain shelf for later. Mindfulness and grounding techniques can be great tools for sharpening our focus for these moments.

Focus can also be helpful when we find ourselves stuck in our integrated masculine energy. In that state, we often daydream about the past achievements that contributed to our success or worry about taking risks in the future. With mindfulness, we can keep our attention on the present moment, maintaining connection to the people and opportunities in front of us.

Release perfectionism.

Perfectionism is decidedly antihuman. If we were already perfect as is, we would have no reason to put so much effort into our personal growth. It's helpful to embrace the attitude that we're all works in progress. Life is a messy adventure, and all we can do is our best. It's just not realistic to demand a peak-integration standard of ourselves at all times. Lowering our expectations can help us get on a level of operation that we're actually capable of achieving. We can leverage radical self-acceptance, self-love, and self-compassion to align our expectations with our true potential.

Failure is inevitable, particularly while we're actively working to create success in life. There will always be times when we come up short of where we want to be, and for people stuck in their integrated feminine, this can be destabilizing. We can aim to develop a level of resilience that keeps us from sinking below sea level after failure occurs. Remember, every single person you admire has made copious mistakes in the past. You can reframe failure as a source of learning and incorporate the lessons of your negative experiences in the future.

Define specific, realistic goals.

Letting go of perfectionism enables us to identify goals we know we can reach. Think about what you want to accomplish and set a workable timeline for how you can make it happen. The more specific you can get here, the better. Let's say, for instance, that you want to get a master's degree. Which programs appeal to you? How long will it take you to work through the process? How much will it cost? Do you have the time, energy, and money to make it happen within the next five years? Take everything into account and ensure it's all possible before solidifying your commitment. Visualization can be a great tool for mentally mapping out our path into the future.

Create a strategy and take a step.

Action without a plan can feel random and overwhelming when we're stuck in our integrated feminine energy. We're much more likely to fail when we lack a clear strategy for how to move forward. Take the time and energy to work out how you'll handle the series of tasks you need to accomplish in pursuit of your larger goal. Form a routine that fits within the timeline of your goal and develop that muscle on a daily basis. Even if you can only commit to one small task per day, you'll still be moving forward consistently. Plan on working at a pace that won't require you to overextend yourself.

Look at your strategy and begin to move through it one step at a time. When you're feeling overwhelmed or tempted to procrastinate, focus on the next step you have to take rather than your entire to-do list. It's not possible to get everything done at once. The process of creation takes time, patience, and dedication. If whatever step you're working on starts feeling too difficult, break it down into smaller steps. You might even enlist the help of an accountability partner or coach. Whatever you do, keep going.

Deepen your devotion.

Rather than focusing on the results you want to achieve, focus on the process and what you love about it. Make your craft a source of fulfillment and joy. If it helps, connect back to your purpose by keeping your *why* in mind. You chose your goal for a reason, so do what you can to remain tuned into the passion and meaning behind it. If you're a mechanic, you might derive satisfaction from fixing things that are broken. If you're a teacher, you might be fulfilled by the lightbulb moments you create for your students. Sometimes, it's the little things that carry us forward in the long run. If you can, connect with a community of like-minded people who share your love of what you do. We all benefit from supportive peers we can bounce ideas off of.

Form, demonstrate, and communicate strong boundaries.

To remain in action over time, you'll need to protect the energy of your mind, body, and spirit. Remember that the masculine energies of this world always seek to distract, possess, and dominate the feminine, especially in its integrated form. People will want your time and attention as you work toward your goals, so it's important to define and adhere to your boundaries. Setting strong boundaries with others can take time and practice. We have to get good at being honest with ourselves and others about what we need. When this becomes a habit, we can protect ourselves and remain in integrity, aligned with our purpose.

Maintain a healthy balance.

Once you're no longer stuck in the top-left quadrant, you can begin to find your groove and maintain the action you're taking to continue moving forward. This is a great place to be if you can sustain balance around the work you're doing and still find time to rest and enjoy your free time. Find a point of equilibrium that feels healthy for you and stay within that window of productivity. Before you know it, you'll be knocking out the goals on your list with increasing efficiency. It helps to create balance in all the major areas of your life. This includes your purpose and relationships, but also your spiritual, physical, mental, and financial health. When you're integrated, you're in the habit of devoting enough time and energy to the aspects of your life that need your attention, which leads to stability and satisfaction.

Nurture your relationships.

If you find yourself stuck in the top-right quadrant of the chart, disconnected from others emotionally, you can work to nurture your energetic relationship with yourself and others. You can come to a place of harmony while remaining in service to others, allowing you to share your gifts with the world as your authentic self. Ultimately, we are interdependent rather than independent, and fostering strong connections contributes to everyone's well-being. Group counseling and support groups offer safe forums for practicing healthy connection in our relationships.

Develop a growth mindset.

Rather than working to cross some imaginary finish line in one short sprint, approach life as a marathon full of ups and downs that allow us to grow. We're allowed to make mistakes, be wrong, change our minds, and go through hard times along the way. Releasing perfectionism can help us take the risks necessary for continuous personal development that contributes to our integration.

To avoid getting stuck in our integrated masculine, it helps to remain open to new avenues of learning. We can enrich ourselves by challenging and updating our beliefs when we hear new information that refutes our biases. Adjusting and refining our perspective over time is crucial if we want to grow. It also helps to learn, practice, and adopt new skills that can benefit us in some way. These steps all reconnect us with our feminine energy and revitalize our *why*.

Seek external guidance.

You might choose to hire a coach or find a mentor who can help you maintain your integrated masculine energy. External support can help you reprioritize your goals, values, and overall direction when you're feeling lost. People you trust who have experience in your field can also point out blind spots you may not be seeing in yourself.

Set regular check-ins.

It's helpful to create an accountability-focused process to help you reevaluate the dynamics of your masculine energy on an ongoing basis. Checking in with yourself about your choices and pursuits can help you stay connected to your feminine energy and prevent you from going on autopilot. These check-ins can be done monthly, quarterly, or annually, depending on your goals.

Once we're able to thrive in our integrated masculine energy while maintaining a connection to our integrated feminine, peak integration becomes possible for us. We combine love-based thoughts and feelings with love-based action to experience fulfillment on a level that makes all our efforts worth it. This energy permeates some of our best, most memorable experiences. Mastering the skill of uniting our feminine and masculine energy allows us to build and sustain the fulfilling life we all yearn for. We can enjoy supportive relationships, good mental health, continuous growth, and alignment with our purpose. When this becomes your status quo, you'll have more freedom to kick back and enjoy the fruits of your labor. You won't have to worry it might all fall apart because you'll feel confident in how you manage your energies.

Now that we've covered what you can do to get unstuck from the four quadrants of the energy chart, you might be wondering how to handle situations where *others* are stuck. Next, we'll talk about ways to navigate our interactions when challenges arise.

CHAPTER 14

Helping Others Rise

"The most common way people give up their power
is by thinking they don't have any."

—ALICE WALKER

Regardless of how much progress we make in our quest to make integration our status quo, we will always encounter those who are still stuck below sea level. They may be struggling with addiction, entangled in a toxic relationship, navigating mental health challenges, or simply feeling lost in regard to their purpose. This is not a cause for judgment. We all learn and grow at different rates as we walk our respective paths. At the same time, we shouldn't feel called to take on the work of saving anyone else. Codependent tendencies will only pull us down below sea level in the long run.

We can't change people. This is a hard pill to swallow, especially when it comes to those we love, but it's a crucial lesson to learn when we're working to stay integrated. Rather than trying to do the impossible, we can help people struggling with disintegration by setting an integrated example they can follow and support them in ways that are healthy for us. If all goes well, they may begin taking steps to integrate in their own life.

When Others Are Stuck in the Disintegrated Masculine

It can be frustrating and frightening to deal with someone who's perpetually stuck in their disintegrated masculine energy. While we can't "fix" anyone or solve their problems for them, we can provide compassionate support while maintaining self-protective boundaries. This is a messy endeavor, but necessary if we're going to succeed in maintaining the relationship.

The prerequisite to this interrelational work is respect from the other person. When we have their respect, we can engage with their disintegrated masculine energy fruitfully. By contrast, we only waste our time and energy by engaging with the "you can't tell me shit" crowd. Never lean in to offer empathy while you're being disrespected. Only come to the table when the other person is willing to do their part. The following steps can help you move forward from there.

Don't take their energy personally.

It's easy to internalize other people's behavior and make it about ourselves. We might blame ourselves for angering them, not understanding that their emotions are their responsibility, not ours. Understand that the other person's issues aren't about you, but about a feminine energy trigger that hasn't been explored or expressed. By depersonalizing the emotions of others, we can avoid attaching ourselves to their disintegrated energies.

Boundary work is an essential tool for drawing a line in the sand between ourselves and others. We need to develop a clear sense of what we are and aren't responsible for. Compassion for ourselves and others goes a long way in these situations too. We can feel empathy for their struggles without taking on their pain as our own.

Remove yourself when your boundaries are crossed.

People stuck in a pattern of disintegrated masculine behavior often struggle to respect the boundaries of others, especially when healing is new to them. You have to be willing to walk away from situations where your boundaries are violated. This teaches others what you will and won't tolerate in a way that protects your safety. Our boundaries are paper thin unless we're willing to enforce them. Rock-hard boundaries are perceived when we communicate clearly and keep to our word.

Going low or no contact with those who violate our boundaries can protect us from further harm by that person. Figure out how much time and closeness you can tolerate while keeping your best interests in mind.

Call out harmful behavior.

Don't allow yourself to be manipulated, dismissed, ignored, or intimidated. People under the spell of dark-yang energy are often unaware of how deeply their maladaptive coping mechanisms impact those around them. Point to the behaviors that hurt you and make it known that you're not okay with how you're being treated. Be open and honest about what you're experiencing from the standpoint that your feelings matter just as much as theirs.

Nonviolent Communication (NVC) is an approach based on the principles of nonviolence and humanistic psychology. This tool allows us to receive and express communication empathically through focus on observations, feelings, needs, and requests. Rather than saying, for instance, "I hate how you're always late," we can say, "I feel stressed when you're late because I worry we won't have enough time to get everything done." Looking into these techniques can help us discuss difficult issues in ways others are more likely to connect with.

Avoid enabling or people-pleasing.

Many of us were raised to offer help to people who are struggling or to put the needs of others ahead of our own. These conditioned responses are dangerous when the person we're dealing with is stuck in their disintegrated masculine, as avoiding accountability is often their primary goal. Abandoning ourselves or enabling disintegrated behavior, like anger problems or addiction, does nothing to solve the problem in the long run. The other person is unwell, but they must take responsibility for themselves if they're to make progress and uphold their end of the relationship.

Therapy and support groups for partners of people stuck below sea level, like Codependents Anonymous, are great tools for folks who struggle with enabling or people-pleasing tendencies. You might also seek out resources for survivors of abuse.

Protect your energy.

Regardless of how things go with the other person, you need to be able to take care of yourself. Protect your energy and engage in things that bring you joy. Keep your commitments with friends, family, and colleagues. Create safety and relaxation in your own life. It's easy to let the disintegrated masculine in others pull you down, but you can't help them or anyone else if you're setting yourself on fire to keep others warm. Put yourself first as the main character of your life.

The best tool in these situations, as counterintuitive as it may seem, is a healthy dose of selfishness. As much as we decry and shame selfishness in our society, putting everyone else's needs before our own becomes destructive to everyone involved.

When Others Are Stuck in the Disintegrated Feminine

We have the power to provide the support and encouragement our loved ones need to rise out of the disintegrated feminine. It's not possible for us to solve their problems for them, but we can provide compassionate support while maintaining self-protective boundaries. By helping those we care for when they're at their lowest, we demonstrate a level of compassion that feels increasingly hard to come by in adulthood. Be a balloon. This involves pulling others into a higher energetic vibration through the creation of positive feelings.

This interrelational work is best approached from a place of unconditional positive regard, the frame from which most therapists and counselors are trained to operate. In this state, we can hold space for people who are suffering and give them a safe connection where they can be themselves, tears and all. We don't have to wallow with them or absorb their upsetting energy. It's enough to simply accept them as they are and be there with them as they work through their stuff. If this begins to feel overwhelming, set gentle boundaries and take space for yourself. Never drown in order to keep others afloat.

Offer the support you can manage.

People stuck in disintegrated feminine energy tend to isolate themselves from the world, which ends up amplifying their feelings of hopelessness, keeping them stuck. Your support can deliver the shift in perspective and energy needed to reconnect with the world, feel their value, and remember their inherent potential. Whatever you have to offer can be of huge benefit, whether that's a loan to help ease financial worries, a reassuring hug, or an empathetic environment where they can share their feelings. Hold space for them in a way that helps them access emotional safety. Be a secure attachment for them by sticking around when times are tough. Having people who care for us in our lives helps us feel hope that everything will be okay eventually, no matter how dark the present moment may be.

Validate their experience.

Our encouragement can feel hollow if we're not validating the feelings of the loved one we're trying to help. "Don't worry, be happy! It'll all work out!" This sentiment is difficult to believe or appreciate when we're unable to see our path out of darkness. The better option is to meet our suffering loved ones where they're at by validating how they're currently feeling. "I understand how hard it is to be in this position. I've been there before. It's so stressful." Active listening and empathy are key tools here. If you haven't been in a similar situation, you can say something like, "Hey, I've never dealt with this before, but I can imagine it must be painful." Validating the pain of others helps them feel seen and open to expressing the truth of what they're dealing with. This creates a strong emotional connection, earning us their trust and making them more likely to hear our encouraging suggestions.

Gently challenge disintegrated thinking.

People stuck in feelings of hopelessness are likely caught in black-and-white, all-or-nothing thinking. They've lost sight of the light within themselves and others and reverted to extreme, inaccurate, and limiting beliefs.

"I'm a failure."

"It's pointless to try."

"I've never done anything right."

"Nothing's ever going to get better."

"Nobody likes me."

People clinging to such beliefs need help finding comfort in the gray area of nuance that lies between polar extremes. You can provide this assistance by gently challenging statements that reflect black-and-white thinking. "You're not a failure! I've seen you accomplish amazing things in the past. Remember that job interview you aced last year? You're just going through a rough patch. Everyone does." With this nuanced and compassionate perspective, you can reflect a brighter, more accurate version of reality back to the other person.

Help raise their vibe.

The sensation of the emotions present in our body provides the basis of our thinking. Survival-focused emotions like fear and anger disable the parts of the brain responsible for executive functioning. By lifting the mood, you give your loved one a chance to quiet the part of the brain keeping them in survival mode. Tell them what you love, admire, or appreciate about them. Make them laugh or watch a funny show together. Make art together and get their creative juices flowing. Play high-vibe music that lifts their mood and gets them moving. You might even attend a "laughter yoga" class together. These activities will reawaken their neocortex and shift how their brain is operating.

Hold your energetic boundaries.

When we lack boundaries around our energy, it's easy to get bogged down by the disintegrated feelings of the people around us. Understand that you don't need to get stuck in sadness, anxiety, or anger to connect with a person who is stuck in those emotions. You can meet them where they are and provide them with support while maintaining an attitude of hope, abundance, and expansion. Remain above sea level so your loved one can meet you there as they make the hard climb to the surface. Make space for self-care and use tools like Nonviolent Communication to express your needs when necessary.

At this point, you've learned all there is to know about how to create the optimal conditions for peak integration in your life. It's time to conclude this book by examining what peak integration feels like and how we can ignite sparks to create it.

CHAPTER 15

Capturing Peak Integration

"The self expands through acts of self-forgetfulness."
—MIHALY CSIKSZENTMIHALYI

O n the night of the 2007 Super Bowl, rain poured down on Dolphin Stadium in Miami Gardens, Florida. Halftime show producer Don Mischer called Prince, the artist they'd booked to play the show, and asked whether he was okay to go on in spite of the weather. Prince had only one question. "Can you make it rain harder?"

The show went on, and Prince gave one of the most epic performances of his career, surrounded by soaking fans singing along in joy. Rather than being knocked off track by the unexpected storm, he embraced every aspect of the moment and told the universe to bring it on. He had so much confidence and passion for his work that he was able to let go of control and show up in a seemingly effortless flow of excellence. His brilliance as an individual elevated the collective energy around him, transforming challenges into shared moments of connection. This is the nature of peak integration.

I've experienced this state while giving speeches before. Each time, I had practiced so much and trained so hard to refine my public speaking skills that I was able to show up fully in the moment. Nothing could throw me off, whether it was a child crying in the audience or a cell phone ringing. I was in my element and had found my flow.

As creators, we all get here at some point once we've worked hard enough on our goals. We can be expert musicians, architects, engineers, doctors, athletes, teachers, or coaches. Any act of devotion can elevate us here. At a certain point, we become so adept at our craft that our art becomes embodied. Our skills can be seen and felt in our energy. We lose doubt over whether we have what it takes to live our purpose and click into a state of flow wherein we feel free, unburdened in spirit, able to connect in joy. We learn to transmute our fear into love.

Peak integration is the highest expression of devotion to self and others—a life where personal alignment fuels collective transformation. It's about living with purpose, where every internal breakthrough drives outward action. This isn't just self-improvement; it's a relentless commitment to connection, love, and the well-being of all. It's understanding that real power comes from balancing our inner vision with external impact, embodying compassion through bold action. To live in peak integration is to fuse our highest potential with a fierce dedication to creating a world where both we, and those around us, can thrive. This is the ultimate form of love and commitment—a life of purpose, driven by connection and justice for all.

What It Feels Like

Within the space of peak integration, we feel undaunted, confident that whatever we're doing is the right thing at the right time. It feels like safety, harmony, fulfillment, peace, and seamless connection to self and others. We can be fully in the moment, loving whatever's happening and showing up with complete presence, unclouded and whole. We are connected to the cosmic energetic sea of the Divine and have access to it all. Our limited beliefs fall away, and we feel we can do anything; we are now the superheroes of our own stories. We lose track of time, not by way of distraction or dissociation, but because we are connected to our passion for our creations.

We must know that like all feelings, peak integration is temporary and ephemeral. It will pass, and we will return to our cycles through the four quadrants of the chart. This is no cause for disappointment, as all four energies of our feminine and masculine are there for us to master. There is gold hidden in the lessons provided by each, and if we learn to apply them to our lives, we can widen our capacity for peak experiences moving forward.

We're not meant to park ourselves in any particular energy or eternally chase unnatural ideas of perfection. We're dynamic beings, brought here to flow through all the energies of existence, continually discovering the awe-inspiring depths of ourselves, one another, and our collective connection to the universe through shared consciousness. There's no shame to be had in any of our experiences. All of it offers the lessons needed for the growth necessary to become our highest self.

Ultimately, peak integration is about serving our purpose by delivering our most precious gifts to the world. We're helping others connect at macro and micro levels. We're making our eternal mark on the fabric of existence. There are countless combinations of ways to carry this out, but yours will be entirely unique to you. You'll inspire others by virtue of living in love, creating a domino effect that sends love crashing into the hearts of those around you. You will accomplish all this from a playful place of empowered imperfection, free of worry about looking foolish or making mistakes. Singers who miss a note can still belt out an opera. Athletes can miss shots and still play the best game of their lives. We can let go, lock into our gifts, and channel them into the world for the benefit of all. This is what we've come here to do.

The ultimate form of integration is to unite fear with love in our spiritual practice. These elements create the polarity pulling at us all, creating engaged tension between us. We move through existence conquering one fear after another while traveling toward the North Star of our fundamental belief in the power of love. Our fear can isolate us as we attempt to run and hide from it—from ourselves—to eradicate it from our lives. I thought I could pray the fear away when I was younger, but I needed instead to confront and learn to channel it differently.

Transformational change comes when we shift our perspective of our fear, looking to it as a teacher instead of an obstacle. We can turn our inner demons into source energy used for understanding, empathy, and personal growth. Each of us has the chance to choose love over fear in this life. It is the dance between these energies that weaves together the moments of our inner light's journey through consciousness.

Mastery on All Sides

Accessing peak integration requires us to first master all sides of the subject matter of our craft. We must develop the set of skills necessary to pivot in the face of any challenge while living our purpose. As a public speaker, I work to develop my cadence, timing, presentation, and emotional connection with my audience. A basketball player, by contrast, works to understand the rules and history of the game. They learn every possible move they can make in every circumstance while they're on the court. Having a sense of every option available to us brings us through tough moments with an ease that only occurs at the expert level.

In addition to mastering our subject of interest, we must also master our own energy for peak integration to occur. We can learn to control our thoughts, emotions, attention, actions, and choices, which we can then incorporate into our work with our craft.

Finally, we can learn to embrace all possibilities of what might occur in our external environment, even those that could seemingly work against us. Another example would be a comedian with the ability to remain in their power in the face of heckling during a performance.

In 2006, comedian Bill Burr took part in The Opie and Anthony Traveling Virus Comedy Tour. During a show in Philadelphia in front of a belligerent crowd, Burr responded to widespread booing with over eleven minutes of pure, uncensored vitriol. By the end of his epic rant, the crowd was cheering his name, grateful for the hate-filled roast. At no point did Burr lose control, a stark contrast to comedian Michael Richards of *Seinfeld* fame, who responded that same year to hecklers at a show with a meltdown consisting of racial slurs and insults.

Yet another example of peak integration was seen in Lebron James when he returned to Cleveland after leaving the Cavaliers in 2010 to join the Miami Heat. In the face of vicious treatment, with crowd members calling him a traitor to his hometown, Lebron dominated on the court, leading to an epic 38-point performance. Like Darth Vader, he allowed external hate to fuel his power. Like in Prince's halftime show, Bill Burr's Philly rant, or Lebron's return to Cleveland, peak integration is an energy available to those who commit to their craft at the highest level.

Living in What Is

The same laws of peak integration that apply to our craft apply to the self as well. Jim Beebe, my therapist and mentor, once wrote an essay titled "A Path to Living in What Is," wherein he stated the following:

> When you need something in your world to be different
> than it is, then you are discontent and that need controls
> you. Now, this can be an extremely difficult concept to get
> our minds around. To see my life as exactly what I need it
> to be can run so contrary to what my feelings tell me.

It can feel nearly impossible to embrace and own the aspects of our lives that inspire the most pain. I've come to realize that when it comes to my own life, I needed the dark moments to connect with the unique fingerprint of my purpose here. My dad's death, my destructive choices, the agony that took place amid the blessings—all of it made me who I've become.

When we live life as if every challenge is unfair and that we don't deserve the suffering we encounter, our disintegrated energy not only impacts how we feel, but also how we handle life as a whole. With a reframed emotional mindset, we can surrender to what is, allowing it to carry us forward. We can never have all the answers or live in perfection, but we can always rely on our higher power to provide us with direction, no matter where we are.

Parting Thoughts

With mastery over our inherent gifts, we can realize our vision of a connected world that aligns more closely with our internal experience. There is a path to achieving this that allows us to access a state of flow, peace, and wholeness, and it is through the four quadrants of the energy chart. Use it and watch change blossom in all areas of your life.

The stark reality is that this revolution must happen now if we're to recover from the division plaguing our world. The work of integration, carried out on a societal level, would have pervasive implications for our collective future. The challenges we face moving forward are dire. Climate change, food insecurity, natural disasters, unchecked AI activity, and the prospect of global war all lie ahead of us as existential threats. Mastery over our own energy at a level that collectively unites us is crucial if we're to survive. We have no choice but to adapt together as a species. I pray you find your own personal sense of empowerment in this book and feel moved to contribute to this movement in whatever way suits your purpose.

The most important takeaway here is that whenever you find yourself energetically stuck, there is always a way out that can lead you in a better direction. When times are tough for you or someone you know, and you're not quite sure what to do, I invite you to return to this book as a reference for solutions. In part I, we examined the impact of masculine and feminine energy in various cultural contexts. Part II showed us how these energies show up in our everyday lives. Part III provided concrete steps and tools for moving on from stuckness in each of the four quadrants of the chart. Now, it's time to go out into the world and connect with others working toward integration. Express your masculine and feminine energy in ways that help you show up in the world as your optimal self.

In a recent conversation with a close friend who works as a sommelier, I asked her what it was that she loved so much about wine. Her answer was simple: "I love it because I'll never know all there is to know about it." That statement and its sentiment can be applied to everything we desire, including love itself.

I will never stop learning about my parents and their impact on my life. I'll never stop learning about the trauma I've experienced or battling the issues I battle. There will always be more to learn about myself and my partner. More to learn about my mission and purpose in this life. I strive to make the choice to embrace and love all of this. If I were to think I had arrived at some all-knowing state at any point in my life, I would no longer be able to grow in my relationship with it.

As a collective, we can choose never to stop learning about one another. There is always more to discover. We can decide to have empathy for the trauma others have been through. We can decide to see and appreciate the inherent gifts in every experience and interaction. We can decide to set a higher bar of spiritual agreement and understanding. And we can only see that basis of understanding through connection.

When we choose to observe disintegration appropriately in its segmented expressions, we can evaluate it against the sense of fundamental truth resonant in us all. Truth is not found in division. Truth is not Black. Truth is not White. It doesn't vote Democrat or Republican. Truth is found in Peak Integration.

Healing is painful—and many people will choose not to integrate during their lifetime. Even if everyone in the world bought this book and followed its teachings, some readers would still choose hate and division. No matter what choices we make in the name of our sovereign power, we will still cycle through all quadrants of the energy chart. We will always be confronted by hate, confusion, and fear. Use this. *All* of it, no matter how taboo it may seem. Use every experience available to you as fuel for your purpose.

Love what is.

Use it.

Embrace it.

Transmute it.

Breaking Free:
The E-B-C-P Action Plan

Clearly define the life area where you feel stuck.

Self-Assessment

- Dominant Emotion: What is the primary emotion you experience in this area?

- Core Beliefs: What underlying beliefs are shaping your emotions and actions?

- Behavior Patterns: What habitual behaviors are reinforcing the situation?

Emotion-Belief-Choice-Pursuit Pipeline

EMOTION	BELIEF	CHOICE	PURSUIT
(Dominant emotion)	(Underlying belief)	(New choice)	(Desired action)

Action Plan

- Weekly Commitments: Outline specific steps to shift your beliefs and behaviors.

- Support Network: Identify individuals who can offer support and encouragement.

- Obstacle Anticipation: Consider potential challenges and develop coping strategies.

Integration and Growth

- Mindfulness Practice: Cultivate present-moment awareness.

- Self-Compassion: Treat yourself with kindness and understanding.

- Continuous Learning: Seek knowledge to expand your perspective.

Activity: Balancing Energy in the 7 Areas of Life

The goal of this exercise is to identify imbalances in masculine and feminine energy within each life area, ultimately leading to a deeper understanding of one's integration potential.

AREA OF LIFE	FEMININE ENERGY QUESTIONS	MASCULINE ENERGY QUESTIONS
Physical	How do I feel about my body? Are there any body image issues or self-criticism?	How do I take care of my physical body? Do I prioritize physical activity and nourishment?
Emotional	What emotions do I struggle with? How do I express my emotions?	How do I manage my emotions? Do I suppress or overreact to emotions?
Intellectual	How do I connect with my intuition and inner wisdom?	How do I apply knowledge and logic in my life? Do I over-intellectualize or avoid learning?
Social	How do I connect with others on an emotional level? Do I feel seen and heard?	How do I initiate and maintain relationships? Do I dominate or withdraw in social settings?
Spiritual	How do I connect with my inner self and spirituality? Do I trust my intuition and inner guidance?	How do I express my spirituality in the world? Do I engage in spiritual practices or community?
Occupational	How do I feel about my work? Does it fulfill me emotionally?	How do I perform my job duties? Am I assertive and goal-oriented?
Financial	How do I feel about money? Do I have a healthy relationship with money?	How do I manage my finances? Do I have a clear financial plan?

Acknowledgments

My path has been shaped by the generosity, wisdom, and unwavering support of so many remarkable people, and I want to express my deepest gratitude. To Bill Duffy, Craig Chretien, and Ken Norton Jr., men of unmatched character and integrity—you have led by example, grounding me with your wisdom and steady guidance. Thank you to my surrogate auntie, Jamese, and to my cousins who have forever felt like siblings—Treaven, Geneva, Christian, Ranada, Jayden, and Atif. Thank you, Alethea Espino; your dedication to our numerous conversations, brainstorming sessions, and collaborative efforts helped shape the original structure of the energy chart. Thank you to those who entrusted me with your heartfelt stories to enrich this material—especially Shein, Anita, Cyd, Shannon, Thomas, Kevin, Steve, and Fariba. Lessie Schrider, your unapologetic feedback gave this manuscript the honesty it needed. Rose Friel, your wisdom and guidance made the daunting world of book publishing feel far more navigable. Maggie Langrick, your belief in me and my message has been invaluable. And to the entire Greenleaf Publishing team—especially HaJ Chenzira-Pinnock, Lee Reed-Zarnikau, Jen Glynn, Emma Watson, Elizabeth Brown, Claudia Volkman, Alyse Mervosh, Jonathan Lewis, and Neil Gonzalez—thank you for helping me share my vision.

To Dickinson State University, you were a beacon during a challenging time in my life. Coach Ty Orton, Patti Carr, Margaret Marcussen, and Dr. Eric Grabowsky, your kindness and encouragement gave me strength when I needed it. Daniel "Daryl" Casey, my brother in spirit, your loyalty and friendship are gifts I try to never take for granted. Thank you to my Toastmasters family at Gettin' Toasty #147 for your invaluable help and support in me finding my voice. Thank you to my business partners, Lea Kozin and Les Krone, for your belief in me and your commitment to build something special together. Stephanie Dang, Dajana Zeljkovic, Ralice Remy, and Ruth Arzate, my sisters in spirit, you have been a constant source of support, and I'm grateful for your presence in my life. Bobby "Big Country" Shields, thank you for being another bright example of what it means to be a good man. To Niyi and Ibe, words can't express my gratitude for our friendship. Thank you, Janet Wolfe, Kate King, and Megan Greeley, for your consistent support. Jim Beebe, MFT, and Jim H., my sponsor—both of you have helped me find my way when I felt lost. Your guidance through some of my hardest truths gave me the strength to rebuild and move forward with purpose.

To ACG and family, I am undeserving of the grace and forgiveness that you've extended—even in the many moments when I fell short. Your willingness to extend that to me has been a profound lesson in humility and growth. To those who've helped me fuel my purpose—Stan Lathan, Dr. Mark Goulston (RIP), Alonzo Fulgham, Ann McNeil, and so many others—your belief in me has pushed me forward through any moment of doubt. Sunset Sound Recording Studio, thank you for opening your doors to bring this book to life in your legendary space. And profound thanks to Indie, for being a guiding light through nearly every shadowed moment.

I am deeply grateful to Doug Teitelbaum, whose support and generosity were instrumental in bringing this book to fruition.

Special thanks to God, You, Peggy, and Prince.

Endnotes

Chapter 1

1. Maria H. Couppis and Craig H. Kennedy, "The Rewarding Effect of Aggression Is Reduced by Nucleus Accumbens Dopamine Receptor Antagonism in Mice," January 8, 2008, *Psychopharmacology*, https://pubmed.ncbi.nlm.nih.gov/18193405/.

Chapter 2

1. Robert Plutchik and Henry Kellerman, editors, *Emotion: Theory, Research, and Experience, Volume 1, Theories of Emotion* (New York: Academic, 1980).

2. Stephen W. Porges, "Orienting in a Defensive World: Mammalian Modifications of Our Evolutionary Heritage: A Polyvagal Theory," *Psychophysiology*, July 1995, https://pubmed.ncbi.nlm.nih.gov/7652107/.

3. Three Initiates, *The Kybalion: A Study of the Hermetic Philosophy of Ancient Egypt and Greece*, 1908 (Yogi Publication Society, 1940).

4. "Marie-Louise von Franz—The Process of Individuation (Full Essay)," posted July 14, 2021, by Individuation Portal, YouTube, https://www.youtube.com/watch?v=9wJMXwIC0gw&t=12s.

5. Anthony Stevens, *Jung: A Very Short Introduction* (Oxford University Press, 1994), 70–85.

6. C. G. Jung, *Mysterium Coniunctionis* (Princeton University Press, 1977).

7. Laurynas, "The Ultimate Secret of Feminine and Masculine Polarity," November 10, 2020, Medium.com, https://throughmindbodyspirit.medium .com/the-ultimate-secret-of-feminine-and-masculine-polarity-aa729f96ac27.

Chapter 3

1. Ellyn Maese, "Almost a Quarter of the World Feels Lonely," October 24, 2023, Gallup blog, https://news.gallup.com/opinion/gallup/512618/ almost-quarter-world-feels-lonely.aspx.

2. The CIA-Contra-Crack Cocaine Controversy: A Review of the Justice Department's Investigations and Prosecutions, https://oig.justice.gov/ sites/default/files/archive/special/9712/ch01p1.htm.

3. Stefan Felder, "The Gender Longevity Gap: Explaining the Difference Between Singles and Couples," February 2006, *Journal of Population Economics*, https://www.researchgate.net/ publication/24059308_The_gender_longevity_gap_Explaining_the_ dierence_between_singles_and_couples.

4. Richard Frye, Carolyn Aragao, Kiley Hurst, and Kim Parker, "In a Growing Share of US Marriages, Husbands and Wives Earn About the Same," April 13, 2023, Pew Research Center, https://www.pewresearch .org/social-trends/2023/04/13/in-a-growing-share-of-u-s-marriages- husbands-and-wives-earn-about-the-same/.

5. Patrick Clapp, "The Disproportionate Impact of the COVID-19 Pandemic on Women in the Workforce," February 14, 2023, United States Census Bureau, https://www.census.gov/data/academy/webinars/2023/ impact-of-the-covid-19-pandemic-on-women-in-the-workforce.html.

6. Sian Cain, "Women Are Happier Without Children or a Spouse, Says Happiness Expert," May 25, 2019, *The Guardian*, https://www.theguardian.com/lifeandstyle/2019/may/25/ women-happier-without-children-or-a-spouse-happiness-expert.

7. Nicole Andrejek, Tina Fetner, and Melanie Heath, "Climax as Work: Heteronormativity, Gender Labor, and the Gender Gap in Orgasms," January 31, 2022, *Sage Journal*, https://www.ncbi.nlm.nih.gov/pmc/ articles/PMC8847982/.

Chapter 5

1. Barrie Davenport, "39 Unhealthy Signs of a Dysfunctional Family," September 1, 2023, Live Bold and Bloom, https://liveboldandbloom .com/09/relationships/dysfunctional-family.

2. Jana Švorcová, "Transgenerational Epigenetic Inheritance of Traumatic Experience in Mammals," National Library of Medicine, https://www .ncbi.nlm.nih.gov/pmc/articles/PMC9859285/.

3. Rachel Yehuda, "How Parents' Trauma Leaves Biological Traces in Children," July 1, 2022, *Scientific American*, https://www.scientificamerican.com/article/ how-parents-rsquo-trauma-leaves-biological-traces-in-children/.

Chapter 6

1. Julianne Holt-Lunstad, Timothy B. Smith, and J. Bradley Layton, "Social Relationships and Mortality Risk: A Meta-Analytic Review," July 27, 2010, *PLoS Med*, https://journals.plos.org/plosmedicine/ article?id=10.1371/journal.pmed.1000316#:~:text=What%20Do%20 These%20Findings%20Mean,affect%20mortality%2C%20the%20 researchers%20conclude.

2. "Dunbar's Number: Why We Can Only Maintain 150 Relationships," October 9, 2019, BBC.com, https://www.bbc.com/future/ article/20191001-dunbars-number-why-we-can-only-maintain-150- relationships.

Chapter 7

1. Michael Tavon on Twitter, March 16, 2022, https://x.com/michaeltavon/ status/1504223796005568512.

2. Amir Levine and Rachel Heller, *Attached: The New Science of Adult Attachment and How It Can Help You Find—and Keep—Love* (New York: TarcherPerigee, 2012).

3. Rainer Weber, Lukas Eggenberger, Christof Stosch, and Adreas Walther, "Gender Differences in Attachment Anxiety and Avoidance and Their

Association with Psychotherapy Use—Examining Students from a German University," June 22, 2022, Behavioral Sciences, https://www.ncbi.nlm.nih.gov/pmc/articles/PMC9312160/#:~:text=This%20is%20also%20evident%20in,research%20%5B42%2C43%5D.

4. Charisse Cooke, "The Anxious-Avoidant Dance: What Happens When Insecure Attachment Styles Combine?", April 18, 2024, welldoing.org, https://welldoing.org/article/anxious-avoidant-dance-what-happens-when-insecure-attachment-styles-combine.

5. Gary Chapman, *The 5 Love Languages: The Secret to Love That Lasts* (Chicago: Northfield Publishing, 1992).

Chapter 8

1. Quoted in Richard Schickel, *The Stars* (New York: Dial Press, 1962).

2. Lindsey Gibson, *Adult Children of Emotionally Immature Parents: How to Heal from Distant, Rejecting, or Self-Involved Parents* (Oakland, CA: New Harbinger Publications, 2015).

Chapter 9

1. E. Mohandas, "Neurobiology of Spirituality," January–December 2008, *Mens Sana Monographs*, https://www.ncbi.nlm.nih.gov/pmc/articles/PMC3190564/#:~:text=This%20cognitive%20process%20most%20probably,et%20al.%2C%202001.

2. Viktor E. Frankl, *Man's Search for Meaning: An Introduction to Logotherapy* (Boston: Beacon Press, 1959), 63–65.

3. Lou Papineau, "Prince on Prince: The Best Quotes From the Man Himself," February 20, 2017, *The Current*, https://origin-www.thecurrent.org/feature/2017/02/20/prince-on-prince-the-best-quotes-from-the-man-himself.

Chapter 10

1. Malcolm Gladwell, *Outliers: The Story of Success* (New York: Little, Brown and Company, 2008), 35–40.

2. Nick Offerman Closes The 20th Annual Webby Awards," posted May 17, 2016, by The Webby Awards, YouTube, https://youtu.be/yfKKEszdxZI?si =JwhgcLc76hW1OEil.

Chapter 11

1. Bessel A. van der Kolk, *The Body Keeps the Score: Brain, Mind, and Body in the Healing of Trauma* (New York: Penguin Books, 2014).

Chapter 12

1. Tammi R.A. Kral, Brianna S. Schuyler, Jeanette A. Mumford, Melissa A. Rosenkranz, Antoine Lutz, and Richard J. Davidson, "Impact of Short- and Long-Term Mindfulness Meditation Training on Amygdala Reactivity to Emotional Stimuli," July 7, 2018, *Pub Med Central*, https://www.ncbi.nlm.nih.gov/pmc/articles/PMC6671286/.

Chapter 13

1. Becky Kane, "The Science of Analysis Paralysis," todoist.com, https://todoist.com/inspiration/analysis-paralysis-productivity.

2. Ted J. Kaptchuk et al., "Placebos Without Deception: A Randomized Controlled Trial in Irritable Bowel Syndrome," *PLoS ONE* 5, no. 12 (2010): e15591, https://doi.org/10.1371/journal.pone.0015591.

About the Author

PIERCE J. BROOKS is a two-time TEDx speaker, coach, and transformative leader who has turned personal struggle into a purposeful mission: helping others embrace the power of uniting their duality. Drawing from his work with coaching startups, corporations, and sports teams, Pierce empowers individuals to integrate vulnerability with strength and discipline with reflection. *Peak Integration* is the culmination of his work and evolution—a framework for mastering internal and external energies, transcending limitations, and living with purpose.